Endorsements for the Second Edition

"The issue is not, argue Farkas and Schou, a confrontation between post-truth and rationality, but a question of democracy, implying a clash between different interpretations of truth, which in turn requires adequate and egalitarian opportunities for discourse and exchange for its constantly reiterated search for agreements and compromises. These qualities are usually absent in most societies. However lively current debates over post-truth and fake news, this vital dimension is usually overlooked. This is a book that not only deserves to be widely read, but which should also inspire movements and campaigns."

Colin Crouch, *Professor Emeritus at the University of Warwick, UK, External scientific member of the Max Planck Institute for the Study of Societies at Cologne.*

"One of the most original studies on liberal democratic politics today, Farkas and Schou's book offers a stunning discourse analysis of the ways we talk about fake news and alternative facts, revealing how these ways of talking profoundly shape our political imaginaries in a manner reductive and perilous for democracy itself. But more than a compelling exploration of how discourses on post-truth work and why they matter, the book is also invaluable as a resource for the reinvention of democratic politics by placing people's voices and public deliberation at the heart of the political process. This is a contemporary classic and I cannot recommend it highly enough to anyone – scholar, student, journalist or concerned citizen – seeking to understand the challenges of our media-saturated world."

Lilie Chouliaraki, *Professor and Chair in Media and Communications in the Department of Media and Communications at LSE, UK.*

"*Post-Truth, Fake News and Democracy: Mapping the Politics of Falsehood* is a clear-eyed critique of the new political imaginaries of "post-truth worlds," which have dominated popular and scholarly discourse since 2016. Johan Farkas and Jannick Schou systematically demonstrate how these discourses have limited not only how we conceptualize the relationship between democracy, information, and digital media, but the possible solutions. Instead, scholars must grapple with the legacy of political manipulation in liberal democracy, contextualizing the current moment within longer, and messier, histories. The book is a call to decouple academic work from trends, hot takes, and think pieces about "infodemics" and "fake news," enabling us to rethink our assumptions about democracy and imagine more radical futures."

Alice E. Marwick, *Associate Professor in the Department of Communication, Co-Director of The Center for Information, Technology, and Public Life, University of North Carolina at Chapel Hill, USA.*

"A wonderful scholarly polemic that argues that 'fake news' and 'misinformation' are not new but hard-wired into a media system that is skewed by the distortions and exclusions of corporate power and liberal democracy. It maps out in a comprehensive and accessible fashion both the problems and some of the radical democratic solutions we need for a meaningfully accountable media. Essential reading to make sense of post-truth discourses."

Des Freedman, *Professor of Media and Communication Studies, Head of Department and Co-Director of the Goldsmiths Leverhulme Media Research Centre, Goldsmiths, University of London, UK.*

Endorsements for the First Edition

"This is a book that needed to be written. Through an impressive empirical mapping and discourse theoretical analysis of recent post-truth and fake news discourses, the authors identify, and problematize, how democracy in these discourses is articulated as a technocratic order based on "the rule by truth." In the process, and with the help of historical contextualization, Farkas and Schou expose the reactionary anti-democratic imaginary within the discourses, and consequently open space to once more envision democracy in terms of "the rule by the people." This incredibly insightful and important book is a must read for all students, scholars, and proponents of democracy."

Lincoln Dahlberg, *Researcher in Media Politics and Digital Democracy.*

"Few deny the emergence and importance of post-truth politics, fake news, and the changing impact of the public and social media on democratic politics, though it is difficult to find compelling diagnoses and alternatives. In *Post-Truth, Fake News and Democracy*, Johan Farkas and Jannick Schou provide a compelling diagnosis of the contemporary discourses on "post-truth" through an in-depth analysis of news articles, commentaries, academic publications, policy briefs, and political speeches. Carefully linking empirical research and critical political philosophy, the book successfully challenges those who call simply for greater truth and rationality by outlining a deeper conception of democracy, and its attendant institutions and practices. This is an important and path-breaking contribution that responds to a pressing issue in contemporary society and politics."

David Howarth, *Professor and Director of the Centre for Ideology and Discourse Analysis, University of Essex, UK.*

Post-Truth, Fake News and Democracy

The new edition of *Post-Truth, Fake News and Democracy* offers an updated overview and critical discussion of contemporary discourses around truth, misinformation, and democracy, while also mapping cutting-edge scholarship.

Through in-depth analyses of news articles, commentaries, academic publications, policy briefs, and political speeches, the book engages with the underlying normative ideas that shape how fake news is being addressed across the globe. Doing so, it provides an innovative, critical contribution to contemporary debates on democracy, post-truth, and politics.

- Three new chapters: Chapter 2 provides an outline of the scholarly field of research into fake news; Chapter 5 examines how issues of fake news and (mis)information have become intertwined with contemporary crisis events; and Chapter 9 presents democratic alternatives to post-truth solutionism.
- A new foreword by Professor Sarah Banet-Weiser.
- Fully updated examples and studies from contemporary events, including the COVID-19 pandemic, the United States Capitol attack, and the Russian invasion of Ukraine.
- Extended discussions on the causes of democratic decline, currently proposed solutions to fake news, and democratic alternatives to our current predicament.

Interesting, informative, and well documented, *Post-Truth, Fake News and Democracy* continues its commitment to understand and engage with the current state and future of democracy.

Johan Farkas is a postdoctoral fellow at the University of Copenhagen. He is part of the project "Tell Me the Truth: Fact-Checkers in an Age of Epistemic Instability" funded by the Carlsberg Foundation.

Jannick Schou holds a PhD from the IT University of Copenhagen. He is the author of several monographs on questions of politics, citizenship, and democracy.

Post-Truth, Fake News and Democracy

Mapping the Politics of Falsehood

Second Edition

Johan Farkas and Jannick Schou

NEW YORK AND LONDON

Designed cover image: Getty Images – Nastasic

Second edition published 2024
by Routledge
605 Third Avenue, New York, NY 10158

and by Routledge
4 Park Square, Milton Park, Abingdon, Oxon, OX14 4RN

Routledge is an imprint of the Taylor & Francis Group, an informa business

© 2024 Johan Farkas and Jannick Schou

The right of Johan Farkas and Jannick Schou to be identified as authors of this work has been asserted in accordance with sections 77 and 78 of the Copyright, Designs and Patents Act 1988.

First edition published by Routledge 2020

ISBN: 978-1-032-56302-2 (hbk)
ISBN: 978-1-032-56303-9 (pbk)
ISBN: 978-1-003-43487-0 (ebk)

DOI: 10.4324/9781003434870

Typeset in Times New Roman
by Newgen Publishing UK

Contents

Foreword

A feminist reading

In 2016, Oxford Dictionaries named "post-truth" as the word of the year. As Farkas and Schou elegantly argue in this book, this moment marked a time when the "traditional" gatekeepers of the truth – mainly journalists and public intellectuals – were routinely having their thoughts, opinions, and arguments – indeed, their "truths" – questioned, challenged, and dismissed. This questioning of the truth apparently unleashed a number of mobs (especially online mobs), where, as the authors detail, "so-called malicious actors and misinformed citizens have started to spread lies, deception, hate, propaganda, and fake information on a previously unseen scale. All these phenomena are claimed to be indicative of a brand-new political age or paradigm in which 'Truth' and 'Reason' are superseded by echo chambers, filter bubbles, emotions, and individual gut feelings."

I share, with the authors, deep skepticism about this dynamic. While surely it is the case that there has been an uptick in hate, deception, lies, and fake information in the contemporary moment, especially in the online world, my skepticism lies with the idea that somehow before this moment, there was a kind of pure, unadulterated truth that was freely available and legitimate to all. Similarly to the authors, it is less important to me to point out how some version of the truth has been diminished (if not outright obliterated), and more important to theorize the "specific set of ideas they [the lies and the deception] serve to produce and bring into existence." But it is also important to highlight the ways in which the "truth" itself – before the contemporary post-truth crisis – was never organized around a binary of truth versus falsity. Truth has always been radically, culturally contingent.

While "post-truth" was the word of the year in 2016, "feminism" was the word of the year in 2017. Yet, there is very little mention of feminism – or gender as a specific constituency of the post-truth – in writings about post-truth. The potential connection between the two has not been deeply acknowledged, despite them both reaching fever pitch at the same time in the same political climate (see Banet-Weiser & Higgins, 2023). The same world that gave way to the renaissance of popular feminism also gave way for the rise of the contemporary crisis of post-truth. They are part of the same cultural ecosystem.

As many scholars have pointed out, examples of post-truth abound, mostly tied to state or global politics, and mostly articulated on a media platform, whether that is on mainstream media or social media. Indeed, the public anxiety about truth claims and who can and should be a truth teller has as a core logic the apparent relationship between truth and democracy, as well as the relationship between a rational subject and truth. This relationship is seen to be profoundly disrupted in the current moment.

The whole concept of misinformation, the core expression of the post-truth crisis, depends on an assumption that the "information" that the prefix "mis" qualifies somehow represents the "truth." While "truth" is an often contested concept, it has nonetheless always depended on the assumption that certain actors tell the truth and that these actors have been authorized with the mantle of veracity in their understandings of the world and of themselves. Yet the idea that this is a contemporary problem belies a long history, one that suggests that the game is rigged differently at different historical moments, and that for women and people of color, the game has always been rigged.

That is, the conception of truth and notions of believability in the West have historically been inextricable from whiteness and masculine subjectivity. The public outcry about what the post-truth crisis diminishes offers an alibi for the apparent diminishing of white masculinist debate. The truth has always depended on those who are authorized to *define* it. That is, the concern around post-truth has become urgent when those who have defined the truth historically – primarily white, privileged men – begin to witness *their* truths beginning to be questioned, eroding, when *they* are potentially not believed.

Thus, the post-truth "crisis" is often framed as the downfall of hitherto functional "rationality" in politics, the death of expertise and Enlightenment values. As Farkas and Schou meticulously explain, "democracy" is the normative foundation for this crisis. And, despite the contemporary focus on misinformation and the "post-truth," with scores of books and articles published focusing on this apparently novel "crisis," (some more historical and critical than others), I think, along with the authors, that it is crucial to have historical specificity when considering the relationship between gender, the post-truth, and misinformation: with roots in the Enlightenment and ideas of "masculine rationality," women were understood as governed by their emotions, subjective in their understandings of the world, not even capable of speaking the truth – thus, always already the bearers of misinformation. Women, that is, are not victims of the contemporary crisis of the post-truth; in many ways, their subjectivity has been culturally constructed *as* post-truth. In this context, men's "truths" have long been positioned as universal while women's truths have been positioned as incidental, subjective, and unique, even in the most "rational" corners of the natural sciences (e.g., gender bias in medical research, exclusion of women from drug trials, heart attack symptoms, to mention only a few examples).

The detailed arguments in this book help to clarify and historicize this moment; the contemporary misogynistic backlash against women in all realms of life, whether sexual violence, politics, or education, finds a home in what Farkas and Schou call a "post-truth world." As the authors contend, the concerns around post-truth – misinformation, disinformation, outright lies – are proclaimed to be a crisis in knowing, in subjectivity, in democracy, they are seen as an affront on all of these ontological and indeed scientific claims of being and knowing. Yet this has been the material context for women for centuries. In other words, the relationship between misogyny, post-truth, and misinformation is not a new one. The authors point out that the contemporary post-truth "crisis" is one that is partly built on nostalgia, for a time when democracy was apparently based in unassailable truths, "thus erasing long historical struggles of disenfranchised groups, such as women and racial minorities, to be acknowledged as part of the democratic populace." Yet it is not only that the struggle for marginalized folks to be acknowledged as part of democracy is erased in the contemporary lament about post-truth, but that the very subjectivity of women and people of color to be seen as authentic beings, capable of truth-telling, has been denied for centuries; as Imani Perry has argued, people of color were long denied status even as persons, let alone acknowledged as part of a democracy (Perry, 2018). As Kathryn Higgins and I have recently argued in our book, *Believability,* men – but especially white men in positions of power – have historically occupied a central position as ideal believable subjects. They are seen as objective, while women are always already subjective. Within the context of sexual violence, for example, the mandate for objectivity at the heart of the Western understanding of truth operates as a mechanism of domination. It simultaneously "locks out" the knowledge of particularized subjects from the realm of truth while "locking in" the truths particular to Anglo-European contexts and white men's experiences of them.

We see this dynamic with the heightened visibility of the extreme right, key actors in the current environment of misinformation. Extreme right movements, from neo-fascism to white Christian nationalism, use misogyny as a core logic to their politics and their misinformation campaigns; it is not merely a strategy or tactic but rather these movements are frequently based on misogyny as a set of discourses and practices that aim to "reset" the gender balance back to its "natural" patriarchal relation (see Bratich, 2023). At the center of the circulation of current forms of misinformation are digital media and communication platforms, which centrally use misinformation to mobilize citizens and communities. A key strategy of the extreme right is recuperation: men's rights organizations in digital culture are filled with false campaigns about how women and feminists have not only destroyed society, but emasculated it.

The gendered logic of misogynistic misinformation campaigns is that of a zero-sum-game: men lose, become invisible, when women win and become more visible. Conservative populist movements take a particular shape in a contemporary crisis in hegemonic masculinity, a crisis brought on by global economic collapse (as men lose their jobs and future security), by more visible efforts to diversify workplaces and cultural spaces (exemplified by a few visible successful women in technology fields), and by increasing popular feminist activism.

Farkas and Schou help guide us with some of the specifics of the current moment, those that mobilized choosing these two cultural and discursive practices – the post-truth and feminism – as words of the year. What are the post-truth and feminism responding to, in the early aughts? Post-truth characterizes a very contemporary cultural moment that responds to increased digital circulation of dis/misinformation. Contemporary feminism, also in digital circulation, is most often a response to misogyny. Yet, although feminist theories have long explored the ways in which women's bodies, affects, practices and ideologies have been framed as subjective compared to the "objective" masculine spheres, and although both misogyny and misinformation have been growing concerns in the contemporary digital era, the relationship between these two contemporary discursive practices hasn't been thoroughly explored in scholarship (there are key exceptions, such as Gilmore, 2017; Hewa, 2021; Marwick & Lewis, 2017).

Thus, we need to consider the historical relationship between misogyny and misinformation if we are going to truly grasp the cultural and political significance of the post-truth moment. Misogynistic disinformation campaigns haven't received the same kind of attention as, say, "fake news" or the crisis of the post-truth, perhaps because misogyny itself is so normalized. And, while Farkas and Schou do not offer a fully-fledged analysis of misogyny and post-truth, this book is importantly generative for thinking through contemporary debates around truth, information, and rationality within wider historical contexts and struggles for power, including misogyny and structural sexism.

Thus, as the authors carefully argue and clarify, democracy is not about the "truth" but about *people*; and in this sense democracy has always depended also on the exclusion of people who are othered culturally, politically, and socially. For me, it is those dynamics, the historically different truths that the authors point out are the product of social and political struggles, that need our urgent attention. This is, as Farkas and Schou say, quoting Gramsci, a moment of the interregnum. The new moment of this world, yet to be born, must be one that challenges the exclusivity of what we have known as democracy.

Sarah Banet-Weiser
Philadelphia, PA USA
6 July 2023

References

Banet-Weiser, S. & Claire Higgins, K. (2023). *Believability: Sexual Violence, Media and the Politics of Doubt*. Cambridge: Polity Books.

Bratich, J.Z. (2023). *On Microfascism: Gender, War, Death*. Philadelphia: Common Notions Press.

Gilmore, L. (2017). *Tainted Witness: Why We Doubt What Women Say About Their Lives*. New York: Columbia University Press.

Hewa, N. (2021). The Mouth of the Internet, the Eyes of the Public: Sexual Violence Survivorship in an Economy of Visibility. *Feminist Media Studies, 22*(8), 1900–2001. https://doi.org/10.1080/14680777.2021.1922483

Marwick, A. & Lewis, R. (2017). Media Manipulation and Disinformation Online. Data & Society. https://datasociety.net/library/media-manipulation-and-disinfo-online/

Perry, I. (2018). *Vexy Thing: On Gender and Liberation*. Durham: Duke University Press.

Acknowledgments

This book deals with contemporary discourses in and around questions of truth, democracy, and politics. It charts the formation of a new political battlefield revolving around ideas such as fake news, alternative facts, and post-truth, providing a staunch critique of the limitations of these continuously developing ideas. With this book, we argue that not only have contemporary concerns around democracy and truth been severely limited in their understanding of what democracy is. They have also taken for granted that democratic practices are almost solely about truth, rationality, and consensus. This need not be the case. Indeed, it *should* not be the case. And so, with this book, we want to suggest that our current democratic moment should not lend itself to claiming more *true* politics but more *democratic* politics.

In writing this book – both the first edition, which came out in 2019, and now the second installment – we have often felt like chasing a constantly moving target. Both public debates and political interventions move fast, often in unexpected directions. This also means that we have continuously had to amend our arguments to keep up to date with the newest developments. For some, the Sisyphean task of following the shifting boundaries of a continuously moving field might seem like an argument against writing this book. Should we not have waited, it might be asked, until things were more settled? On the contrary, our point in writing this book is precisely that things are not yet settled and that there is still room for thinking, acting, and doing otherwise. The book attempts to do so, often in an explicitly polemic tone, by intervening in contemporary academic and political dialogues. There is a pressing need for critical scholars to engage with our democratic moment. They must do so in an effort to demand deeper, better, and more inclusive democratic institutions and societies. While parts of this book may thus be rendered obsolete in due time, we nonetheless believe that its basic message will continue to resonate for the foreseeable future. Democracy always needs our care, concern, and attention.

Many of the ideas presented in this book date all the way back to conversations started in 2015. Back then, we had become increasingly interested in understanding new forms of political manipulation on digital platforms. In particular, we had looked into how fake accounts on Facebook were being deployed to tactically discredit and antagonize ethnic and religious minorities. At the end of 2016, things seemed to suddenly change, as fake news became a ubiquitous term in the public imagination. Yet, somewhat contrary to our previous work, what caught our attention was not how such news actually operated, but the kind of performative impact the concept of fake news seemed to have. Indeed, it seemed to us that fake news, alternative facts, post-truth, and similar ideas were being used as new political imaginaries in a struggle over the very future of democracy. This book is our attempt to understand this field of struggle, which has continued to capture public and political discourse ever since. Only by knowing the stakes of these conflicts might it become possible to imagine other futures and alternatives for democratic practices.

In this second edition of the book, we have had the opportunity to revisit and refine the arguments presented in the original rendition. Not only have we added new empirical material to the book, diving into the intricacies of a number of new and pressing cases; we have also had the opportunity to flesh out some of the arguments of the first edition in much greater detail. In this way, the second edition combines the core arguments and structure of the first while also adding a series of new chapters and nuances.

For invaluable comments, feedback, and encouragement along the way, we would like to thank our colleagues at the IT University of Copenhagen, Malmö University, and the University of Copenhagen. A special thanks to the librarians at the Malmö University Library for helping us assemble our archive. We would like to thank international colleagues who have engaged with our work and invited us to speak about the first edition of this book. Thanks to our editor at Routledge, Natalja Mortensen, and to Charlie Baker for making this book become possible. Thanks to Professor Sarah Banet-Weiser for writing the new foreword. Finally, and most importantly, we would like to thank our families and friends for love and support.

Chapters 4 and 6 include arguments presented in Farkas, J. & Schou, J. (2020). Post-Truth Discourses and their Limits: A Democratic Crisis?, In G. Terzis, D. Kloza, E. Kużelewska & D. Trottier (Eds.), *Disinformation and Digital Media as a Challenge for Democracy* (pp. 103–126). Intersentia. Chapter 5 expands upon arguments in Farkas, J. & Schou, J. (2018). Fake News as a Floating Signifier: Hegemony, Antagonism and the Politics of Falsehood. *Javnost – The Public*, 25(3), 298–314. Finally, some arguments overlap with those presented in Farkas, J. (2023). *This is Not Real News: Discursive Struggles over Fake News, Journalism, and Democracy* [Doctoral thesis, Malmö University]. Malmö University Press.

We take full responsibility for any errors, mistakes, or omissions.

Johan Farkas & Jannick Schou
July 2023

Part I

Preparing for the post-truth journey

1 Introduction

The fake news virus

In late 2019 and early 2020, a new and highly uncertain viral threat started to surface around the globe. The disease soon came to be known under the now ubiquitous name COVID-19 and evolved into the as-of-yet most significant pandemic of the 21st century. As the virus spread globally, it simultaneously moved to the top of political agendas, with policymakers debating not only its consequences for public health, but also for the economy, security, and much more. This development was reflected at the annual *Munich Security Conference*, a forum in which policymakers, intellectuals, and business actors discuss the state and future of international security policy.

On 15 February 2020, Tedros Ghebreyesus, Director of the World Health Organization (WHO), spoke on the dangers of COVID-19. In what were to become a highly publicized moment, Ghebreyesus warned the international crowd of the dangers of an emergent *infodemic*:

> We're not just fighting an epidemic; we're fighting an infodemic. Fake news spreads faster and more easily than this virus, and is just as dangerous.... . We call on all governments, companies, and news organizations to work with us to sound the appropriate level of alarm ... . Now more than ever is the time for us to let science and evidence lead policy. If we don't, we are headed down a dark path that leads nowhere but division and disharmony.
>
> (Ghebreyesus, 2020)

With Ghebreyesus' speech, the notion of the *infodemic* was swiftly propelled into the mainstream, becoming a common trope across politics, journalism, and academia. To many intellectuals, it came to be seen as a "threat to one of the pillars of democracy – transparency and truthful information" (Pedrazzani et al., 2021, p. 181) and a catalyst for "panic, fear, and chaos within the society" (Gupta et al., 2022, p. 670). If governments and media conglomerates did not act promptly – a number of prominent voices argued – democracy would soon

DOI: 10.4324/9781003434870-2

be facing an existential peril from misinformed masses, trapped in alternative realities dominated by fake news.

In response to this new rhetorical figure, governments across the world began to implement emergency measures, often involving direct and unmasked restrictions on free speech. Human rights groups were soon to warn that this development would hurt democracy more than it would protect it (Human Rights Watch, 2020, 2021). These warnings were, however, largely ignored.

Despite its meteoric rise to the top of policy agendas, the core ideas contained within the notion of the infodemic were far from new. Indeed, what was perhaps most intriguing about the sudden ubiquity of this concept was that – by and large – the fear, symbolism, and solutions surrounding the infodemic had already dominated public discourse for years. In 2016, then-US presidential candidate, Hillary Clinton, had proclaimed that there was an "epidemic of malicious fake news" jeopardizing "our democracy and innocent lives" (cited in Taylor, 2016). In 2017, the CEO of Apple, Tim Cook, had stated that fake news was "killing people's minds" (cited in Rawlinson, 2017). And in 2018, Indian politician, Subramanian Swamy, had called fake news a "cancer" in need of "surgery" (Press Trust of India, 2018).

One of the perhaps most vocal expressions of these ideas in the period before COVID-19 came from French president, Emmanuel Macron. In 2018, before the Joint House of the US congress, Macron had proclaimed that "[t]o protect our democracies, we have to fight against the ever-growing virus of fake news, which exposes our people to irrational fear and imaginary risk... Without reason, without truth, there is no real democracy because democracy is about true choices and rational decisions. The corruption of information is an attempt to corrode the very spirit of our democracies."

In addition to echoing political rhetoric from before COVID-19, the solutions to the infodemic also channeled and rehashed ideas from before 2020. Already in 2017, a number of governments had implemented a wave of "anti-fake news laws" that human rights groups criticized for harming free speech and democratic participation (Henley, 2018).

Rather than capturing a novel threat, then, the infodemic represented yet another iteration of an already pervasive set of ideas and discourses in late capitalist states; namely that societies worldwide face an existential threat from fake news, alternative facts, and misinformation, spreading like viruses and corrupting the minds of millions. Fear of the infodemic was only a fragment of an already existing *zeitgeist* of fear that continues to captivate political discourse. Then as much as now, it seems that everywhere one looks, there is no shortage of politicians, scholars, and public intellectuals lamenting the impending death of democracy, as supposedly hard facts and rationality are drowned out by misinformation, fake news, and lies. According to some, as exemplified by the French president, the very *spirit* of democracy is corroding.

Indeed, whether labeled as an infodemic, post-truth era, post-factual society, or misinformation age, a prevailing narrative of our time has become that scientific evidence is no longer trusted, medical evidence is sidestepped, and proper journalism is under attack from fake news farms, troll factories, social bots, and deepfakes. These discourses argue that the rise of social media platforms, such as Facebook, TikTok, and WeChat, has been a catalyst for a seemingly endless flood of misinformation and deception. Traditional gatekeepers of truth, such as editors, journalists, and public intellectuals, have supposedly lost their monopoly on public issues. In this process, so-called malicious actors and misinformed citizens have started to spread lies, deception, hate, propaganda, and fake information on a previously unseen scale. All these phenomena are claimed to be indicative of a brand-new political age or paradigm in which "Truth" and "Reason" are superseded by echo chambers, filter bubbles, emotions, and individual gut feelings. This amounts to an epochal rupture in the very fabric of democracy. The foundations of our political system are cracking up. Democracy is doomed, unless these destructive trajectories are interrupted and changed for the better through drastic measures.

Often, a series of seemingly disparate events – from the re-election of Narendra Modi as Prime Minister of India in 2019, global vaccine hesitancy movements in 2020, the US Capitol Attack in 2021, the war in Ukraine in 2022, to the Brazilian Congress attack in 2023 – are lumped together as proof of a profound crisis of truth. It is precisely this supposed crisis that is so often used to legitimize decisive and far-reaching political action.

This book seeks to investigate and critically examine these contemporary narratives and discourses about democracy, politics, and truth. Grappling with these potent ideas, currently circulating at rapid speed in late capitalist democracies, it systematically details the emergence of what we term as *post-truth worlds*. We use this concept as an overall frame of reference, useful for capturing a still developing and continuously expanding field of political struggle and contestation. This field revolves around explaining *how, why,* and *in what ways* democratic practices are currently being put under dire pressure.

Post-truth worlds, in our understanding, can be seen as discursive formations or political imaginaries produced, disseminated, and adopted across the globe, always nested within specific socio-political contexts with real-world consequences. With this book, we want to move into these worlds. We want to explore their internal discursive logics: that is, the ideas they contain and the implicit normative premises that structure them. Why is it, we ask, that contemporary democratic states and societies are currently said to be facing an immense crisis of truth? How has the seemingly unstoppable barrage of fake news and alternative facts – flooding the gates of democracy and inaugurating an era of post-truth politics – been conceptualized and linked to wider political issues? And what are the dominant normative ideas that continue to inform our current ways of thinking and acting upon questions of truth, democracy, and politics?

To answer these questions, we use a substantial amount of space in this book on presenting an empirical mapping of the current terrain of political struggle over the stakes and ideas in contemporary post-truth worlds. Indeed, a large portion of this work is taken up by a relatively detailed discourse analysis of the kinds of claims made as to how democracy, truth, and politics influence each other. In wanting to interrogate this continuously morphing *politics of falsehood* (Farkas & Schou, 2018), we are not interested in evaluating or assessing whether or not or to what extent current debates around truth, deception, and democracy are accurate or not. We do not aim to say whether democracies *really* are facing an "information nightmare" (Filibeli, 2020). Instead, we want to take contemporary concerns seriously by understanding these as performative interventions seeking to give meaning to and influence our democratic moment in profound ways. Whether they accurately represent the world or not is, for us, less important than the specific set of ideas they serve to produce and bring into existence. At its core, this book can thus be seen as a study in political conceptual history, albeit with a contemporary twist.

In proposing this shift in analytical focus – from looking at conditions of truth to discourses on truth – this book differentiates itself quite substantially from existing accounts of post-truth politics and the infodemic. In recent years, there has been no shortage of commentators and intellectuals decrying the onslaught of fake news and post-truth. A veritable industry of post-truth alarmism has sprung up, decrying the *"War on Truth"* (d'Ancona, 2017), *"Death of Truth"* (Kakutani, 2018), *"Infocalypse,"* (Schick, 2020), *"How Bullshit Conquered the World,"* (Ball, 2017) and *"How We Lost the Global Battle Against Disinformation"* (Stengel, 2019). Similarly, legacy media outlets across the world have disparaged the new age of disinformation by publishing a wealth of articles, op-eds, and commentaries, dedicated precisely to the decline of democracy and truth.

In the academic landscape, too, there is a growing movement focused on questions in and around fake news, infodemics, and post-truth. Notable recent contributions include titles such as *Lie Machines: How to Save Democracy from Troll Armies, Deceitful Robots, Junk News Operations, and Political Operatives* (Howard, 2020), *Cheap Speech: How Disinformation Poisons Our Politics – and How to Cure It* (Hasen, 2022), and *Foolproof: Why We Fall for Misinformation and How to Build Immunity* (van der Linden, 2023). As already hinted at, our aim with this book is to do something different than what is attempted in these existing interventions. We want to understand the new political discourses, ideas, and grammars around post-truth, fake news, and alternative facts. Rather than saying what is true and what is fake, we want to turn this issue into an empirical set of questions. In this sense, we hope to take stock of the current debate surrounding these issues, unpacking contemporary anxieties, visions, and ideals about democracy and politics. In so doing, we will not only understand our existing situation better; we might also begin to understand the limits and problems of post-truth worlds and start carving out other ways of thinking and acting about truth and democracy.

Democracy in decline? Core arguments

This book is an attempt to unpack contemporary post-truth worlds by exploring discussions on truth, democracy, and falsehood, diving into their political logics and implicit normative ideas. We seek to think with and, importantly, *beyond* these existing worlds. Based on a systematic empirical mapping of the state of debate, we aim to produce new political openings, allowing us to envision other ways of imagining the state of democracy. In this sense, the book has both empirical and critical ambitions. It hopes to fuse detailed empirical studies with political philosophical discussions on democracy, politics, and capitalism.

The critical ambition is in large part formed through an engagement with the existing state of affairs. This is an engagement that is both historical and political. Our aim is not to "debunk" or "expose" existing discourses as ideological veils or smokescreens, but, more modestly, to suggest that their rendering of the world is not complete. They have severe blind spots and lack crucial connections to wider historical developments taking place since the middle of the last century. Not only does the notion of the post-truth era come with an implicit nostalgia for a never existing "truth era" of democracy, thus erasing long historical struggles of disenfranchised groups, such as women and racial minorities, to be acknowledged as part of the democratic populace. The idea of a post-truth era also fails to acknowledge that democracy, as a political system, has never only been about truth in the first place. In doing so, it neglects that contemporary democracies were by no means in a stable condition before the supposed villains of post-truth suddenly knocked them off their course.

Formulated in the most straight-forward way, this book will argue that current discourses about the fate of democracy have tended to presuppose a very particular understanding of what counts as *true* and *false*. In so doing, they have also tended to smuggle in an implicit, yet nonetheless incredibly pervasive and strong, model of how proper democracies ought to function. They have claimed certain forms of power as being natural and supposedly inherent to democracy as a form of governance and political ordering, namely political power grounded in rationality and reason. We will argue that this current way of thinking about democracy – which has become almost completely hegemonic in contemporary political debates – is both politically charged and normatively risky. What it essentially does is to equate the idea of democracy with those of reason, rationality, and truth *tout court*. Reason and truth become the primary conditions for democracy to exist in these discourses: democracy *is* truth, it *is* reason. In this narrative, what is threatening democracies worldwide is falsehoods – pure and simple. To re-establish the former (that is, democracy) one must eliminate the latter (that is, falsehoods).

This type of argument is certainly not without precedent, neither historically nor in a contemporary light. Indeed, in what can best be described as a strange foretelling of the current state of democracy, the German philosopher and staunch defender of rationality, Jürgen Habermas, argued already in 2006 that "[a] 'post-truth democracy'... would no longer be a democracy" (Habermas, 2006, p. 18). Similarly, the history of democratic thought is littered with philosophers and political theorists linking democratic practices to truth-telling, rationality, consensus, and reason.

Yet, to claim that democracy is identical to truth – or even the conditions of possibility for truth to exist – is also to take for granted the highly contested and complex history of democracy itself. It is to gloss over the fact that what democracy is has never been static or fixed but continuously evolving and disputed. As is well known, the practice and idea of democracy constitutes what we might call an *essentially contested concept* whose contents and meaning have shifted greatly over time. Democracy has never just been one thing alone, instead remaining an object of political and social struggle. Even so, if one were to distill a common kernel from democracy, it is questionable whether a system of truth would be it. Turning to the etymological roots of democracy reveals a different story, as David Held (2006, p. 1, original emphasis) so succinctly recounts:

> While the word "democracy" came into English in the sixteenth century from the French *démocratie,* its origins are Greek. "Democracy" is derived from *dēmokratía*, the root meanings of which are *demos* (people) and *kratos* (rule). Democracy means a form of government in which, in contradistinction to monarchies and aristocracies, the people rule.

Far from a question of truth, the etymological roots of democracy reveal its intimate connection to the people – and rule by the people. Beyond this initial definition, the history of democracy as a concept and a form of governance is complex and multilayered. Over time, competing definitions and ideas about the ways in which democracy is best organized has continued to roam back and forth. Different styles and forms of democracy have emphasized distinct patterns of political participation, rights, and obligations. Though varying in terms of its concrete implementation, most liberal democracies today are based on representative forms of democracy in which citizens get to vote for (different) political parties at periodic elections. This is a system of delegation in which citizens, through their vote, elect politicians to represent their interests. While this style of democracy is dominant in advanced capitalist countries, often based on minimal forms of direct engagement and everyday influence, it is certainly not the only way of organizing a democratic system. Indeed, throughout history there has been (and continues to be) much more direct forms of democracy, emphasizing rule by the people as not just a periodic occurrence but integral to mundane life. Moreover, one ought to remember the distinct influence by social movements, political activists, and civil society on the concrete historical development of democracy, whether for the better or worse.

The tension sketched out above between a system of delegation and political expertise, on the one hand, and popular sovereignty and the people, on the other hand, continues to form an important dynamic in most liberal democracies. In this context, the political philosopher Chantal Mouffe (1993, 2005) has argued that liberal democracies are *not* constituted as singular orders but are carriers of what she terms as *the democratic paradox*. For Mouffe, this democratic paradox resides precisely in the fact that contemporary democracies are the product of liberalism – with its emphasis on rights, individualism, and law – and the democratic tradition, which has historically been linked to ideas about equality, participation, and popular sovereignty. Liberal democracy has to balance these counteracting forces, she suggests, and its success is in many ways dependent on its ability to do so.

We will return to these discussions on the political philosophy and history of democracy in the third part of the book. We will do so to give a critical response to contemporary ideas about a crisis of truth, offering a quite different portrayal of democracy than what is dominant in post-truth worlds. Based on our empirical dissection of the current terrain of struggle, we want to argue that the proliferation of ideas about fake news and the ambushing of reason should not, at least not primarily, be understood as a "truth crisis." There is a series of deep-seated problems facing liberal democracies, but the rise of fake news and alternative facts is not the biggest of our problems. In fact, solving the post-truth crisis could very well *add* to our current predicament – at least in the way it is currently imagined. Why is that? Because a large majority of those proclaiming that a truth crisis is destroying liberal democracies all seem to view evidence, reason, and hard facts as the *only* solution to contemporary democratic problems. To save democracy, these voices argue, we need to once again secure the solid ground of reason that has begun to shatter. The supposedly natural connection between truth and democracy must be restored.

This is a dangerous path. A large part of this book is dedicated to showing why. As this book will try to demonstrate, this kind of *truth-based solutionism* is all too often no solution at all. It carries within it a dangerous seed that obscures what we perceive to be the core promise or even utopia of the democratic tradition: namely that popular sovereignty and rule by the people *is* possible. Post-truth worlds often end up as attempts to undo the democratic paradox by throwing the democratic tradition to the wayside. Democracy, we want to argue in this book – particularly following radical democratic and pluralist political thinkers like Chantal Mouffe, Ernesto Laclau, Wendy Brown, and Jacques Rancière – is not just about facts, reason, and evidence. It never has been. Democracy and politics are instead about the interlocking exchanges between the individual and the people, as well as the competing political ideas about how society ought to be structured that emerges from this interplay. We cannot deduce how we want to live together. There is no single formula for the composition of the political community. What remains proper to a well-functioning democracy is not so much its ability to navigate based on reason and truth, but its ability to include and give voice to different political projects and groups. Democracy is about different visions for how society should be organized. It is about clashes of opinions, affect, and emotions.

As we will demonstrate in this book, it is precisely these elements that continue to be denied and obscured within current solutions to the alleged post-truth crisis. To make matters worse, these solutions often add insult to injury by combating the very thing they are trying to save: to cure democracy, anti-democratic or even authoritarian measures are prescribed. Responding to this development, we believe that what we need now, perhaps more than ever, is not necessarily more truth. We need spaces for the enactment of politics proper.

This book should be seen as a staunch defense of democracy, not as the sole rule of reason, but as the rule of the people. Saving democracy is, we will argue, not about arming against fake news and disinformation – at least not primarily. It is instead, and perhaps more importantly, about creating genuine spaces for politics: that is, spaces for contestation, for political difference, and for pluralism. Doing so implies imagining other futures than those currently promoted under the banner of truth and rationality. It requires the construction of a new Left politics that can adequately address key societal issues and concerns.

In short form, these are the core arguments set up in this work. We will show how a certain imaginary has gripped large parts of the world and why its implicit ideas about the nature of democracy are problematic. We will furthermore suggest that other paths are possible, even necessary, if we want to reclaim the democratic tradition. While we are currently trapped within the confines of specific post-truth worlds, there is nothing to suggest that our history is programmed in advance. There is always room for resistance: that is, for thinking and doing otherwise. This book hopes to contribute to this endeavor.

Approach and clarifications

Before embarking on our investigation into and out of contemporary post-truth worlds, we want to make our approach to this matter as clear as possible by tackling certain questions in advance. We do not seek to dispute or deny the threats posed by misinformation, lies, and deception. We do not claim that false information and propaganda techniques are harmless. They do real harm to real people. We know this, since we have contributed to exploring this in a number of studies, examining the intricacies of political deception and conflict in digital media. This includes studies of racism on fake Facebook pages (Farkas, Schou, & Neumayer, 2018a, 2018b), Russian interference in the 2016 US elections (Bastos & Farkas, 2019; Farkas & Bastos, 2018), manipulation through "mimicked news" in online tabloid media (Farkas & Neumayer, 2020b), and connections between 20th and

21st century propaganda (Farkas, 2019; Farkas & Neumayer, 2020a). This work has sought to contribute to understanding how contemporary media ecologies foster both new means of deception and struggles against these.

In conducting this research, we have become increasingly concerned about the kinds of conversations we – as academics, citizens, and participants in public debate – are currently having. Or *not* having. A conversation that is currently missing forms the core of this book: that is, the fate of democracy as *dēmokratía*, rule by the people, rather than rule by truth.

In this context, we might as well make clear from the beginning that we have both been formed by a quite particular way of thinking about democracy. This has in large part been fueled by participatory, pluralistic, and open ideas about what democracy is and should be, about who should be allowed to speak and be heard (Laclau & Mouffe, 2014; Mouffe, 1993, 2005; Rancière, 2014). Being faced with on-going discussions on how to handle and reconstruct liberal democracies, it seems to us that such democratic ideas have been thrown in the bin. Yet, moving seamlessly from the preposition that we should combat false information and deliberate deception to wanting to reinstate the privilege of truth is a complete non-sequitur to us. The two are not mutually exclusive. It *is* possible to both be worried about new capabilities of digital technologies *and* wish for more participatory and inclusionary forms of democracy. In fact, as shall be argued here, this pairing might be the only way forward if democracy is to survive.

As captured by the title of this book, most of its chapters are taken up by in-depth discussions and analyses of current discourses perpetuated at rapid speed across social media, news headlines, scholarly articles, policy briefs, and presidential speeches. Indeed, much of this book presents a close textual analysis, grappling with the particular ways in which language is mobilized to express and articulate certain visions about the conditions and faith of democracy. To claim that such an investigation only sheds light on language and discourses, however, would be to artificially limit the scope and breadth of the arguments developed here. While our analysis does focus on the deployment of language and construction of texts, these should not be seen as freely floating entities that can simply be divorced from material circumstances, contexts, and practices (Laclau & Mouffe, 2014). Language not only reflects our way of understanding and acting in the world but is also recursively involved in bringing those very worlds into existence. To deconstruct the mounting political grammar currently promoted about the post-truth era, particularly in the so-called Western world, is also to lay bare the hegemonic cognitive schemes and institutional structures that guide contemporary political actions, policy measurements, and interventions. Engaging with these is furthermore a means of taking part in hegemonic struggles over the very meaning and modalities of the world itself.

As a consequence, this book does not claim any neutral high-ground or universal position of reason. This does not mean that the book resides in the often-caricatured realm of *post-modernism*, a strange portrayal of a position in which truth and reason are said to be cast aside as completely relative, arbitrary, and groundless. We instead take the challenge inaugurated by post-structuralist writers seriously, not least the work of Laclau (1990, 2005), by occupying a middle-ground best captured by the term *post-foundationalism* (Marchart, 2007). Inspired particularly by the writings of Laclau, but also Chantal Mouffe, Jacques Derrida, and Oliver Marchart, this is a position that – at one and the same time – denies the possibility of any stable and unshakeable ground underlying social reality *and* affirms the possibility of multiple grounds that seek to install a precarious and temporary foundation. Phrased somewhat differently, such a position takes issue with the idea of any transcendental universal Truth (capital T) that cuts across and goes beyond geographies, epochs, subjectivities, species, and (perhaps even) planets. Instead, it argues that there have historically been *different truths* (lowercase t) that have been the product of social and political struggles. These competing truths are not mere smokescreens or ideological veils but situated world-making efforts around which particular forms of life have grown out. We are never operating without ground, yet no ground is ever eternal and firm. In the political realm, there can be no absolute or universal site of political legitimacy. All politics is about competing (antagonistic) ways of understanding and giving meaning to the world. The very object of politics remains the mobilization and hegemonization of the field of social meaning.

These political philosophical coordinates will be developed further throughout this book, particularly in Chapter 3. For now, we simply use them to say that just as the world of politics is not a world of the universal nor is that of research and academic knowledge. We are also situated within certain conceptions and apprehensions of what the world is and could be. Indeed, as our analysis showcases, far from just describing an already assembled world, researchers play an important role in making things, such as post-truth, infodemics, and fake news, come into being at all. They take part in performing, producing, and constructing the very meaning of these ideas. This should, however, not make us give up in advance or forfeit any kind of normative commitment. Instead, as David Howarth has so succinctly insisted, it should prompt us to engage in political struggles alongside other political actors. As Howarth (2000, p. 123) states by reference to the work of Laclau and Mouffe:

> Critical discussion of Laclau and Mouffe's project for radical democracy have centred on their supposed relativism. If there are no ultimate grounds for defending and justifying any set of values and beliefs, how can they expect to argue for radical democracy? This sort of "enlightenment blackmail," as Foucault (1984, p. 43) puts it, implies that unless one has or invokes absolute foundations to defend a political project, then one has no ground whatsoever. However, just as most competitors in a game cannot predetermine its outcome yet are still willing to play, so Laclau and Mouffe can argue their case for radical democracy without assuming it to "trump" any opposition

proposal. In other words, it is the actual proposals they (and others) put forward which must be evaluated and not the conditions of possibility for making any judgment at all.

It is precisely from this sort of position – both critical of the normative *and* deeply normative – that we want to think through current ideas of post-truth and fake news. We want to do so to argue for different ways forward than those that are currently precluded and obscured by dominant political discourses. Doing so is rooted in the firm belief that what is currently at stake is not just a battle over what is true and what is fake. This is an entirely one-sided framing of the problem, and it is precisely this framing that is all too often set by news headlines, public intellectuals, and politicians alike. In our view, reducing the current political moment to a crisis of truthfulness is in itself a deeply political act serving to obscure a whole set of important democratic issues that could be discussed – that *need to be* discussed. This includes questions about how democracies ought to function. What kind of society we want to live in. Who holds power over what resources. What kinds of bodies are allowed to speak. Who are recognized as equals and treated as life worth living. If we can forge even a few intellectual entry points for engaging with these questions during the course of this book, our efforts have not been in vain.

Outline of book

The book is organized in three core parts, the first of which you have already embarked upon. In Part I, *Preparing for the Post-Truth Journey*, we present the tools we use to navigate the complex terrain of post-truth worlds. Spanning three chapters, Part I outlines the aims of the book, its theoretical and methodological foundations, and the state of existing research into fake news, post-truth, and related phenomena.

Part II is called *Into Post-Truth Worlds*. Here, we systematically unpack the ideas, solutions, and problematizations currently conjured up in public discourse across the world. We look at the interventions and anxieties linking democracy to questions of post-truth, fake news, infodemics, and alternative facts, examining the implicit normative ideas about democracy contained in these. In this sense, Part II – which also spans three chapters – contains the main empirical portion of this book. It presents a detailed exploration of the political terrain that is still developing around the state of democracy, truth, and politics.

Part III, named *Out of Post-Truth Worlds,* takes up the mantle from Part II, but shifts gears slightly. Instead of attending to the political worlds currently being constructed, this chapter seeks to critically analyze their premises through the lens of critical and pluralist political philosophy. Doing so, we want to argue that, rather than deepening democratic practices, contemporary post-truth worlds have relied on ideas closely connected to *post-political* and *post-democratic* trajectories. Arguing that democracy is more or less solely about truth, consensus, and rationality, they have served to undermine the voice of the people and popular sovereignty. This is problematic not only because it denies the constitutive role of the people, but also insofar as it can serve to create a self-propelling feedback loop. As a counterproposal to this model, we suggest that ideas offered by radical political philosophers, concerned with deepening democratic institutions and reclaiming these from the grips of the capitalist market, can serve as powerful alternatives. The book ends by arguing that we are currently situated in a democratic moment, what Gramsci (1992) named as *the interregnum*. This is a time in which the old system seems to be failing but no firm model has been devised for the future. We close the book by arguing that such a moment provides an opening for once again contesting the hegemony of capitalism, while working towards more inclusive, democratically open, and just societies. At the very least, this might be the kind of utopia we need to invoke to once again start believing in a better and more democratic future.

References

Ball, J. (2017). *Post-Truth: How Bullshit Conquered the World*. London: Biteback Publishing.

Bastos, M., & Farkas, J. (2019). "Donald Trump is my President!" The Internet Research Agency Propaganda Machine. *Social Media + Society, 5*(3). https://doi.org/10.1177/2056305119865466

d'Ancona, M. (2017). *Post-Truth: The New War on Truth and How to Fight Back*. London: Ebury Press.

Farkas, J. (2019, 25 January). Disguised Propaganda on Social Media: Addressing Democratic Dangers and Solutions. *Brown Journal of World Affairs, 25*(1). http://bjwa.brown.edu/25-1/disguised-propaganda-on-social-media-addressing-democratic-dangers-and-solutions/

Farkas, J., & Bastos, M.T. (2018). IRA Propaganda on Twitter: Stoking Antagonism and Tweeting Local News. In *Proceedings of the 9th Annual International Conference on Social Media and Society*, 281–285.

Farkas, J. & Neumayer, C. (2020a). Disguised Propaganda From Digital to Social Media. In J. Hunsinger, L. Klastrup & M. M. Allen (Eds.), *Second International Handbook of Internet Research* (pp. 707–723). Dordrecht: Springer. https://doi.org/10.1007/978-94-024-1555-1_33

Farkas, J., & Neumayer, C. (2020b). Mimicking News: How the Credibility of an Established Tabloid is Used When Disseminating Racism. *Nordicom Review, 41*(1), 1–17. https://doi.org/10.2478/nor-2020-0001

Farkas, J., & Schou, J. (2018). Fake News as a Floating Signifier: Hegemony, Antagonism and the Politics of Falsehood. *Javnost – The Public, 25*(3), 298–314. https://doi.org/10.1080/13183222.2018.1463047

Farkas, J., Schou, J., & Neumayer, C. (2018a). Cloaked Facebook Pages: Exploring Fake Islamist Propaganda in Social Media. *New Media and Society, 20*(5) 1850–1867. https://doi.org/10.1177/1461444817707759

Farkas, J., Schou, J., & Neumayer, C. (2018b). Platformed Antagonism: Racist Discourses on Fake Muslim Facebook Pages. *Critical Discourse Studies*, *15*(5), 463–480. https://doi.org/10.1080/17405904.2018.1450276

Filibeli, T.E. (Ed.). (2020). *Information Nightmare: Fake News, Manipulation and Post-Truth Politics in the Digital Age*. Berlin: Peter Lang.

Foucault, M. (1984) "What is Enlightenment?" In P. Rabinow (ed.) *The Foucault Reader* (pp. 32–50). Harmondsworth: Penguin.

Ghebreyesus, T.A. (2020, 15 February). *Munich Security Conference*. World Health Organization. www.who.int/director-general/speeches/detail/munich-security-con ference

Gramsci, A. (1992). *Selections from the Prison Notebooks*. London: Lawrence & Wishart.

Gupta, A., Li, H., Farnoush, A., & Jiang, W. (2022). Understanding Patterns of COVID Infodemic: A Systematic and Pragmatic Approach to Curb Fake News. *Journal of Business Research*, *140*, 670–683. https://doi.org/10.1016/j.jbusres.2021.11.032

Habermas, J. (2006). Religion in the Public Sphere. *European Journal of Philosophy*, *14*(1), 1–25. https://doi.org/10.1111/j.1468-0378.2006.00241.x

Hasen, R.L. (2022). *Cheap Speech: How Disinformation Poisons Our Politics – and How to Cure It*. New Haven: Yale University Press.

Held, D. (2006). *Models of Democracy*. Stanford: Stanford University Press.

Henley, J. (2018, 24 April). Global crackdown on fake news raises censorship concerns. *The Guardian*. www.theguardian.com/media/2018/apr/24/global-crackdown-on-fake-news-raises-censorship-concerns

Howard, P.N. (2020). *Lie Machines: How to Save Democracy from Troll Armies, Deceitful Robots, Junk News Operations, and Political Operatives*. New Haven: Yale University Press.

Howarth, D. (2000). *Discourse*. Buckingham: Open University Press.

Human Rights Watch. (2020, 6 May). Ethiopia: Free Speech at Risk Amid Covid-19. *Human Rights Watch*. www.hrw.org/news/2020/05/06/ethiopia-free-speech-risk-amid-covid-19

Human Rights Watch (2021, 11 February). Covid-19 Triggers Wave of Free Speech Abuse. Hrw.Org. www.hrw.org/news/2021/02/11/covid-19-triggers-wave-free-spe ech-abuse

Kakutani, M. (2018). *The Death of Truth: Notes on Falsehood in the Age of Trump*. New York: Tim Duggans Books.

Laclau, E. (1990). *New Reflections omn the Revolution of our Time*. London: Verso.

Laclau, E. (2005). *On Populist Reason*. London: Verso.

Laclau, E., & Mouffe, C. (2014). *Hegemony and Socialist Strategy: Towards a Radical Democratic Politics*. London: Verso.

Macron, E. (2018, 25 April). Address to the U.S. Congress. *CNN*. http://transcripts.cnn.com/TRANSCRIPTS/1804/25/ctw.01.html

Marchart, O. (2007). *Post-Foundational Political Thought: Political Difference in Nancy, Lefort, Badiou and Laclau*. Edinburgh: Edinburgh University Press.

Mouffe, C. (1993). *The Return of the Political*. London: Verso.

Mouffe, C. (2005). *The Democratic Paradox*. London: Verso.

Pedrazzani, A., Maraffi, M., Guglielmi, S., Biolcati, F., Chiesi, A. M., Sani, G. M. D., Ladini, R., Molteni, F., Segatti, P., & Vezzoni, C. (2021). Is Democracy Effective

Against Coronavirus? An Analysis of Citizens' Opinions in Italy. *Partecipazione e Conflitto, 14*(1), 176–201. https://doi.org/10.1285/i20356609v14i1p176

Press Trust of India (2018, 11 April). Fake News Like Cancer, Needs Surgery, Says BJP Leader Subramanian Swamy. *Financial Express.* www.financialexpress.com/india-news/fake-news-like-cancer-needs-surgery-says-bjp-leader-subramanian-swamy/1129137/

Rancière, J. (2014). *Hatred of Democracy*. London: Verso.

Rawlinson, K. (2017, 11 February). Fake News is Killing People's Minds, Says Apple boss Tim Cook. *The Telegraph.* www.theguardian.com/technology/2017/ feb/11/fake-news-is-killing-peoples-minds-says-apple-boss-tim-cook

Schick, N. (2020). *Deep Fakes and the Infocalypse: What You Urgently Need To Know*. London: Monoray.

Stengel, R. (2019). *Information Wars: How We Lost the Global Battle Against Disinformation and What We Can Do About It*. New York: Grove Atlantic.

Taylor, J. (2016, 8 December). "Lives Are At Risk," Hillary Clinton Warns Over Fake News, "Pizzagate." NPR. www.npr.org/2016/12/08/504881478/lives-are-at-risk-clinton-warns-over-fake-news-pizzagate

van der Linden, S. (2023). *Foolproof: Why Misinformation Infects Our Minds and How to Build Immunity*. London: 4th Estate.

2 An expanding field

Approaches, concepts, provocations

Alongside its meteoric rise in public debate, the concept of fake news – and the wide chain of ideas surrounding this term – has become widely adopted in academic research. Indeed, as Freelon and Wells (2020) conclude, fake news and disinformation have rapidly become *"the* defining political communication topic of our time" (p. 145). From being a marginal concept used mainly by scholars studying news parodies (Tandoc et al., 2018), fake news has become a catch-all term used to describe a range of phenomena, including "fabrication, manipulation, propaganda, and advertising" (ibid., p. 141).

As a simple search on Google Scholar shows, "fake news" was mentioned in no less than 34,500 publications in 2022, down from a peak of over 40,000 in 2020 (Google Scholar, 2023c, 2023b). That is more than a 70-fold increase since 2012, where the term only appeared in 462 publications (Google Scholar, 2023a). Figure 2.1 depicts the rise of scholarship into "fake news," "disinformation," "post-truth," and the "infodemic" from 2015 to 2022 (as heuristically probed through Google Scholar). This chart illustrates how rapidly academics have adopted all four concepts as staples in the literature. While "fake news," "disinformation" and "post-truth" rose to rapid prominence after 2016, the idea of the "infodemic" did so following 2019. These dates connect, of course, to important events in newer political history, not least the Brexit referendum in the United Kingdom and election of Donald Trump as 45th President of the United States in 2016 as well as the outbreak of COVID-19 in 2019. These connections will be explored in much more detail in the second part of the book. For now, we simply want to highlight how explosive the interest in fake news has been, with 2020 marking a hitherto peak in scholarly hype, while tens of thousands of texts are still being published to this day. Adding to this, we want to draw attention to the ways in which a whole array of new concepts has continuously been brought to the table in attempts to capture the same phenomena. Indeed, it seems that every so often new and increasingly fanciful terms have been deployed to understand the current situation.

The academic fields that have sprung up around fake news and related concepts have provided plenty of data about new forms of falsehoods,

DOI: 10.4324/9781003434870-3

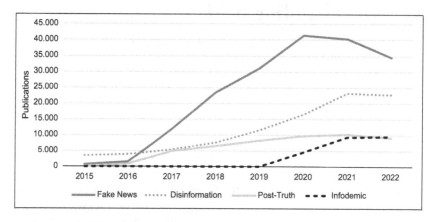

Figure 2.1 Google Scholar results for "fake news," "disinformation," "post-truth," and "infodemic," 2015 to 2022.

Source: Google Scholar (https://scholar.google.com/), retrieved 28 February 2023.

fabrications, and malicious information. Yet, despite thousands of publications, there is still little to no consensus on the precise meaning of notions such as fake news, post-truth, or the infodemic, let alone agreement on the historical and structural foundations of these phenomena. As numerous scholars have pointed out – and as will become clear throughout this chapter – research has all too often tended to view fake news as a distinctly novel phenomenon with little to no historical context or antecedents. In so doing, researchers have tended to smuggle in and haphazardly apply overly universalist and superficial forms of analysis. As Hedrick, Karpf, and Kreiss (2018) conclude: "So many analyses of fake news, Russian fake accounts on Facebook, and bots after the 2016 election have occurred in a vacuum, often ignoring the deeper political, social, and cultural contexts from which they have emerged" (p. 1059). Not only has a lack of contextual engagement hampered our ability to understand and engage with our present political predicament; it has also provided us with poor conceptual as well as practical tools for challenging the present situation. By approaching fake news as a completely new societal threat, scholars have tended to neglect "the deeper challenges to democracy emerging from the structural transformations of the public arena" (Jungherr & Schroeder, 2021, p. 10).

Willingly or not, many of the ideas propelled and intellectually legitimized by research has had such close affinity with those produced by journalists, policymakers, intelligence agencies, and tech giants that it can be difficult to discern where one field stops and another begins. For this reason, it is far from a coincidence that our empirical engagement with post-truth worlds – that is, the effort undertaken in this book to critically engage with the morphing set of normative ideas surrounding the issues of fake news, truth, and democracy – tackles academic research as being *on par* with a host of other fields inhabiting these worlds. Far from neutral observers of reality, academic researchers have been instrumental in laying out the normative coordinates through which our current predicament is so often articulated. To put it simply: scholarship can never simply explain or observe an already assembled world "out there." It is always implicated in producing the very categories and concepts through which the social world is viewed. This has been especially apparent in our present case where many of the concepts (and ensuing hype and fear) deployed by media, journalists, and policymakers have originated in or been promoted by the academic field.

In this chapter, we want to provide a brief yet panoramic overview of the expanding field of research dedicated to understanding post-truth, fake news, and associated phenomena. We do so not only to situate the present enquiry within a wider intellectual backdrop, but also to offer a series of provocations as to how we might grapple with our present democratic moment in other ways than those currently dominating the literature. These provocations are meant to substantiate the need for distinctly different conceptual approaches than the current hegemonic ones. In so doing, it may serve as common intellectual ammunition for all those who – like us – have become increasingly weary of the dominant explanations about the present state of democracy across academic, journalistic, and political thinking.

Starting with a brief introduction to historical concerns around propaganda and manipulation, we first want to showcase how recent scholarly works often echo concerns from the early 20th century, though this is rarely acknowledged or reflected upon. Second, we will highlight how contemporary research follows a historic trend of trying to find an "untainted" or apolitical vocabulary to describe political manipulation and falsehoods. This, we argue, has led to a complex mess of overlapping concepts, each of which have become politically entangled in their own right. Third, and finally, we want to offer four provocations for future research, calling for historical perspectives, epistemic vigilance, critical engagement, and rejection of "magic bullets."

Historical antecedents I: from propaganda to fake news

Long before fake news became an academic buzzword, propaganda had been studied and theorized throughout the 20th century. As noted by Sproule (1997), World War I "popularized the term *propaganda* and made coordinated social influence a matter of general public interest" (p. 22, original emphasis). In the wake of the Great War, journalist and public intellectual, Walter Lippmann, argued that "a revolution" was taking place in (then) contemporary United States. New forms of propaganda, he claimed, was changing society in ways that were "infinitely more significant than any shifting of economic power… . Under the impact of propaganda, not necessarily in the sinister meaning of the word alone, the old constants of our thinking have become variables" (Lippmann, 1922, p. 248). Thanks to the technological rise of mass communication – that is, radio, newspapers, and the telegraph – coupled with intellectual breakthroughs in psychoanalysis, political actors could now *manufacture consent* in new and highly effective ways (Lippmann, 1922). A growing industry of persuasion had emerged that, according to Lippmann (1922), challenged the fundamental assumption that liberal democracy revolves around people's rational participation in public debate and decision-making.

Lippmann was far from alone in holding these ideas. In 1920, psychologist Raymond Dodge argued that, while propaganda had previously been "relatively mild and inoffensive... all that is changed now. Propaganda as the great art of influencing public opinion, seems to be a permanent addition to our social and political liabilities" (p. 241). In line with this sentiment, political scientist Harold Lasswell wrote in 1927 that propaganda had an "ever-present function" in "modern life" due to "the rapid advent of technological changes" (p. 631). As a result of mass media and growing societal complexity, he claimed, "we live among more people than ever, who are puzzled, uneasy, or vexed at the unknown cunning which seems to have duped or degraded them" (Lasswell, 1938, p. 2, originally published in 1927).

Fast forward a hundred years. If we compare the writings of Lippmann, Dodge, and Lasswell to those of present-day scholars, we find many similarities in their descriptions of the state of liberal democracy. According to a myriad of present-day intellectuals, the adoption of new technologies – now in the form of digital media – has "ignited an unprecedented circulation of false information in our society" (Ceron et al., 2021, p. 1) that threatens "people's abilities to know what is true" (Barzilai & Chinn, 2020, p. 2). While manipulation is "not a new phenomenon, the means by which it is spread has changed in both speed and magnitude" (Burkhardt, 2017, p. 2). As a result, democracy has supposedly entered a "'post-truth era' where misinformation abounds, scientific facts are increasingly called into question, and trust in science is being eroded" (Compton et al., 2021, p. 2).

What becomes clear from this brief comparison is that – similar to ideas circulating around a hundred years ago – intellectuals today also warn us that liberal democracy is turning an unprecedented and dangerous corner, as technology gives rise to new forms of mass persuasion and manipulation. What this should tell us, more than anything, is not that the same old thesis has been true all along. Instead, it highlights how that which might seem new and unparalleled often has deep historical roots. Beyond the flashy veneer of current academic buzz, we find intellectual tropes and conceptual interventions that are far from new.

One notable difference between then and now, however, is the vocabulary used. Whereas early 20th century intellectuals primarily debated the role of "propaganda" in modern societies, present-day scholars tend to talk about "fake news," "disinformation," "misinformation," "post-truth," and "infodemics." This change can, on the one hand, be explained by the simple passing of time; languages change and new words come into fashion. On the other hand, it also points to a more significant theoretical point, namely that the continuous production of new academic concepts has in itself been underpinned by a very particular concern: the search for an *untained*, even pure and innocent, concept. This is something we will address in the following.

Historical antecedents II: the search for an untainted concept

In 1928, Edward Bernays – later designated as the "grandfather of public relations" (Davis, 2000, p. 284) – wrote that propaganda was a "perfectly wholesome word, of honest parentage, and with an honorable history" (Bernays, 1928, p. 22). To spread propaganda, Bernays (1928, p. 22) argued, meant to influence "the relations of the public to an enterprise, idea or group," a practice performed daily by politicians, companies, public institutions, and citizens. Propaganda was in itself a neutral endeavor, which could serve noble purposes, such as strengthening trust in government and help the public make informed decisions. On the flipside, propaganda could also be used for more sinister purposes, something that had to be addressed by creating moral guidelines for practitioners and countering bad forms of propaganda with good ones.

Bernays was not alone in defending propaganda as a neutral term (Sproule, 1997). Already in the 1920s, however, this defense was an uphill battle. After World War I, propaganda had quickly come to have "an ominous clang in many minds" (Lasswell, 1938, p. 2, originally published in 1927). In 1926, British politician Lord Ponsonby described propaganda as "the defilement of the human soul [which] is worse than the destruction of the human body" (cited in Taylor, 2003, p. 1). Propaganda had become synonymous with nefarious forms of manipulation – practices that solely eroded the pillars of democracy. This sinister meaning was strengthened during and after World War II (Jowett & O'Donnell, 2015), as propaganda became intimately linked to fascism and Nazism (Taylor, 2003). Eventually, the term primarily became something that political actors would never admit to using themselves but might accuse their opponents of doing (ibid.).

If we once again fast-forward, this time to 2016, fake news quickly became adopted as a ubiquitous concept, used to indicate that "*something*" was "amiss in the digital public sphere" (Creech, 2020, p. 953, original emphasis). Alongside its popularity among scholars and journalists, politicians also started using the term, not only to describe digital threats against democracy, but also to attack perceived political opponents. This strategy was made (in-)famous by Donald Trump who accused critical journalists of spreading or embodying fake news. In response to this development, some scholars began arguing for the abandonment of the term, urging their colleagues to "stop talking about fake news"

(Habgood-Coote, 2018, p. 1033) and instead use "more precise language" (Freelon and Wells, 2020, p. 146). Others argued that academics should "keep talking about fake news... sorting out what is 'essential' to this phenomenon" (Pepp et al., 2022, pp. 471–472).

Despite disagreement, the underlying premise across these academic debates have remained relatively coherent. At its core, debates about the usefulness of "fake news" have revolved around a certain desire to move away from tainted language and instead use clear-cut and objective concepts when trying to distinguish facts from fiction. As mentioned, this desire is nothing new, as earlier scholars also argued for abandoning the negative "baggage" surrounding the term "propaganda" and "start thinking in more objective terms" (Taylor, 2003, p. 2).

As such, the hunt for an untainted concept has a long history and continues to dominate scholarship. Rather than using fake news, some scholars have proposed the term "information disorder," arguing that fake news should be avoided since it is "woefully inadequate to describe the complex phenomena of information pollution" and has been "appropriated by politicians around the world" (Wardle & Derakhshan, 2017, p. 5). Others have proposed the term "junk news," arguing that it is better suited for capturing "the full range of con-spiratorial, sensationalist, extremist, and factually incorrect political news and information" (Howard, 2020, pp. 86–87). Others still have argued for the use of "disinformation" due to its clearer and less political meaning (Freelon & Wells, 2020). Finally, coming full circle, others have encouraged colleagues to instead "diagnose speech as propaganda" (Habgood-Coote, 2018, p. 1051), returning us to the vocabulary of the 20th century.

The problem with the search for a clear, neutral, and apolitical alternative to fake news is that there is fundamentally no way to engage in distinctions between societal truths and falsehoods without also engaging with historical and political struggles. There is no way to arrive at an "untainted" concept that is not already part of political attacks and accusations or that will not become so in the future. Instead, the search for an apolitical concept only creates a continuous stream of new, overlapping terms, the next of which always seems just around the corner.

When looking at the etymology of prevalent terms in public and academic discourse, this pattern becomes painfully clear. Disinformation, for example, derives from the Russian word *dezinformácija* (*дезинформация*), which was used by the KGB (Merriam-Webster, n.d.). According to some prominent accounts, the term was coined by Joseph Stalin himself who picked it due to its French-sounding origins, which was useful for associating the West with nefarious manipulation tactics (Pacepa & Rychlak, 2013).

The notion of the "Big lie," which has also been used by both scholars and journalists in connection to fake news and the post-truth era (Albrecht, 2023; Hasen, 2022; Kellner, 2018; Wodak, 2022), was originally coined by Adolf Hitler in *Mein Kampf* (*große Lüge* in German). Hitler used this term to accuse Jews of being responsible for Germany's defeat in World War I (Cavanagh, 2022; Peters, 2018). Drawing on anti-semitic conspiracy theories, such as the *Protocols of The Elders of Zion*, Hitler accused Jewish people of spreading lies so colossal that people would believe them due to their inability to imagine anyone engaging in such outrageous forms of deception (Cavanagh, 2022).

What these histories reveal is that, whether we talk about "propaganda," "fake news," "disinformation," or the "Big lie," these terms all have deeply political histories and troubled legacies. Every new term will almost automatically become involved in political struggle. Rather than trying to circumvent such political dimensions by using new "objective" definitions, we argue that the practice of studying manipulation and falsehoods needs to be embraced as a fundamentally *political* one. For us, this means studying how and why different actors mobilize propaganda, fake news, and disinformation – as both overlapping phenomena and contested signifiers – in wider political projects and historical battlegrounds. It urges us to understand the conditions of production and circulations of these concepts. Finally, it forces us to critically reflect upon how our own scholarly work is always already part of social formations used to legitimize and uphold specific relations of power.

The current state of fake news research

When probing into contemporary academic literature on fake news, one quickly faces a peculiar paradox: despite thousands of recent publications, few studies address the political entanglements, legacies, and histories of fake news within wider societal struggles (Egelhofer & Lecheler, 2019; Wright, 2021). Indeed, academics often neglect the political signification of fake news entirely, focusing on the topic as a new form of universal *content,* rather than an iteration of existing forms of manipulation or as a new form of political *discourse.* Part of the reason for this, it seems to us, is that research into fake news and post-truth, although spanning a range of different academic disciplines, has relied on strikingly similar premises and narratives about truth, democracy, and technology.

As we will elaborate upon later in this book, a dominant assumption across academic engagements with fake news and post-truth has been that democracy has entered a completely new "misinformation age" (O'Connor & Weatherall, 2019), "post-truth era" (Visvizi & Lytras, 2019), "post-factual state" (McIntyre, 2018, p. 74), or "infodemic crisis" (Artieri, 2023, p. 22). The tacit assumption is that we now live in the aftermath of an epochal rift in the fabric of democracy where falsehoods spread "like wildfire across the globe" (Carson, 2020, p. 146) and citizens are trapped in "political bubbles on the attention market [that] may also be described as a collective loss of reality" (Hendricks & Vestergaard, 2019, p. 44). Civilization has crossed a tipping point and stepped into a brand-new reality, academics have often assumed, making historical perspectives more or less irrelevant since they cannot explain the *novelty* or *universality* of our contemporary moment. As a result of these assumptions, academics have tended to neglect historical and situated perspectives, opting primarily for trying to flesh out the "proper" meaning of our new epoch as well as developing new methods for detecting, classifying, and potentially removing "bad content" and "nudging people to reason" (Effron & Helgason, 2022, p. 4).

Thankfully, some critical research has begun to emerge, dedicated to "moving beyond a narrow focus on fake news" (Wright, 2021, p. 645) and engaging with "the phenomenon as a political one" (Monsees, 2023, p. 163). This work examines the political and historical signification of fake news and related phenomena in geo-political contexts spanning Europe (Egelhofer et al., 2021; Monsees, 2020), Africa (Tully, 2022; Wasserman, 2020), the Middle East (Dehghan & Glazunova, 2021), Asia (Lim, 2020; Neo, 2020; Rauchfleisch et al., 2022), and North America (Bratich, 2020; Creech, 2020; Marwick et al., 2021; Mejia et al., 2018). What this research shares is a focus on the historical and discursive legacies and implications of our supposed post-truth moment. In so doing, it has helped in addressing how both contemporary and past knowledge gatekeepers and centers of power have leveraged notions of propaganda, fake news, and so forth to legitimize certain political outcomes and assert dominance over who gets to act as a truth-sayer. We see this book as a contribution to this emergent critical field.

Four provocations for future research

With this panoramic overview of the state of research in mind, we want to offer four provocations for future research. These directly inform our analytical approach and serve to showcase how this book is as much an empirical excavation as it is a theoretical and political intervention. These provocations are both meant to be a critique of the current state of affairs and a signpost for how we might do things differently. We deliberately frame these as *provocations* so as to signal that they are intended as bold and expressive statements, outlining a set of overarching problems that (to our mind) haunt contemporary research. On close scrutiny, there are always more nuances to things. There are always academics doing otherwise. As such, the aim here is not to claim that existing research has all but failed – far from it.

As we have highlighted throughout this chapter – and will continue to do in the rest of this book – we are already seeing a proliferation of approaches that are much better suited for undertaking the task of understanding fake news than those dominating the field just a few years ago. Still, the large majority of research remains underpinned by conceptual apparatuses, theoretical assumptions, and methodological approaches that we find problematic and – in the end – normatively risky.

Provocation 1: history needs to be brought to the forefront

In labeling fake news and post-truth as distinctly novel phenomena, researchers have all too often ignored the complex historical legacies of political manipulation in liberal democracies. They have tended to neglect how governments and corporations throughout the 20th century have continuously engaged in – what used to be called – propaganda to legitimize political ends, whether this be wars against enemy "Others" or non-action against corporate harms (e.g., tobacco and fossil fuel). By not engaging with the legacy of these strategies throughout the history of modern liberal democracies, contemporary fake news researchers still "might not even know what the real problem is" (Monsees, 2023, p. 163), since what is proclaimed to be distinctly new often turns out to have clear historical precedents.

As Professor of History, Sophia Rosenfeld, writes in her book, *Democracy and Truth: A Short History*, bringing history to the forefront reminds us that "truth and its opposites are always implicated in questions of power – and thus truth is never fully divorced from politics and social conflict" (Rosenfeld, 2019, p. 20). Instead of assuming that truth used to be a shared, apolitical common good within liberal democracies, going back in time allows us to ask critical questions about who has benefitted from existing truth-telling regimes and who have historically been marginalized and excluded from participating in knowledge production and supposedly "rational" debate (Chambers et al., 2004; Forde & Bedingfield, 2021; Mejia et al., 2018). Doing so brings to the foreground how going back to the "good old times" of truth-saying is not a universal cure for anything. If we wish to strengthen democracy, we need to understand and engage with how democratic values, such as participation, collectivity, and egalitarianism, have been continuously shaped by relations of power. We need to be attentive to how our present moment has deep historical roots that have shaped and continue to shape contemporary institutions. Moreover, we need to recognize that concepts in and of themselves have complex histories: they are formed over time through highly layered processes of meaning-making. Deploying particular concepts thus requires us to exhibit epistemic vigilance throughout our academic practice.

Provocation 2: epistemic vigilance must be brought back into the table

Research on fake news, disinformation, and associated phenomena has tended to work in close proximity to the work of journalists, policymakers, tech companies, and other parts of society, with ideas crossing the symbolic borders of each field at often breakneck speed. Not only that, academia has also tended to uncritically overtake conceptual narratives and empirical concerns found in other domains with little to no regard for the historical and political context of their emergence. What ought to be an *object of analytical inquiry* has all too often become *an analytical objective*. Phrased somewhat differently: it seems to us that research has tended to uncritically accept and absorb narratives and vocabularies deployed by the very domains it ought to critically study.

This problem is far from new. In *The Rules of Sociological Method,* one of the founding texts of sociology, Emile Durkheim (1982, originally published in 1895) precisely warned against explanations that do not break with the inherited common sense, instead uncritically overtaking the *prenotions* circulating at any particular point in time. Taking his cue directly from this exposition, Pierre Bourdieu has also, throughout his work, argued for the need for epistemological vigilance, so as to go beyond borrowing the *folk concepts* and *spontaneous sociologies* easily offered to researchers from the sites they are studying. In *The Craft of Sociology: Epistemological Preliminaries,* Bourdieu, alongside Jean-Claude Chamboredon and Jean-Claude Passeron, argues that "epistemological vigilance is particularly necessary in the social sciences, where the separation between everyday opinion and scientific discourse is more blurred than elsewhere" (1991, p. 13). Extending and updating these ideas, sociologist Loïc Wacquant (2022) has recently provided an important conceptual study of the rise and fall of the idea of the "underclass." Doing so, he offers a critique of what he deems as *normalized empiricism*: a form of social science that "borrows its categories unfiltered from the social world, it is driven by data collection and mining, and, paradoxically, it is maximally distant from the phenomenon" (2022, p. 7). This critique is, he furthermore notes, "a *clarion call against epistemic promiscuity* – the tendency of scholars to deploy a mix of instruments of knowledge and criteria of validation circulating in different universes (science, journalism, philanthropy, politics and public policy, everyday life), without duly checking their origins, semantic span, logical coherence, and the social unconscious they carry" (p. 9, original emphasis).

To our mind, researchers seeking to understand our contemporary democratic moment ought to take careful notes from these ideas. The point here is not to say that scientific discourse is necessarily more true, pure, and objective (in whatever sense of these words one prefers); but that one cannot have any hope of understanding, let alone explaining, for example, the rise of fake news and post-truth if one blindly imports these concepts as if they were neutral, ahistorical, and unbound to particular conditions of production. Concepts are never merely neutral. They have histories that are deeply entangled in power relations and politics. Epistemic vigilance is thus imminently a call for conceptual *reflexivity*, urging us as researchers to not only be aware of the ideas we import into our own discourse, but also to acknowledge the deeply normative element involved in all conceptual work as such. The work undertaken in this book is precisely a contribution to such an endeavor, diving into the conceptual intricacies of contemporary post-truth worlds.

Provocation 3: the magic bullets must be unloaded

When studying fake news and post-truth, researchers have often assumed – implicitly or explicitly – that false information and manipulation work like "magic bullets" that are shot into the brains of passive audiences. As Associate Professor Alice Marwick (2018) notes, this type of assumption has a long history in public and academic discourse around media technologies, despite being both empirically unsubstantiated and thoroughly criticized for decades. When talking about fake news today, academics and public intellectuals often imply that "people – the audience – make up an undifferentiated mass; that media affects all people the same way; and that it has the impact that the creators intended" (Marwick, 2018, p. 482). This is seen in both the ways in which the post-truth era is framed as a crisis and in research designs seeking to understand its implications.

Many prominent studies of the "effects" of fake news and post-truth turn out to simply be studies of what researchers have known for decades; namely that information does not work like a magic bullet. Scholars have, for example, exposed people to false headlines about COVID-19 vaccines and found (to no surprise) that this does not suddenly change their inclinations towards getting a vaccine (de Saint Laurent et al., 2022). Others have exposed US citizens to political messages from "trolls" on Twitter and found that this does not suddenly turn liberals into conservatives or vice versa (Bail et al., 2019). Of course, reaffirming old conclusions in new studies has its merits. Still, the problem with much contemporary research is that, by relying on a magic bullet theory of information, many studies cannot conclude much about how manipulation actually works. By being trapped within the confines of the magic bullet, such research can only affirm how manipulation (or opinion formation in general) does *not* work. Breaking free of these self-imposed constrictions would require situated, structural, and longitudinal approaches that are currently underrepresented.

What is notable and also slightly discouraging about much of the current research into fake news is that knowledge about the limits of "magic bullet experiments" predate this scholarship by decades. Already in the 1960s, French sociologist Jacques Ellul (1965) criticized experiments into – what was then termed – propaganda, arguing that short-term exposure studies were "completely useless to draw conclusions from… about the efficacy of real propaganda" (p. 266). The main problem, Ellul (1965) argued, is that people's minds simply cannot be significantly altered by being exposed to a few pieces of propaganda. By trying to isolate the effects of manipulation, exposure studies take place under conditions that "are the very opposite of propaganda," occurring "in a vacuum" with "no crowd effect, no psychological tension, no interaction of individuals caught in a mass and exciting each other" (p. 265). In this way, we can, once again, see how a lack of historical engagement has often limited the state of fake news scholarship, paving the way for a reproduction of errors and false starts of the past.

Provocation 4: fake news solutionism needs critical engagement.

As a final provocation, we want to highlight the conspicuous lack of critical research into the political implications of contemporary discourses around fake news and post-truth. Whether it be so-called anti-fake news laws, intelligence agency task forces, private–public partnerships, or social media company initiatives, millions of citizens across the world are experiencing wide-ranging and ongoing political consequences of prominent "solutions" to fake news. Still, only few researchers have looked into their ramifications and implications for democracy and human life (for notable exceptions, see Cunliffe-Jones et al., 2021; Lim, 2020; Neo, 2020).

The urge for critical research is not a simple one – not least because it forces us to define what we mean by critical research in the first. As is well known, critical research comes in many forms, theoretical as well as methodological. Our point here is not to define how and in what ways one ought to do proper critical research. Much more modestly, we want to suggest that there has been a distinct lack of research interested in how the concrete measurements being rolled out across many countries in order to combat misinformation and fake news have had a very real impact on citizens. There has been an almost complete shortage of scholarship interested in how deeply sedimented forms of power – economic, legal, and otherwise – have been imbricated in the production of contemporary discourses that not only describe the world, but also have material consequences for human co-habitation.

In many countries, governments have directly used the fake news debate to legitimize measures previously labeled as undemocratic, but which are now "construed as aligned with global democratic norms" (Neo, 2020, p. 1919). These developments have not only remained underexplored in research, but – as we will unpack later in this book – have even been legitimized by scholars.

Critical scholarly engagement, then, is in our view tantamount for understanding our contemporary moment and imagining other potential solutions. One should not accept the epistemological mind-game set up by too much research, claiming that unless one has technical solutions to proper political problems, one should not criticize the status quo. Nor should we accept the idea that discursive research, concerned with unpacking the formation of meaning, cannot take a normative approach to contemporary issues without undermining itself. It is a completely false contradiction, as we will explore further in the coming chapter.

Summing up and moving closer to our journey

Conducting research on contemporary issues is always interlaced with a series of difficult choices, particularly when the issues under scrutiny are politically charged and fiercely debated. Nowhere has this been more apparent than when looking at the present research on democracy, fake news, misinformation, and related phenomena. In the wake of pressing political debates, a whole array of scholars have hastened to the staunch defense of democracy. Yet, while armed with new and shiny concepts, one more fanciful and undertheorized than the other, some important components seem to have been lost along the way. Not only has the complex history and antecedents to our present moment tended to be almost completely forgotten; research has also tended to overtake (or be overtaken by) the very things it ought to explain. It has taken at face value that democracy is under siege by fake news and that Truth (with a capital T) has waned in the process. To our mind, this has left us open to conceptual blinkers and given very little intellectual ammunition for engaging with our democratic practices, ideals, and institutions in any meaningful way.

One of our key motivations for writing this book has been to intervene in the present state of affairs – in academic research as well as wider political discourses – and to carve out alternative ways of thinking about the state and future of democracy. In this endeavor, we are thankfully not alone. We are part of an emergent – and hopefully growing – critical line of scholarship. With the present set of provocations in mind, we turn in the next chapter to how we approach the project undertaken in this book – both methodologically, theoretically, and ontologically. Our claim is that post-foundationalist discourse theory provides us with an important backpack of tools that we can use to explore and carve out the contours of post-truth worlds.

References

Albrecht, M.M. (2023). *Trumping the Media: Politics and Democracy in the Post-Truth Era*. London: Bloombury Academic.

Artieri, G.B. (2023). Infodemic Disorder: Covid-19 and Post-Truth. In G. La Rocca, M.-E. Carignan, & G.B. Artieri (Eds.), *Infodemic Disorder: Covid-19 Coping Strategies in Europe, Canada and Mexico* (pp. 15–30). Cham: Palgrave Macmillan.

Bail, C.A., Guay, B., Maloney, E., Combs, A., Hillygus, D.S., Merhout, F., Freelon, D., & Volfovsky, A. (2019). Assessing the Russian Internet Research Agency's Impact on the Political Attitudes and Behaviors of American Twitter Users in Late 2017. *PNAS, 117*(1), 243–250. https://doi.org/https://doi.org/10.1073/pnas.1906420116

Barzilai, S., & Chinn, C.A. (2020). A Review of Educational Responses to the "Post-Truth" Condition: Four Lenses on "Post-Truth" Problems. *Educational Psychologist, 55*(3), 107–119. https://doi.org/10.1080/00461520.2020.1786388

Bernays, E.L. (1928). *Propaganda*. New York: Horace Liverlight.

Bourdieu, P., Chamboredon, J-C., & Passeron, J-C. (1991). *The Craft of Sociology: Epistemological Preliminaries*. Berlin: Walter de Gruyter.

Bratich, J. (2020). Civil Society Must Be Defended: Misinformation, Moral Panics, and Wars of Restoration. *Communication, Culture & Critique, 13*(3), 311–322. https://doi.org/10.1093/ccc/tcz041

Burkhardt, J.M. (2017). Combating Fake News in the Digital Age. *Library Technology Reports, 52*(8), 5–33. www.journals.ala.org/index.php/ltr/issue/viewFile/662/423

Carson, A. (2020). *Investigative Journalism, Democracy and the Digital Age.* London: Routledge.

Cavanagh, E.D. (2022). Countering The Big Lie: The Role Of The Courts In The Post-Truth World. *Cornell Law Review, 107,* 64–94. www.cornelllawreview.org/2022/06/26/countering-the-big-lie-the-role-of-the-courts-in-the-post%E2%80%91truth-world/

Ceron, W., de-Lima-Santos, M.F., & Quiles, M.G. (2021). Fake News Agenda in the Era of COVID-19: Identifying Trends Through Fact-Checking Content. *Online Social Networks and Media, 21,* 1–14, https://doi.org/10.1016/j.osnem.2020.100116

Chambers, D., Steiner, L., & Fleming, C. (2004). *Women and Journalism.* London: Routledge.

Compton, J., van der Linden, S., Cook, J., & Basol, M. (2021). Inoculation Theory in the Post-Truth Era: Extant Findings and New Frontiers for Contested Science, Misinformation, and Conspiracy Theories. *Social and Personality Psychology Compass, 15*(6), 1–16. https://doi.org/10.1111/spc3.12602

Creech, B. (2020). Fake News and the Discursive Construction of Technology Companies' Social Power. *Media, Culture & Society, 42*(6), 952–968. https://doi.org/10.1177/0163443719899801

Cunliffe-Jones, P., Diagne, A., Finlay, A., & Schiffrin, A. (2021). Bad Law – Legal and Regulatory Responses To Misinformation In Sub-Saharan Africa 2016–2020. In P. Cunliffe-Jones, A. Diagne, A. Finlay, & A. Schiffrin (Eds.), *Misinformation Policy in Sub-Saharan Africa: From Laws and Regulations to Media Literacy* (pp. 105–218). London: University of Westminster Press.

Davis, A. (2000). Public relations, business news and the reproduction of corporate elite power. *Journalism, 1*(3), 282–304. https://doi.org/10.1177/146488490000100301

de Saint Laurent, C., Murphy, G., Hegarty, K., & Greene, C.M. (2022). Measuring the effects of misinformation exposure and beliefs on behavioural intentions: a COVID-19 vaccination study. *Cognitive Research: Principles and Implications, 7*(1), 1–19. https://doi.org/10.1186/s41235-022-00437-y

Dehghan, E., & Glazunova, S. (2021). "Fake news" Discourses: An exploration of Russian and Persian Tweets. *Journal of Language and Politics, 20*(5), 741–760. https://doi.org/10.1075/jlp.21032.deh

Dodge, R. (1920). The Psychology of Propaganda. *Religious Education: The official journal of the Religious Education Association, 15*(5), 241–252. https://doi.org/10.1080/0034408200150502

Durkheim, E. (1982). *The Rules of Sociological Method.* Washington: The Free Press.

Effron, D.A., & Helgason, B.A. (2022). The Moral Psychology of Misinformation: Why We Excuse Dishonesty in a Post-Truth World. *Current Opinion in Psychology, 47,* 1–6. https://doi.org/10.1016/j.copsyc.2022.101375

Egelhofer, J.L., Aaldering, L., & Lecheler, S. (2021). Delegitimizing the Media? Analyzing Politicians' Media Criticism on Social Media. *Journal of Language and Politics, 20*(5), 653–675. https://doi.org/10.1075/jlp.20081.ege

Egelhofer, J.L., & Lecheler, S. (2019). Fake News as a Two-Dimensional Phenomenon: A Framework and Research Agenda. *Annals of the International Communication Association, 43*(2), 97–116. https://doi.org/10.1080/23808985.2019.1602782

Ellul, J. (1965). *Propaganda: The Formation of Men's Attitudes*. New York: Vintage Books.

Forde, K.R., & Bedingfield, S. (2021). *Journalism and Jim Crow: White Supremacy and the Black Struggle for a New America*. Champaign: University of Illinois Press.

Freelon, D., & Wells, C. (2020). Disinformation as Political Communication. *Political Communication, 37*(2), 145–156. https://doi.org/10.1080/10584609.2020.1723755

Google Scholar. (2023a). *"Fake News," 2012–2012*. Google Scholar. https://scholar.google.com/scholar?q=%22fake+news%22&hl=en&as_sdt=0%2C5&as_ylo=2012&as_yhi=2012

Google Scholar. (2023b). *"Fake News," 2020–2020*. Google Scholar. https://scholar.google.com/scholar?q=%22fake+news%22&hl=en&as_sdt=0%2C5&as_ylo=2020&as_yhi=2020

Google Scholar. (2023c). *"Fake News," 2022–2022*. Google Scholar. https://scholar.google.com/scholar?hl=en&as_sdt=0%2C5&as_ylo=2022&as_yhi=2022&q=%22fake+news%22&btnG=

Habgood-Coote, J. (2018). Stop Talking About Fake News! *Inquiry: An Interdisciplinary Journal of Philosophy, 62*(9–10), 1033–1065. https://doi.org/10.1080/0020174X.2018.1508363

Hasen, R. L. (2022). *Cheap Speech: How Disinformation Poisons Our Politics – and How to Cure It*. New Haven: Yale University Press.

Hedrick, A., Karpf, D., & Kreiss, D. (2018). The Earnest Internet vs. the Ambivalent Internet. *International Journal of Communication, 12*, 1057–1064. https://ijoc.org/index.php/ijoc/article/view/8736

Hendricks, V.F., & Vestergaard, M. (2019). *Reality Lost: Markets of Attention, Misinformation and Manipulation*. Cham: Springer Open.

Howard, P.N. (2020). *Lie Machines: How to Save Democracy from Troll Armies, Deceitful Robots, Junk News Operations, and Political Operatives*. New Haven: Yale University Press.

Jowett, G.S., & O'Donnell, V. (2015). *Propaganda and Persuasion* (Sixth Edition). London: SAGE Publications.

Jungherr, A., & Schroeder, R. (2021). Disinformation and the Structural Transformations of the Public Arena: Addressing the Actual Challenges to Democracy. *Social Media and Society, 7*(1). https://doi.org/10.1177/2056305121988928

Kellner, D. (2018). Donald Trump and the Politics of Lying. In M.A. Peters, S. Rider, M. Hyvönen, & T. Besley (Eds.), *Post-Truth, Fake News: Viral Modernity & Higher Education* (pp. 89–100). Singapore: Springer.

Lasswell, H.D. (1927). The Theory of Political Propaganda. *The American Political Science Review, 21*(3), 627–631. https://doi.org/10.2307/1945515

Lasswell, H.D. (1938). *Propaganda technique in the World War*. New York: Peter Smith.

Lim, G. (2020). *Securitize/Counter – Securitize: The Life and Death of Malaysia's Anti-Fake News Act*. Data & Society. https://datasociety.net/library/securitize-counter-securitize

Lippmann, W. (1922). *Public Opinion*. New York: Harcourt, Brace and Company.

Marwick, A. (2018). Why Do People Share Fake News? A Sociotechnical Model of Media Effects. *Georgetown Law Technology Review, 2*(2), 95474–95512. https://doi.org/10.1177/1464884917730217

Marwick, A., Kuo, R., Jones Cameron, S., & Weigel, M. (2021). *Critical Disinformation Studies: A Syllabus*. Center for Information, Technology, and Public Life (CITAP). The University of North Carolina at Chapel Hill. https://citap.unc.edu/critical-disinfo

McIntyre, L. (2018). *Post-Truth*. Cambridge, MA: MIT Press.

Mejia, R., Beckermann, K., & Sullivan, C. (2018). White Lies: A Racial History of the (Post)truth. *Communication and Critical/Cultural Studies*, *15*(2), 109–126. https://doi.org/10.1080/14791420.2018.1456668

Merriam-Webster. (n.d.). *Disinformation*. Merriam-Webster.com. Accessed April 24, 2023, from www.merriam-webster.com/dictionary/disinformation

Monsees, L. (2020). "A War Against Truth" – Understanding the Fake News Controversy. *Critical Studies on Security*, *8*(2), 116–129. https://doi.org/10.1080/21624887.2020.1763708

Monsees, L. (2023). Information Disorder, Fake News and the Future of Democracy. *Globalizations*, *20*(1), 153–168. https://doi.org/10.1080/14747731.2021.1927470

Neo, R. (2020). A Cudgel of Repression: Analysing State Instrumentalisation of the "Fake News" Label in Southeast Asia. *Journalism*, *23*(9), 1919–1938. https://doi.org/10.1177/1464884920984060

O'Connor, C., & Weatherall, J.O. (2019). *The Misinformation Age: How False Beliefs Spread*. New Haven: Yale University Press.

Pacepa, M., & Rychlak, R.J. (2013). *Disinformation: Former Spy Chief Reveals Secret Strategies for Undermining Freedom, Attacking Religion, and Promoting Terrorism*. New York: WND Books.

Pepp, J., Michaelson, E., & Sterken, R. (2022). Why we should keep talking about fake news. *Inquiry: An Interdisciplinary Journal of Philosophy*, *65*(4), 471–487. https://doi.org/10.1080/0020174X.2019.1685231

Peters, M.A. (2018). Truth and Truth-Telling in the Age of Trump. *Educational Philosophy and Theory*, *50*(11), 1001–1007. https://doi.org/10.1080/00131857.2017.1376510

Rauchfleisch, A., Tseng, T.-H., Kao, J.-J., & Liu, Y.-T. (2022). Taiwan's Public Discourse About Disinformation: The Role of Journalism, Academia, and Politics. *Journalism Practice*. Advance online publication. https://doi.org/10.1080/17512786.2022.2110928

Rosenfeld, S. (2019). *Democracy and Truth: A Short History*. Philadelphia: University of Pennsylvania Press.

Sproule, M.J. (1997). *Propaganda and Democracy: The American Experience of Media and Mass Persuasion*. Cambridge: Cambridge University Press.

Tandoc, E.C., Lim, Z.W., & Ling, R. (2018). Defining "Fake News": A typology of scholarly definitions. *Digital Journalism*, *6*(2), 137–153. https://doi.org/10.1080/21670811.2017.1360143

Taylor, P.M. (2003). *Munitions of the Mind: A History of Propaganda from the Ancient World to the Present Era*. Manchester: Manchester University Press.

Tully, M. (2022). Responses to Misinformation Examining the Kenyan Context. In H. Wasserman & D. Madrid-Morales (Eds.), *Disinformation in the Global South* (pp. 179–192). Hoboken: John Wiley & Sons.

Visvizi, A., & Lytras, M.D. (Eds.). (2019). *Politics and Technology in the Post-Truth Era*. Bingley: Emerald Publishing.

Wacquant, L. (2022). *The Invention of the "Underclass": A Study in the Politics of Knowledge*. London: Polity.

Wardle, C., & Derakhshan, H. (2017). Information Disorder: Toward an interdisciplinary framework for research and policy making. *Report to the Council of Europe*, 108. https://rm.coe.int/information-disorder-toward-an-interdisciplinary-framework-for-researc/168076277c

Wasserman, H. (2020). Fake News from Africa: Panics, Politics and Paradigms. *Journalism*, *21*(1), 3–16. https://doi.org/10.1177/1464884917746861

Wodak, R. (2022). Shameless Normalization as a Result of Media Control: The Case of Austria. *Discourse and Society*, *33*(6), 788–804. https://doi.org/10.1177/0957926522 1095419

Wright, S. (2021). Discourses of Fake News. *Journal of Language and Politics*, *20*(5), 641–652. https://doi.org/10.1075/jlp.21058.wri

3 Political theory in post-factual times

To enter into contemporary post-truth worlds, we need to bring the proper equipment and gear. We do not necessarily need an already established map of where we are going. Indeed, what we are trying to do in this book is precisely to enter into still unknown terrain. Be that as it may, we do need to bring a conceptual and ontological backpack to be able to navigate the territory. How are we to understand and engage with contemporary discourses on truth, democracy, and politics? And how can we begin to make sense of the normative ideas contained therein? In an attempt to grapple with these questions, this chapter presents a set of key analytical tools for engaging with contemporary discourses in and around questions of post-truth, fake news, and democracy. It does so not by outlining a series of strong concepts that we then more or less mechanically apply to the situation at hand. Instead, we opt for a lighter approach, focusing on how we might make sense of and interpret specific political struggles and forms of meaning. The purpose of this chapter, then, is to lay out a series of concepts for unpacking and engaging with the scenery of contemporary post-truth worlds. While the link between this conceptual backpack and the object of our analysis might not seem obvious at first, its importance will hopefully become clear as the book progresses. The chapter proceeds in three main steps. We start out by presenting the main theoretical resource drawn on in this book, namely post-Marxist discourse theory, particularly in its post-foundationalist variant developed by Laclau and Mouffe (2014, see also Laclau, 1990; Mouffe, 2005; Marchart, 2007, 2018). In our description of this work, we will emphasize its relational focus, outlining how it is concerned with understanding the ways in which social reality is constructed through hegemonic struggles. Based on these ideas, we will then dive into a discussion of discourse theory and its relation to the proclaimed post-truth moment of our time. What does it mean, we ask, to analyze and engage with questions of truth in our present era? What kind of normative yardstick (or lack thereof) are we working with in this study? Finally, we present some methodological remarks, outlining how we have mapped contemporary post-truth worlds. Doing so, we describe how we collected our archive of empirical material that includes media articles, academic articles,

DOI: 10.4324/9781003434870-4

books, policy initiatives, and political speeches. We also reflect on some of the inherent tensions involved in understanding post-truth worlds through such an approach. Rather than pretending that there is any sort of finality to our account, we instead want to foreground its contingencies and limitations. All of this sets the scene for our travel both into and out of post-truth worlds in Parts II and III of this book.

Discourse theory and its development

Our approach takes its central theoretical concerns from the work of post-Marxist scholars Ernesto Laclau and Chantal Mouffe – or what has been dubbed the Essex School of Discourse Analysis (Townshend, 2003). In doing so, we draw on what has been labeled *post-foundational political thought* (Marchart, 2007, 2018; Marttila, 2016), which attempts to grasp the political signification of meaning without relying on essentialist or universalistic assumptions about the constitution of Society, Humanity, Nature, or Truth. In 1985, Laclau and Mouffe published their much-debated work *Hegemony and Socialist Strategy* (Laclau & Mouffe, 2014). Causing both controversy and heated discussion, this book sought to overcome the fairly rigid economic determinism and class essentialism still haunting parts of (European) critical theory at the time (Sim, 2000). It did so by synthesizing key insights from a wealth of (then) contemporary currents, including figures such as Derrida, Gramsci, Lacan, and Althusser. Offering a way out of the economistic or class-centric impasse at the time, Laclau and Mouffe sought to describe social reality as a continuously developing field of hegemonic struggles. Such struggles, they maintained, revolve around the con-struction and fixation of discourses: that is, what they took to be particular ways of not only representing social reality but making it come into being as such. Laclau and Mouffe described social reality as the outcome of ongoing articu-latory practices. Thinking through relationships in this way also means that no container, such as "Society," "Economy," or "Class," can explain or encapsulate *all* social relations. Society is not a closed totality from which all other relations can be deduced. Indeed, society itself represents an "impossible object of ana-lysis," as it is always "overflowed by a surplus of meaning" (Howarth, 2000, p. 103).

Leaving behind fixed explanatory containers – seemingly capable of describing all social relations with little regard for local, situated, and embodied practices – means dispensing with any ideas of history as a progressive unfolding of a closed systemic logic. Social relations constitute an antagonistic battle-ground where concrete and historical relationships of power, coercion, and con-sent play out. These relationships are contingent in the sense that, given other historical circumstances, they could have been otherwise. Yet, they are not arbi-trary insofar as they rely on particular historical developments taking place over time, making certain ways of ordering relationships more probable than others.

To us, Laclau and Mouffe's work provides a productive confrontation with fixed ideas about how to explain and interpret human existence and co-habitation. Laclau and Mouffe aim to fundamentally destabilize and question any and all concepts, particularly those claiming to be neutral, universal, and essential. The radical challenge they pose is the following: if we cannot assume there is any such thing as, for example, a Society, Economy, or (transcendental) Subject, then how can we go about describing social and political ordering? While today some of their arguments may seem less controversial than in the 1980s, they still ask us to leave behind much of the conceptual baggage from research on democracy and politics. We cannot assume that democracy, for example, has any substantial or essential meaning. Instead, we need to dive into the concrete struggles through which any democracy is understood, constructed, and institutionally reproduced. We need to understand the specific ways any such thing as democracy has developed in the first place.

Since the 1980s, both Laclau and Mouffe have published extensively on a variety of topics. Up until his death in 2014, Laclau honed in on issues of populism, subjectivity, and politics, developing (what had then become known as) *discourse theory* as a conceptual and theoretical enterprise (Laclau, 1990, 2005, 2014). Mouffe, meanwhile, continues to tackle questions of democracy, pluralism, and political change, not least in her work on radical democracy and agonistic pluralism (Mouffe, 1993, 2005, 2013, 2018). At the same time, a veritable school has developed around Laclau (and Mouffe), as prominent scholars like David Howarth, Jason Glyson, Aletta Norval and Yannis Stavrakakis (amongst others) have continued the intellectual project begun in the 1980s in exciting and highly original ways.[1]

For our present purposes, one of the most important conversations developing from their work centers on the issue of *post-foundationalism*. In the mid-2000s, political philosopher Oliver Marchart (2007) pushed the philosophical coordinates established by the Essex School more or less to their logical conclusion. What Marchart suggested, not least in his 2007 book *Post-Foundational Political Thought*, was that, from Laclau's work, a highly original and radical form of post-foundationalist political thought could be established. This post-foundationalist approach, he demonstrated, places contingency at the core of social reality and our experience of it. It does so to suggest that there is no ultimate or final ground from which the world can be deduced or instituted: there is no principle that determines how and in what ways relations and the worlds we inhabit take form. Post-foundationalism thus offers an alternative to the false choice of either foundationalism (the reduction of all relations to singular principles) or anti-foundationalism (the claim that no such principles can be established at all).

For Marchart, the notion of foundationalism is best understood as a kind of umbrella term. It is a way of capturing a particular premise or underlying claim found in some parts of social theory and political philosophy. This premise – which can also be called the "foundationalist claim" – states that all relationships can be understood or even derived from a single and relatively stable foundation. In other words, underlying all of social reality is a set of principles that ultimately determine or give meaning to everything. Importantly, this foundation is not in itself part of the social or political reality that it acts as a foundation for. It is, moreover, not in itself prone to changes, instability, or developments, but remains relatively stable. The foundationalist claim is the idea that underlying social and political relationships are a set of external and firm principles that define and even determine these fields. Marchart mentions *economic determinism* as one example – that is, the idea that the economy is made up of a set of (iron) laws that determine the ways in which all other parts of society function. Yet, there are many other forms of foundationalism out there: for example, the idea found in much early political philosophy that God acts as the underlying principle for all world building. This kind of theorization posits an eternal ground that cannot be challenged and is not in itself changeable as part of the system. In being outside and stable, such foundations *ground* the entirety of systems. They institute and give coherence to the ways in which the world is.

Post-foundationalism simultaneously represents a response and critique to foundationalism. It does so in a manner that must not be misconstrued as anti-foundationalism: the often-caricatured idea that social reality and politics are completely groundless and that in the end everything is completely arbitrary. The problem with this view, besides being largely a straw man, is that in denying foundationalism, it has to invoke and work through foundationalism. The idea that there is no (and never has been any) ground is in itself a foundationalist claim: it posits the complete absence of ground as *the* ultimate ground. What must be developed instead is a genuine alternative, Marchart argues, that goes through a "subversion of the very terrain on which foundationalism operates, a subversion of foundationalist premises – and not their denial" (2007, p. 13).

Post-foundationalism attempts such a subversion by arguing that instead of working with either ultimate grounds or no grounds, social relationships are always operating based on multiple, contingent grounds (in the plural). These grounds are historical through and through and serve to navigate the tension between grounding and groundlessness. Indeed, even though the meaning of relationships can never be fixed, the world does not become completely free-floating, arbitrary, and moldable. In place of ultimate grounds, as said above, we uncover multiple grounds or grounding efforts attempting to make up for the lack. As such, we cannot reduce the world to the unfolding of any singular order, principle, or foundation. Claiming so, however, does not mean moving into anti-foundationalist territory. Instead of subverting the idea of ultimate grounds, post-foundationalism argues that in its place, we find a plurality of contingent, partial, and historically situated grounds. Different worlds have different ways of gaining coherence and meaning. Historically, different grounds have taken each other's place in a continuously developing series, which Derrida, in his famous essay, *Structure, Sign, and Play in the Discourse of the Human Sciences*, enumerates as "*eidos, archē, telos, energeia, ousia* (essence, existence, substance, subject) *alētheia*, transcendentality, consciousness, or conscience, God, man, and so forth" (Derrida, 2001, p. 353, original emphasis). The issue, then, is not between one ground or no ground; it is instead about grounds in the plural:

> [w]hat is at stake in political post-foundationalism is not the impossibility of *any* ground, but the impossibility of a *final* ground. And it is precisely the absence of such an Archimedean point that serves as a condition of possibility of always only gradual, multiple and relatively autonomous acts of grounding.
>
> (Marchart, 2007, p. 155)

To claim that all grounds are contingent means that their particular manifestation – the specific ways in which social relations are grounded in a historic moment – is "neither impossible nor necessary – so that they 'could be otherwise'" (Marchart, 2007, p. 28). What is important to notice in this context is that post-foundationalism does not just claim that certain parts of social reality are more or less contingent. It claims that everything is necessarily contingent. The only thing that is not contingent is contingency itself: contingency is necessary.

Discourses beyond language

Laclau and Mouffe's work, along with its subsequent development, provides us with a crucial infrastructure for moving into post-truth worlds, navigating the political terrain carved out by these discourses. It does so, first and foremost, by offering a series of concepts for using a post-foundationalist ontology to understand and engage with contemporary political struggles. This is not an invitation, in our view, to simply rehearse the already well-known arguments developed by Laclau and Mouffe in the 1980s. Indeed, as Laclau often emphasized himself, "one only thinks *from* a tradition," suggesting that "the relation with tradition should not be one of submission and repetition, but of transformation and critique" (Laclau, 1990, p. 179, original emphasis). Following this argument, our reading of Laclau and Mouffe takes a healthy dose of inspiration from other currents – not least in complexity thinking, political economy, sociology, and critical media studies – and proceeds via a kind of selective eclecticism, fusing together insights from different strands of thought, while maintaining the post-foundationalist ontology.

As noted above, Laclau and Mouffe use the term *discourse* to encapsulate relational systems or configurations of meaning. The basic building blocks for such systems are what they call *moments*, linked together within a relatively stable formation. One way of approaching discourses and discursivity is as world-making efforts: that is, ways of giving meaning to social relations and the different things, people, institutions, and species that form these relationships. The moments that make up any given discourse can be linguistic or textual in nature, but they need not be. Indeed, contrary to the accusations of idealism, what Laclau and Mouffe offer should very much be considered a materialist account (Schou, 2016). This is one that affirms the centrality of institutions, practices, and things, while simultaneously denying the possibility of understanding these prior to their embeddedness in symbolic and relational structures (Laclau & Mouffe, 1987). In this sense, the term discourse might be a poorly chosen word insofar as it mainly connotes language use and speech. As we understand it, Laclau and Mouffe's project is much more radical than this. Indeed, Laclau has repeatedly emphasized this exact point:

> [b]y discourse we should not understand simply speech and writing, i.e. there is nothing specifically linguistic about it. The notion of language has been submitted to sustained critique over the last thirty years and as a result the specificity of an object which was called language in the strict sense has largely dissipated, and language on the other hand is a dimension which constitutes any possible experience. For instance, Wittgenstein's notion of a language game is not involved only in a linguistic dimension; it is a combination of linguistic elements and the action in which these elements are embedded, and the resulting totality of words and actions is what he called a language game *… it is in this sense that discourse is a relational system which can be applied to any possible object.*
>
> (Laclau & Bhaskar, 1998, p. 9, emphasis added)

In this account, discourses are defined as both words and actions, as well as the combined, relational systems that emerge from the interplay between these. In this context, the concept of "meaning" serves an important role, as all relations are seen as always already given, historically situated and institutionally embedded forms of meaning. For humans, there is no escaping meaning, just as there is no point outside meaning. This leads Laclau and Mouffe to reject the distinction between the discursive and the extra-discursive. They do so *not* on the grounds that there is no physical world external to discourse (surely there is), but because this world can never be grasped outside discourses: "the external world is also discursively constituted, not in the sense that it's constituted by the mind of men, but in the sense that any kind of practice is embedded in the elaboration of the linguistic world" (Laclau & Bhaskar, 1998, p. 13).

Any distinction between the discursive and the extra-discursive cannot be maintained, as any and all objects will always already be part of particular relational configurations of meaning. Importantly, this does *not* have anything do with whether there exist things, entities, and processes (such as earthquakes and falling trees) external to discourse.[2] As soon as such events, things, and materialities, enter into discourses, they become part of relational systems of meaning. This also explicitly goes against locating discourses within any all-knowing, rational subject. Discourses cannot be reduced to mental structures but are material through and through. As such, discourses are not to be thought of as merely linguistic, but as relational systems *tout court*. If so, then little stands in the way of stating that Laclau and Mouffe's arguments apply to all actions, ideas, institutions, subjectivities, identities, and social structures. The minimum commitment is, we might say, to think of these in a relational and always already meaningful manner. What remains essential to discourses is not language, speech, or writing but *relations*. It is no incident that discourses are defined in *Hegemony and Socialist Strategy* as the result of "any practice establishing a relation among elements" (2014, p. 91).

As stated, the relational account provided by Laclau and Mouffe suggests that discourses are constituted in and through specific *moments*. This means that there is an openness to social reality insofar as any given discourse represents merely one way of giving meaning to and understanding the world. It is situated in an overflow of potential meaning that cannot be grasped or understood through any one discourse alone. One way of understanding this, using words somewhat unfamiliar to Laclau and Mouffe's work, is in terms of *complexity* and *complexity reduction*. The world is extraordinarily complex and can never be grasped or understood in its "totality" through either actions or words. Instead, to navigate and make sense of the world, actors have to continuously handle and reduce complexity. They do so by limiting the range of potential practices and forms of meaning. This is done in an interplay between actions and words – between social structure and linguistic forms (Sum & Jessop, 2013). Thus, in our somewhat unorthodox reading of Laclau and Mouffe, we take the idea of discourses as an overarching category, comprising different kinds of relational systems of complexity reduction. These facilitate, limit, and constrain the range of actions that can be performed within any given system. They do so in a manner that is never determining but constituted through and within the interplay between singular decisions and sedimented structures. There is, in this sense, both an original *openness* to social reality (it could always be otherwise) and a historical *closure* (it is not otherwise due to historical path-dependencies that accumulate over time).

No closure is ever settled for good, and part of this has to do with the inherent negativity of all forms of discourses. Any moment cannot be grasped as a separate entity, because it can only come into being through its relation to other moments. In this sense, the meaning of any given social construct – an identity, collective, practice, institution, and so forth – is always defined by what it is not. This holds for any moments within a discourse (each are interwoven with a negativity or lack, as they are what they are not) and it goes for any discourse as well. Indeed, for Laclau and Mouffe, all discourses stand in some kind of opposition to other outside discourses: "we" are not like "them," "now" is not like "then," "this" is not like "that" and so forth. This outside, however, is never completely outside, because the inside of the discourse depends entirely on its ability to draw such a frontier or distinction in the first place. In this sense, Laclau and Mouffe follow Derrida in arguing that the outside is always a *constitutive outside* for the inside.

It is from these underlying theoretical premises that Laclau and Mouffe elaborate their account of political struggle and hegemony. Indeed, the major question that follows from their account – emphasizing relations, contingency, and historicity – is why certain discourses become dominant while others fall to the wayside. Here, Laclau and Mouffe treat us to an image of social reality as a battleground between opposing attempts to impose and fixate particular discourses as dominant, self-evident, and natural. The way of doing so is through the mobilization of diverse societal forces, making particular discourses resonate and spread further in social formations than others. The dominance of specific discourses should, as a consequence, be seen as an accomplishment established through ongoing processes of *hegemony*, understood as moral, political, and intellectual power, consent, and leadership. The world is infinitely complex and overflowing with potential meaning yet is constantly fixed and stabilized in such a way that this excess is manageable.

Ontological abyss

Laclau and Mouffe have done more than simply provide a non-essentialist set of tools for understanding and deciphering contemporary political struggles. They have also elaborated a sophisticated *ontology of the political*. Here, we draw particularly on the work of Laclau and the interpretations provided by Marchart (2007, 2018). Doing so allows us to further penetrate what is at stake within discursivity as a form of complexity reduction and meaning making. It allows us to build our approach for studying and investigating contemporary post-truth worlds.

As has been duly noted by a number of critical scholars, Laclau's political ontology hinges on a conceptual distinction between *the political* and *the social*. According to Laclau, his approach is characterized by the "primacy of the political over the social" (1990, p. 33). For Laclau (as well as Mouffe), all relations are constituted by a constitutive lack and exclusion: the present always contains what it is *not* or what it *could have been*. The traces of past alternatives are always somehow there. Yet, how is it, Laclau asks, that (for the most part) we do not sense or experience this exclusion and lack? "[T]he relationship with a postman delivering a letter, buying a ticket in the cinema, having lunch with a friend in a restaurant, going to a concert – where is the moment of exclusion and negativity here?" (Laclau, 1990, p. 33).

To unpack this point, Laclau goes back to the work of the philosopher Edmund Husserl and salvages a set of important concepts from his writings – namely the ideas of *sedimentation* and *reactivation*. In Laclau's reading of Husserl, these two concepts can be thought of as existing in a sort of interplay or ongoing dynamic, where "the routinization and forgetting of origins [is called] 'sedimentation,' and the recovery of the 'constitutive' activity of thought [is called] 'reactivation.'" (Laclau, 1990, p. 34). The idea is that, over time, the contingent foundations for certain institutional practices and forms of life become largely forgotten or routinized. We do not remember why certain relations are formatted or ordered in a certain way, because their origins or genesis have become obscured. For Laclau, this forgetfulness indicates that certain social forms have become *sedimented*.

Sedimentation does not mean that discourses have sprung out of nowhere. Instead, *reactivation* consists precisely in rediscovering the original decisions that lie at the core of these discourses:

> The moment of original institution of the social is the point at which its contingency is *revealed*, since the institution... is only possible through the repression of options that were equally open. To reveal the original meaning of an act, then, is to reveal the moment of its radical contingency – in other words, to reinsert it in the system of real historic options that were discarded.
>
> (Laclau, 1990, p. 34, original emphasis)

The reason, then, why a concert is not perceived in terms of negativity – that is to say, in terms of its contrast to other options that have been repressed, say, for example, communal rituals without division between musicians and audience – is because its origins have been concealed, forgotten, and hidden. While Laclau does not say as much, the tension between sedimentation and reactivation amounts to nothing less than a description of what is typically called structure and agency within social scientific discourse. Laclau is essentially describing how certain forms of discursivity – that is to say, world making and complexity reduction – start out by being more or less completely contingent, over time taking on the guise of being "natural," "objective," and "necessary." One could easily add to this account that sedimentation, as a process, takes place through the inscription of certain discourses (limiting the potential range of meaning and action) into institutional logics, professional identities, embodied modes of being, and subjective forms of life (Sum & Jessop, 2013). In this scheme, reactivation presents itself as a re-opening of social reality that lays bare the contingency of the (seemingly) necessary, allowing for other options to become possible again. Reactivation can take place through critical inquiry but can also spring from within the fabric of everyday life.

It is around these ideas that Laclau develops his ontological difference between the social and the political. In his conceptualization, *the political* represents the instituting moment in which a contingent decision is made between what should and should not be included in any particular discourse (Laclau, 1990). It is the original moment of antagonism, otherness, and struggle. If such decisions are kept and retained, their origins will over time disappear or become concealed, making them part of *the social*. In this sense, *the social* is a broad category encompassing discourses that have become sedimented and seemingly objective. Reactivation – as a rediscovery of the contingency of such objectivity – means rediscovering the political grounds of the social (Laclau, 1990).

What comes out of this distinction, as formulated by Marchart (2007, p. 146), is not just a "theory of 'political signification' but also a 'political theory' of signification." Laclau is not just saying that the distinction between the political and the social holds for political forms of meaning or discourses, but that *all* relations are constituted by this difference. This means that *"all* meaning is, at its roots, political" (Marchart, 2007, p. 147). Moreover, in the account provided by Laclau, the political stands for nothing other than *contingency* and *antagonism*: in other words, the inclusion of some moment rather than others and the suppression of alternatives. To affirm that social reality is best understood through a political ontology, then, is also to affirm the necessity of contingency: "while the conditions of existence of any identity/objectivity/system are *contingent* with respect to the system in question, they are *necessarily* so" (Marchart, 2007, p. 141).

What emerges from these somewhat dense reflections is precisely the idea of post-foundationalist political thought. This tradition affirms, on the one hand, the impossibility of any universal or final ground, from which social reality can be deduced in its totality. Yet it also argues, on the other hand, that *despite* this lack of any firm ground, social reality is constituted by the very attempt to create such grounds. As Marchart (2007, p. 8) neatly summarizes

> in a nutshell, what occurs within the moment of the political, and what can be excavated out of the work of many post-foundational political theorists as an "underlying logic," is the following double-folded movement. On the one hand, the political, as the instituting moment of society, functions as a supplementary ground to the groundless stature of society, yet on the other hand this supplementary ground withdraws in the very "moment" in which it institutes the social. As a result, society will always be in search for an ultimate ground, while the maximum that can be achieved will be a fleeting and contingent *grounding* by way of politics – a plurality of partial grounds.

This claim is more radical than it might seem at first sight in that it advances a *political ontology*. The political is not just a regional category. At its core, all social worlds and practices are always already political. This being political is the underlying premise for any claims about existence. As Marchart (2016) reflects, "[s]uch a radical political ontology is hard to swallow" (p. 321). Indeed, it would seem that Laclau also partly backtracked from these claims, introducing the idea of dislocation as a substitute for antagonism at an ontological level. Here, however, Marchart insists – and we tend to agree with him – that despite

Laclau's own caution, it is conceptually coherent and politically necessary to maintain "a 'maximalist' position regarding the ontological nature of the political" (2016, pp. 322–323). Doing so means affirming that all ontology is political ontology.

Elusive truths

There are different ways of interpreting the implications of a post-foundationalist ontology in terms of normative claims and truth. What is at stake in these assessments is, to a large extent, *how* and *whether* ideas of truth and normativity can be dealt with within a framework that denies any ultimate ground or closure. How is it possible, the questioning goes, to defend certain truth claims against others without presupposing an ontological privileging of particular truth regimes? On what grounds, we might ask, can we defend the view that "[t]o assert that one cannot provide an ultimate rational foundation for any given system of values does not imply that one considers all views to be equal" (Mouffe, 1993, pp. 14–15)?

The starting point for this conversation might be to explicate the implications of a post-foundationalist approach to questions of normativity and facts. From the exposition provided above, we can begin to see how ideas of truth as something solid and stable become much more elusive. With this, questions of normativity also come into play. Indeed, keeping with the premises set out above, Laclau himself argues that the concept and notion of normativity should be expanded significantly. Taking his point of departure in a deconstruction of the classic distinction between the descriptive and the normative, between *the being* and *the ought* as it is found in the work of Kant, Laclau (2014) argues that any idea of facts as somehow pre-existing norms cannot be maintained:

> There are no facts without signification, and there is no signification without practical engagements that require norms governing our behaviour. So there are not two orders – the normative and the descriptive – but normative/ descriptive complexes in which facts and values interpenetrate each other in an inextricable way.
>
> (Laclau, 2014, pp. 127–128)

In this sense, post-foundationalism operates within an expanded understanding of not just the political but also the normative. In many cases, it would seem that these two categories almost collapse, as the instituting moments of the political (i.e., precarious and contingent decisions) are precisely indicative of certain normative dispositions and engagements. What are we to make of these remarks for studying questions of truth, post-truth, and fake news?

One post-foundational approach to the issue of truth could be to denounce the possibility of essentialist Truths, while at the same time affirming the importance of certain fields as producers of qualitatively better forms of knowledge. From such a perspective, one could argue that fields like science and journalism must be strengthened and protected in our current era, not because they have unfettered access to the world "as it is," but because they have developed the best methods for producing reliable knowledge. This type of position is not uncommon to social scientific discourse. One can find a similar argument in the work of sociologist Pierre Bourdieu (2004). He too was skeptical of claims to universality and truth as transcendental foundations, instead opting for investigating how and in what ways certain particularistic interests could take on the guise of universality. Bourdieu was well aware that universalism was the result of particularistic interests, yet also saw how certain agents (within specific fields) would take on the task of advancing "reason and the universal" (Bourdieu, 2004, p. 31). Not least science, art, and aesthetics should, as a consequence, be defended against the impeachment of economic interests. The autonomy of the scientific field, and its ability to produce "universality" through certain scientific practices, should be guarded against the colonization of other fields, Bourdieu argued.

Although there certainly are merits to this kind of account, arguing for the protection of historically significant fields of truth making, we are also wary about it on several fronts. Not only do these types of accounts tend to be implicitly elitist in limiting the progress of (qualitatively different forms of) truth to scientists or specialists (which have historically tended to be White, male, and from the Global North). They also, and more substantially, tend to slide from a historical contingency to a normative necessity: because certain fields have historically established procedures for producing something as true (*historical contingency*), it is argued that these fields should not only be regarded as having a privileged access to truthfulness, but their autonomy should also be defended against intrusion (*normative necessity*). One can well hold this sort of argument on personal grounds, yet its viability as a kind of theoretical logic eludes us somewhat. Yes, different fields produce qualitatively different kinds of knowledge, but this difference does not need to be defined in terms of truth criteria. Whether scientific knowledge – that is to say knowledge produced by the field of science – is accepted as true depends in large part on the extent to which its claims come to resonate with and be accepted by the social formation and the truth regimes of any particular period. There might be good reasons for why this has historically been the case. There might also be good reasons for why this should continue to be so. However, to legitimize this latter option by way of the former – suggesting that because science has historically been able to produce "more-true" truths it should therefore be allowed to do so in the future – misses the power dynamics and political struggles in which this field is implicated. Science is as much a part of the hegemonic struggles to define the terrain of the social as any other field.

In this sense, the truth-telling capacities held by science are as a much a product of discursive battles as any other part of society. If science holds a privileged access to truth (as a discursive construct), this is a historical contingency rather than an empirical necessity: "[A]ny kind of scientific practice, I would say, would have to be hegemonic, that is to say, it has to be proved in front of a tribunal which is constituted by a variety of other practices" (Laclau & Bhaskar, 1998, p. 13). This insight prompts us to critically examine the historical processes through which specific truth-telling regimes have become accepted as such, not least through their reliance upon and interplay with hegemonic economic, racial, and patriarchal formations.

Adding to our hesitation towards equating historical contingency with normative necessity is the fact that nothing dictates that scientific logics can or should be imported directly to the political realm. Indeed, as Chantal Mouffe (1993, p. 14) points out in *The Return of the Political*:

> That a question remains unanswerable by science or that it does not attain the status of a truth that can be demonstrated does not mean that a reasonable opinion cannot be formed about it or that it cannot be an opportunity for a rational choice. Hannah Arendt was absolutely right to insist that in the political sphere one finds oneself in the realm of opinion, or "doxa," and not in that of truth, and that each sphere has its own criteria of validity and legitimacy.

The approach adopted in this book is in this sense both deeply empirical *and* performative. It is empirical insofar as we do not aim to hierarchize or catalog different claims in terms of their truth qualities, opting instead for analyzing their normative implications. Our aim is not to "debunk" particular ideas for not accurately representing social reality or particular events. For us, the question is not whether or in what ways fake news, misinformation, and post-truth phenomena "really do exist" (as somehow independent of meaning). Instead, we argue that, insofar as certain individuals, groups, and institutions speak about and make sense of their world *as if* these phenomena exist, this has very real performative effects. Whether fake news accurately captures what it seeks to portray is beside the point in terms of the effects this concept can have on new political interventions and the mobilization of political forces. In this sense, our account is also performative: it is concerned with the performative force of specific discourses; that is both how they are formed and what their effects are. Once again, we do not make this statement to say that one should not care about the accuracy of discourses around fake news. We are simply stating that in our focus on democratic practices and theory, it does not need to be our entry point.

In deconstructing dominant democratic discourses around post-truth and fake news based on this kind of lens, our aim is not to conclude, which discourse is most "accurate" or "fitting," but to understand their normative underpinnings. At the same time, we maintain that by foregrounding the particular set of democratic ideals currently at play, we can also begin to question these from the viewpoint of radical democratic theory. Doing so, however, does not lend us any universal position outside existing systems. We are also interwoven in tradition and our attempts to intervene in contemporary discourses through a conversation with other imaginaries is not based on what is more or less true. It is rather because we, as subjects inhabiting a tradition, see greater normative worth in some ways of organizing society than in others. Fundamentally, we think democracy – characterized by popular sovereignty, participation, and egalitarianism – matters. Whether this will have any impact or effect depends entirely – as with the discourses we are examining – on the performative effects our own discourse might have.

Methodological approach: mapping the landscape

In this book, we combine empirical analysis with political philosophical discussions. The second (upcoming) part of the book leans towards the empirical side, presenting a wide-ranging mapping of contemporary discourses on fake news, alternative facts, infodemics, and post-truth. The third part then engages in political philosophical discussions around questions of politics and democracy, placing post-truth worlds within a larger historical context and suggesting viable alternatives to the current situation.

Before venturing into post-truth worlds, we dedicate the final part of this chapter to digging deeper into the methodological choices (and issues) we have confronted during our research process. We do so not only in the hope that our research strategy will become transparent to our readers, but also to reflect on some of the inherent problems we have faced. We see this type of open and reflexive approach to methodological questions as being key to the research strategy pursued here.

Operationalizing discourse theory

Methods and methodology have been ongoing topics of debate within discourse theory. Questions of how discourse theory can (and should) inform empirical analysis continue to be a challenge. Not only are there few commonly agreed-upon methodological approaches, there is even disagreement on whether such agreement is something to strive for at all. This has meant that, all too often, discourse theory has been charged with having a methodological weakness or deficit. Even for staunch proponents of discourse theory, such as Tomas Marttila (2016), discourse theory is said to be haunted by a "methodological deficit [which] results from a general absence of systematic elaborations of the relation between the discourse theoretical framework and the design and conduct of empirical inquiries" (p. 3).

While scholars such as Marttila argue that the absence of systematic elaborations of discourse theory in a methodological register represents a weakness, others see it as a strength. In his book, *New Theories of Discourse*,

Torfing (1999) argues that his own lengthy exposition of discourse theory should *not* be used to derive any general or canonical conclusions. Indeed, Torfing (1999, p. 292) even views the production of such instrumental prescriptions as potentially repressive, as any kind of final settlement of the methodological question might serve to shut down alternative approaches.

David Howarth has suggested something similar, arguing that discourse theory is not just an empirical toolkit, but a comprehensive ontological and political endeavor with distinct commitments and normative underpinnings (Howarth, 2005, p. 317). We share this critique of methodology as a supposedly value- and context-free practice, somehow operating independently from the problems being examined. Even so, this methodological critique does not mean that discourse theorists have not attempted to offer methodological and reflexive cues for engaging with empirical cases. They certainly have.[3] While we do not follow any of these attempts wholesale, opting for a somewhat more open-ended approach, we do take central cues from the works of David Howarth and Jason Glynos, explicating how and in what ways discourse theory may be useful for empirical research. They argue that discourse theory offers a *problem-driven research strategy*, rather than pre-selected methods or theories. As such, discourse theory "begins with a set of pressing political and ethical problems in the present, before seeking to analyse the historical and structural conditions which gave rise to them, while furnishing the means for their critique and transgression" (Howarth, 2005, p. 318).

The pressing political problem targeted in this book is the rise of fake news, post-truth, alternative facts, and similar concepts. We are interested in not only *how* these terms have arisen as part of contemporary political struggles, but also the kinds of visions they include for the present and future state of democracy. In this sense, we want to examine the contours of a still developing political grammar, laying bare its normative assumptions and potentials for critique. In doing so, we operationalize discourse theory in its hermeneutic guise, searching for meaning, interpretations, and understandings that are currently produced and circulated. We are interested in how the present historical moment is understood and interpreted by prominent voices in the fields of politics, journalism, and science, and what such meaning-making entail for democracy as a historic construct.

Establishing an archive of data

One of the most important steps in any discourse theoretical analysis concerns the construction of an empirical archive. What documents and types of data should be collected? Are there any formalized criteria for including and excluding certain material? These are but some of the questions facing the establishment of any kind of empirical corpus. As Howarth (2005, p. 337) suggests, there are no clear-cut rules for answering these questions, as they will always be dependent upon the problem being studied and the context(s) engaged with.

In this book, we are in many ways dealing with an open-ended research project, which includes multiple political contexts, nations, outlets, and actors. We are trying to understand the formation of a new discursive landscape that not only transgresses borders and circulates across different types of media, but also operates at different scales simultaneously. As such, there is no neat way to clearly devise a representative sample beforehand. Instead, we have had to rely on an exploratory approach, allowing for a comprehensive data collection. While some might have opted for studying a select number of individual cases, we have chosen to concentrate on hegemonic ideas found *across* different political systems, media outlets, and positions. This has not been based on an *a priori* commitment to doing so, arguing that all discursive positions should necessarily be seen as belonging to the same discourses. Choosing to analyze our material as a set of rather amorphous discourses has been based on our ongoing engagement with and interpretation of our data.

In order to map the discursive landscape, we have assembled an archive consisting of scholarly texts, journalistic articles, books, commentaries from public intellectuals and political figures, as well as documents from different governmental and intergovernmental branches. Our data have been collected on an ongoing basis from 2015 to 2023, accompanied by a systematized archiving in 2018. In the ongoing process, we have closely followed public debates and accumulated academic articles, journalistic commentaries, and public statements related to fake news, alternative facts, and post-truth.

In August and September 2018, we bolstered our data collection through systematic queries on both Google Scholar and ten major Western news outlets, which we had found to be particularly central to the debates.[4] Here, we searched for the terms "fake news," "post-truth," "post-factual," "alternative facts," and "post-factuality." Together with our continuously collected data, we ended up with more than 170 academic publications and over 420 news articles, opinion pieces, and commentaries in prominent outlets written by public intellectuals, journalists, and political actors. Additionally, our database includes a number of policy reports, speeches, and several books on the topic.

In total, our archive contains more than 650 texts, ranging quite substantially in size: from under a single page to several hundred pages in the case of books. Table 3.1 provides an overview of our corpus, including reference examples of the different types of data included. It showcases the diversity of our archive, but also how certain types of data (namely news and research articles) have constituted the quantitatively largest portion of our data material.

Our archive does in no way include all public texts published on post-truth, fake news, or alternative facts. As this is one of the most debated topics of our time, that would hardly be possible. Our archive only covers the tip of the iceberg, and many additional voices could undoubtedly have been included. Even so, we want to maintain that – from a pragmatic and problem-oriented perspective, concerned with intervening in a pressing set of social and political issues – our corpus does provide

Table 3.1 Overview of data based on type, number and examples

Type	Examples	Quantity
Academic books	McNair (2018), Fuller (2018), Howard (2020), Albrecht (2023)	16
News articles (including op-eds and commentaries)	Stelter (2016), Dilworth (2017), Zwirz (2018), Wong (2020), The Economist (2022), Satariano & Mozur (2023)	423
Popular/non-academic books	Ball (2017), Davis (2017), Kakutani (2018), Schick (2020)	8
Policy papers and briefings	European Commission (2018), WHO (2022)	12
Research articles and book chapters	Allcott & Gentzkow (2017), Bennett & Livingston (2018), Hameleers (2020), Pepp, Michaelson, & Sterken (2022) Monsees (2023)	171
Miscellaneous (tweets, web sources, dictionaries)	Cambridge Dictionary (n.d.), Macron (2018), Trump (2017)	31
Total		**661**

Source: Table created by authors.

a productive entry point. While it is certainly not exhaustive, it is one way of diving into an ever changing and expanding political battleground.

Analyzing the data

As stated above, our archive was established alongside and together with our interpretive and analytical work. Against a strictly linear approach to investigating political and social problems, our approach has been iterative: we have continually moved back and forth between data collection, data analysis, and testing out our interpretations through writing and engagements with both academic and non-academic communities. Without wanting to move too deep into further theoretical discussions, our approach has been close to what Glynos and Howarth (2007, 2019) call *the retroductive cycle.* This represents a process in which "as we move from one 'moment' to the next, and back again, revising aspects of our account in light of adjustments made in other moments, we never return to the same spot" (Glynos & Howarth, 2019, p. 118). For this project, our process is characterized by a large portion of analytical openness and flexibility, acknowledging that the justification behind certain choices of method, interpretations, and formulation of arguments is embedded in distinct communities of practice. Rather than being tied to specific reified methods, the legitimacy of our analysis and interpretations rests to a large degree on our ability to formulate these in a compelling way and account for their accuracy, consistency, and rigor.

In the process of working with our collected archive, we have been guided by the important discourse theoretical reflections offered by a number of contemporary writers (Glynos & Howarth, 2007, 2019; Howarth, 2005; Torfing, 1999). Our focus has in particular been on interpreting and understanding dominant meanings and relations found in our material. Without falling back on a positivist and linear image of science – seeing interpretation as the inevitable outcome of predefined analytical processes – we have broadly moved through three major phases, reminiscent of the retroductive cycle. This revolves around *"problematizing* empirical phenomena, *accounting* for these phenomena, and *persuading* – and/or intervening into – the relevant community and practices of scholars and practitioners" (Glynos & Howarth, 2019, p. 118, original emphasis). Table 3.2 provides an overview of our analytical process.

In the first phase, we focused on problematizing the political issue at the core of this book – namely discourses on fake news, post-truth, and their relation to democracy. We did so by gathering empirical material and familiarizing ourselves with the dominant discussions. The aim of this first phase was to devise

Table 3.2 Overview of analytical process

Phases	Description	Activities
Phase 1: Problematization	Problematization of social and political problems under scrutiny: what is the problem? How can we collect data on this problem? What are some of the major discursive voices?	Collection of data, familiarization with material, and establishment of first thematic codes.
Phase 2: Focused analysis	In-depth textual analysis and hermeneutical interpretation of our corpus: What are the dominant discourses and concepts? Which normative ideas are present (and absent)? What kind of subjectivities are framed and produced?	Focused analysis of the material, fleshing out initial codes by in-depth annotation and reading of data; back-and-forth movement between establishing interpretations and testing these empirically.
Phase 3: Reproblematization and intervention	Generalization and reproblematization based on focused data analysis: what major discourses have we found? How can they be engaged with critically? Are there other ways of moving forward?	Presentation of our findings to relevant communities, formulation of counter-hegemonic narratives, and justification of interpretations.

Source: Table created by authors.

a fitting research strategy and construct a fairly systematic collection of data (as described above). Following this problematization, we turned to a focused analysis in the second phase, centered on accounting for the phenomena being studied. Moving back and forth between explanation, interpretation, and theory construction (Glynos & Howarth, 2007), we coded our material. Focusing on discovering and fleshing out major themes, this involved reading through the texts, noting down key signifiers, and establishing major crosscutting arguments. Based on this first and second phase, the third phase revolved around persuasion and intervention. Here, our focus was not only to reproblematize our initial understanding but also to intervene by articulating counter-hegemonic narratives. The narrative presented in this book is a major part of that process, but so are other forms of engagement with scholarly and political communities. This last part thus inserts us, as engaged scholars and analysts, into the very terrain we started out by studying.

As mentioned, the three phases of analysis have not followed a linear structure but rather developed iteratively and hermeneutically. By continuously following debates around fake news, post-truth, and democracy from 2015 to 2023 – while also critically engaging with both academic and non-academic communities – our thinking has continuously evolved and matured in response to shifting and oftentimes paradoxical political developments.

Limitations

As we have already argued, discourse theory eschews any *a priori* commitment to standardized and reified methodological approaches in favor of reflexive and problem-driven research strategies. Doing so also means clearly acknowledging limitations and shortcomings of the adopted approach. Things could have been otherwise, and our way of problematizing the issues under scrutiny is not the only manner in which they could be approached. Here, we would like to bring out five limitations or potential points of critique against our analytical approach.

First, it should be clearly acknowledged that the archive we have assembled is in many ways predominantly Western and even US- and UK-centric, as it mainly targets English-language texts and outlets. This not only raises questions as to the specificity and context of the discourses examined, but also to the generalizability of our findings in other political, cultural, and geographical contexts. To this point, we can only affirm that the discourses examined here are predominantly centered on Europe and the US. That being the case, we have also attempted to include political developments around fake news and post-truth beyond the Western world, including policy changes in countries such as the Philippines, Malaysia, Indonesia, and Kenya. Moreover, while many of the discussions here are taken from English-speaking contexts, the studied discourses have often had both direct and indirect implications for discourses and policy solutions in others parts of the world (Gabbatt, 2018; Lim, 2020). As such, we maintain that our analysis does have relevance beyond the narrow confines of the Western world alone. At the very least, this is our modest hope.

The second concern that should be raised is that we tend to collapse more or less divergent voices into singular discourses. Although we do try to explore the intricacies and complexities of hegemonic discourses around fake news and post-truth, we do not try to provide any form of historical genealogy of the origins and temporal developments of these discourses. This is not our aim. Rather than providing a detailed account of the evolution of discourses over time (undoubtedly an important contribution in its own right), this book seeks to engage with contemporary discourses around post-truth and critically discuss their democratic underpinnings. As such, the discourses studied might not be the only ones currently articulated. Yet, for the purpose of this book, they are sufficient for having a critical discussion around the overall implications of post-truth discourses as democratic imaginaries. To acknowledge this, we deliberately use the term post-truth worlds (in the plural) to indicate that we are dealing with a number of both overlapping and divergent discourses. These cannot be reduced to one monolithic block, although they do share certain underlying democratic ideas and claims, as will be clear over the course of this book. It is precisely these overlapping ideas that constitute the center of our attention.

Third, it could be said that instead of taking the claims presented in post-truth discourses seriously – such as those on the mounting dangers of misinformation, mistrust of expertise, propaganda, and consistent challenges to proper democratic processes – we turn them into a self-contained language game. To our mind, the premise for this critique is off the mark. What we want to understand in this book is the democratic ideals and normative imaginaries contained in post-truth worlds. We do not agree or disagree with concerns about particular forms of false information. Instead, we look at the ways in which these issues are discussed based on certain visions for what counts as a true democracy. Doing so does not mean denying the very real effects of misinformation, lies, and propaganda. Indeed, we have studied this extensively ourselves, both theoretically and empirically (see Farkas, Schou, & Neumayer, 2018a, 2018b; Farkas & Neumayer, 2020; Bastos & Farkas, 2019). This book does not ignore these dangers, but instead takes post-truth discourses seriously as forces of democratic imagination that can have (and are having) very real effects on institutional arrangements, political interventions, and our collective future.

Fourth, we want to pre-emptively underline that discourse theoretical perspectives on fake news and post-truth cannot be exhaustive for critically engaging with these complex political phenomena. Like any theoretical school of thought, discourse theory has blind spots and is more attuned to certain forms of empirical engagement than other. To our mind, situated research exploring the lived experiences and daily practices involved in the formation, reproduction, and circulation of discourses is also imminently needed. In particular, it seems to us that there still remains an important task in developing critical traditions that remain underexplored in the context of fake news, such as post-colonial studies, critical political economy, and feminist theory.

The fifth and final concern we want to highlight here, already probed in the introduction, is that we ourselves fall prey to precisely the kind of relativism that the authors we engage with argue against. As journalist Matthew d'Ancona (2017, p. 107) states in his book, *Post-Truth: The New War on Truth and How to Fight Back*, "post-modern thinkers were the inadvertent prophets of Post-Truth." In this line of reasoning, restoring democracy requires us to step away from so-called post-modern thought in order to re-establish truth. From this perspective, our work might seem as yet another post-modern blinker, escalating the post-truth crisis further by saying that there is no Truth (with capital T). To such a critique, we can only respond that we do not subscribe to simplistic notions of post-modernism, serving as strategic straw men to be picked apart. As noted by Gibbins and Reimer, "[p]ostmodernism is regularly used as a term of derision, indicating a thought that is at best woolly and essentially confused – and at worst misguided and dangerous" (1999, p. 19). It seems that since 1999, not much has changed regarding this straw man. Accordingly, to those who claim that our "position is haunted by the spectre of relativism," we can only say, following Mouffe (1993, p. 14), that "such an accusation makes sense only if one remains in the thrall of a traditional problematic which offers no alternative between objectivism and relativism." Indeed, as we have tried to demonstrate in this chapter, the very ground of objectivity is precisely relativity. Objectivity has a history that is founded on relativity. Adding to this, we will in this book reproblematize this issue by arguing that the problem is not relativism but *the lack thereof.* Indeed, we want to argue that contemporary post-truth voices tend to work with an all too reified and decontextualized understanding of truth, democracy, and the democratic tradition. This has made them unable – or, perhaps, unwilling – to see what we perceive to be the deeply anti-democratic sentiments in their own responses. We hope that this argument will become clear over the course of this book.

With this chapter, we have laid out the theoretical and methodological approach adopted throughout this book. Drawing out central elements from discourse theory, particularly in its contemporary post-foundationalist guise, we have presented the key ontological premises of the present work. Rather than providing clear-cut concepts that can be neatly imposed onto a terrain of political struggle, our theoretical exposition has mainly been located at an ontological level. That is, we have sought to explicate how and in what ways we might begin to talk about and engage with the contemporary production, diffusion, and circulation of ideas about what democracy is and should be. With this approach, we want to focus on discourses of democracy, truth, and politics. We want to understand the normative ideas and rationalities that underpin our collective social and political imagination. How are the state, history, and future of democracy being articulated? And in what ways is that changing due to contemporary concerns over truth, fake news, and facts? It is precisely these questions we turn to next, as we begin our venture into post-truth worlds.

Notes

1 The Essex School is comprised of a more or less loosely coupled set of academics. Prominent contributions (in and around this school) include, in addition to Laclau and Mouffe's own work, *Deconstructing Apartheid Discourse* (Norval, 1998); *Discourse Theory and Political Analysis: Identities, Hegemonies and Social Change* (Howarth, Norval, & Stavrakakis, 2000); *The Politics of Airport Expansion in the United Kingdom: Hegemony, Policy and the Rhetoric of "Sustainable Aviation"* (Griggs & Howarth, 2013); *Logics of Critical Explanation in Social and Political Theory* (Glynos & Howarth, 2007); *New Theories of Discourse: Laclau, Mouffe and Zizek* (Torfing, 1999); *Laclau: A Critical Reader* (Critchley & Marchart, 2004); *Laclau and Mouffe: The Radical Democratic Imaginary* (Smith, 1998); and *Post-foundational Political Thought: Political Difference in Nancy, Lefort, Badiou and Laclau* (Marchart, 2007).

2

> The fact that every object is constituted as an object of discourse has *nothing to do* with whether there is a world external to thought, or with the realism/idealism opposition. An earthquake or the falling of a brick is an event that certainly exists, in the sense that it occurs here and now, independently of my will. But whether their specificity as objects is constructed in terms of "natural phenomena" or "expressions of the wrath of God," depends upon the structuring of a discursive field. What is denied is not that such objects exist externally to thought, but the rather different assertion that they could constitute themselves as objects outside any discursive condition of emergence.
>
> (Laclau & Mouffe, 2014, p. 94, original emphasis)

3 This includes Tomas Marttila's lengthy exposition of Post-Foundational Discourse Analysis in his 2016 book of the same name (Marttila, 2016); Jason Glynos and David Howarth's so-called logics approach, laid out in their 2007 book, *Logics of Critical Explanation in Social and Political Theory*; and Nico Carpentier's attempt to formalize discourse theory into what he dubs discourse-theoretical analysis (Carpentier, 2017).

4 These are BBC News, CNN, Fox News, Reuters, *The Economist*, *The Guardian*, *The New York Times*, *The Washington Post*, *Time Magazine* and *USA Today*.

References

Albrecht, M.M. (2023). *Trumping the Media: Politics and Democracy in the Post-Truth Era*. London: Bloombury Academic.

56   *Preparing for the post-truth journey*

Allcott, H., & Gentzkow, M. (2017). Social media and fake news in the 2016 election. *Journal of Economic Perspectives, 31(2)*, 211–236. https://doi.org/10.1257/jep.31.2.211

Ball, J. (2017). *Post-Truth: How Bullshit Conquered the World*. London: Biteback Publishing.

Bastos, M., & Farkas, J. (2019). "Donald Trump is my President!" The Internet Research Agency Propaganda Machine. *Social Media + Society, 5(3)*. https://doi.org/10.1177/2056305119865466

Bennett, W.L., & Livingston, S. (2018). The Disinformation Order: Disruptive Communication and the Decline of Democratic Institutions. *European Journal of Communication, 33(2)*, 122–139. https://doi.org/10.1177/0267323118760317

Bourdieu, P. (2004). From the King's House to the Reason of State: A Model of the Genesis of the Bureaucratic Field. *Constellations, 11(1)*, 16–36. https://doi.org/10.1111/j.1351-0487.2004.00359.x

Cambridge Dictionary (n.d.). *Fake News*. Accessed 24 April 2023. https://dictionary.cambridge.org/dictionary/english/fake-news

Carpentier, N. (2017). *The Discursive-Material Knot: Cyprus in Conflict and Community Media Participation*. Lausanne: Peter Lang Publishing.

Critchley, S., & Marchart, O. (Eds.). (2004). *Laclau: A Critical Reader*. London: Routledge.

D'Ancona, M. (2017). *Post-Truth: The New War on Truth and How to Fight Back*. London: Ebury Press.

Davis, E. (2017). *Post-Truth: Why We Have Reached Peak Bullshit and What We Can Do About It*. London: Little, Brown.

Derrida, J. (2001). *Writing and Difference* (A. Bass, *Trans.*). 2nd Ed. London: Routledge.

Dilworth, M. (2017, 30 May). Facebook Claims Germany's New Law to Tackle Fake News will Cause Tech Companies to Delete Legal Content. *The Independent*. www.independent.co.uk/news/business/news/facebook-germany-fake-news-law-tech-companies-delete-legal-content-social-media-hate-speech-fine-a7763081.html

The Economist. (2022, 3 November). As Turkey Imposes a Harsh "Disinformation" Law, Critics Fear the Worst. *The Economist*. www.economist.com/europe/2022/11/03/as-turkey-imposes-a-harsh-disinformation-law-critics-fear-the-worst

European Commission (2018). *A Multi-Dimensional Approach to Disinformation*. https://doi.org/10.2759/0156

Farkas, J., & Neumayer, C. (2020). Disguised Propaganda from Digital to Social Media. In J. Hunsinger, L. Klastrup, & M. M. Allen (Eds.), *Second International Handbook of Internet Research* (pp. 707–723). Dordrecht: Springer.

Farkas, J., Schou, J., & Neumayer, C. (2018a). Cloaked Facebook Pages: Exploring Fake Islamist Propaganda in Social Media. *New Media & Society, 20(5)*, 1850–1867. https://doi.org/10.1177/1461444817707759

Farkas, J., Schou, J., & Neumayer, C. (2018b). Platformed Antagonism: Racist Discourses on Fake Muslim Facebook Pages. *Critical Discourse Studies, 15(5)*, 463–480. https://doi.org/10.1080/17405904.2018.1450276

Fuller, S. (2018). *Post-Truth: Knowledge as a Power Game*. London: Anthem Press.

Gabbatt, A. (2018). How Trump's "Fake News" Gave Authoritarian Leaders a New Weapon. *The Guardian*. www.theguardian.com/us-news/2018/jan/25/how-trumps-fake-news-gave-authoritarian-leaders-a-new-weapon

Gibbins, J.R., & Reimer, B. (1999). *The Politics of Postmodernity*. London: SAGE Publications.

Glynos, J., & Howarth, D. (2007). *Logics of critical explanation in social and political theory*. London: Routledge.

Glynos, J., & Howarth, D. (2019). The Retroductive Cycle: The Research Process in Poststructuralist Discourse Analysis. In T. Marttila (Ed.), *Discourse, Culture and Organization: Inquiries into Relational Structures of Power* (pp. 105–126). Cham: Palgrave Macmillan.

Griggs, S., & Howarth, D. (2013). *Politics of Airport Expansion in the United Kingdom: Hegemony, Policy and the Rhetoric of "Sustainable Aviation."* Manchester: Manchester University Press.

Hameleers, M. (2020). My Reality Is More Truthful Than Yours: Radical Right-Wing Politicians' and Citizens' Construction of "Fake" and "Truthfulness" on Social Media – Evidence From the United States and The Netherlands. *International Journal of Communication, 14*, 1135–1152.

Howard, P.N. (2020). *Lie Machines: How to Save Democracy from Troll Armies, Deceitful Robots, Junk News Operations, and Political Operatives*. New Haven: Yale University Press

Howarth, D. (2000). *Discourse*. Buckingham: Open University Press.

Howarth, D. (2005). Applying Discourse Theory: The Method of Articulation. In D. Howarth & J. Torfing (Eds.), *Discourse Theory in European Politics: Identity, Policy and Governance* (pp. 316–349). Basingstoke: Palgrave Macmillan.

Howarth, D., Norval, A.J., & Stavrakakis, Y. (Eds.). (2000). *Discourse Theory and Political Analysis: Identities, Hegemonies and Social Change*. Manchester: Manchester University Press.

Kakutani, M. (2018). *The Death of Truth: Notes on Falsehood in the Age of Trump*. New York: Tim Duggans Books.

Laclau, E. (1990). *New Reflections on the Revolution of our Time*. London: Verso.

Laclau, E. (2005). *On Populist Reason*. London: Verso.

Laclau, E. (2014). *The Rhetorical Foundations of Society*. London: Verso.

Laclau, E., & Bhaskar, R. (1998). Discourse Theory vs Critical Realism. *Alethia, 1(2)*, 9–14. https://doi.org/10.1558/aleth.v1i2.9

Laclau, E., & Mouffe, C. (1987). Post-Marxism Without Apologies. *New Left Review, 166*, 79–106.

Laclau, E., & Mouffe, C. (2014). *Hegemony and Socialist Strategy: Towards a Radical Democratic Politics*. London: Verso.

Lim, G. (2020). *Securitize/Counter – Securitize: The Life and Death of Malaysia's Anti-Fake News Act*. Data & Society. https://datasociety.net/library/securitize-counter-sec uritize

Macron, E. (2018, 25 April). Address to the US Congress. *CNN*. http://transcripts.cnn.com/TRANSCRIPTS/1804/25/ctw.01.html

Marttila, T. (2016). *Post-Foundational Discourse Analysis: From Political Difference to Empirical Research*. Basingstoke: Palgrave Macmillan.

Marchart, O. (2007). *Post-Foundational Political Thought: Political Difference in Nancy, Lefort, Badiou and Laclau*. Edinburgh: Edinburgh University Press.

Marchart, O. (2016). Laclau's Political Ontology. *Contemporary Political Theory*, *15*(3), 318–324. www.doi.org/10.1057/cpt.2016.8

Marchart, O. (2018). *Thinking Antagonism: Political Ontology after Laclau*. Edinburgh: Edinburgh University Press.

McNair, B. (2018). *Fake News: Falsehood, Fabrication and Fantasy in Journalism*. London: Routledge.

Monsees, L. (2023). Information Disorder, Fake News and the Future of Democracy. *Globalizations*, *20*(1), 153–168. https://doi.org/10.1080/14747731.2021.1927470

Mouffe, C. (1993). *The Return of the Political*. London: Verso.

Mouffe, C. (2005). *The Democratic Paradox*. London: Verso.

Mouffe, C. (2013). *Agonistics: Thinking the world Politically*. London: Verso.

Mouffe, C. (2018). *For a Left Populism*. London: Verso.

Norval, A.J. (1998). *Deconstructing Apartheid Discourse*. London: Verso.

Pepp, J., Michaelson, E., & Sterken, R. (2022). Why we should keep talking about fake news. *Inquiry: An Interdisciplinary Journal of Philosophy*, *65*(4), 471–487. https://doi.org/10.1080/0020174X.2019.1685231

Satariano, A., & Mozur, P. (2023, 9 February). The People Onscreen Are Fake. The Disinformation Is Real. *The New York Times*. www.nytimes.com/2023/02/07/technology/artificial-intelligence-training-deepfake.html

Schick, N. (2020). *Deep Fakes and the Infocalypse: What You Urgently Need To Know*. London: Monoray.

Schou, J. (2016). Ernesto Laclau and Critical Media Studies: Marxism, Capitalism, and Critique. *TripleC*, *14*(1), 292–311. https://doi.org/10.2759/0156 10.31269/triplec.v14i1.740

Sim, S. (2000). *Post-Marxism: An Intellectual History*. London: Routledge.

Smith, A.M. (1998). *Laclau and Mouffe: The Radical Democratic Imaginary*. London: Routledge.

Stelter, B. (2016, 1 November). The Plague of Fake News is Getting Worse: Here's How to Protect Yourself. *CNN*. https://money.cnn.com/2016/10/30/media/facebook-fake-news-plague/

Sum, N.-L., & Jessop, B. (2013). *Towards a Cultural Political Economy: Putting Culture in its Place in Political Economy*. Cheltenham: Edward Elgar.

Torfing, J. (1999). *New Theories of Discourse: Laclau, Mouffe and Zizek*. Oxford: Blackwell Publishers.

Townshend, J. (2003). Discourse Theory and Political Analysis: A New Paradigm from the Essex School? *The British Journal of Politics and International Relations*, *5*(1), 129–142. https://doi.org/10.1111/1467-856X.00100

Trump, D. (2017, 18 February). Don't Believe the Main Stream (Fake News) Media. The White House is running VERY WELL. I Inherited a MESS and Am in the Process of Fixing it. *Twitter*. https://twitter.com/realDonaldTrump/status/832945737625387008

Wong, J. C. (2020, 10 April). Tech Giants Struggle to Stem "Infodemic" of False Coronavirus Claims. *The Guardian*. www.theguardian.com/world/2020/apr/10/tech-giants-struggle-stem-infodemic-false-coronavirus-claims

WHO (2022). *WHO policy brief: COVID-19 Infodemic Management.* World Health Organization. www.who.int/publications/i/item/WHO-2019-nCoV-Policy_Brief-Infodemic-2022.1

Zwirz, E. (2018). Trump Fights Fake News with "Awards" for "Most Dishonest & Corrupt Media." Fox News. www.foxnews.com/politics/2018/01/02/trump-fights-fake-news-with-awards-for-most-dishonest-corrupt-media.html

Part II

Into post-truth worlds

4   Prophecies of post-truth

We live in turbulent times. Democracy is in a state of crisis, with fake news flooding the world and alternative facts breaking down the very core of political decision-making. Rational and factual evidence has been cast aside, as political mobs roam social media, using new platforms as potent weapons in a battle against truth-based politics. In its most basic form, this narrative has become one of the dominant portrayals of present-day democratic societies. Scholars, journalists, and policymakers seem to largely agree that democracy is under siege due to a dangerous cocktail of hyper-speed media, right-wing populism, and a withdrawal of trust in the basic pillars of Enlightenment. According to this narrative, rationalism, reason, and facts are being superseded by gut feelings and partisan politics.

At the core of these new prophecies of post-truth lies a very particular mythos, intended to capture not only the current state of democracy itself, but also potential ways of solving and overcoming this crisis of truth. Symptoms, diseases, and cures all coalesce into a more or less single – and largely hegemonic – democratic imaginary. Our purpose with this book is not only to pull apart the inner dynamics of this discourse – demonstrating its implicit normative ideas about the constitution of the political community – but also to suggest that the cure it ordains is in many ways a poison. Indeed, the democratic imaginary examined throughout this second part of the book often turns out to be anti-democratic in nature, focusing more on establishing technocratic and truth-based forms of democracy than restoring genuinely political institutions, popular participation, and the voice of the democratic people.

This chapter takes a first stab at these issues by laying out the hegemonic ideas about post-truth, fake news, infodemics, and post-factuality. It does so by providing a panoramic survey of contemporary scholarly and journalistic debates around these issues, pinpointing the specific vocabulary and discursive worlds they contain and serve to uphold. This will lead, in the following chapter, to a scrutiny of a series of political events that have all been described as symbols or epitomes of post-truth. From the rise of Donald Trump in the US to the COVID-19 infodemic and the information war in Ukraine, a series of

DOI: 10.4324/9781003434870-6

crises have been deeply entangled within contemporary discourses on democracy and truth. This is followed, in Chapter 6, by a mapping of current proposed and implemented solutions to the proclaimed truth crisis of democracy. Taken together, then, this second part of the book lays the foundation for understanding contemporary post-truth worlds and the ideals, anxieties, and hopes contained therein. It dives into the diverse claims currently being made as to how democracy is faring (and how it could be saved), foregrounding the otherwise implicit ideas structuring the stakes of the debate.

A modern-day plague

"A teenager sits at her desk. She is sixteen years old. She wears a VR [Virtual Reality] headset and haptic gloves (that can simulate the sense of touch) and is logged into the latest VR social media platform." So begins a thought-experiment posed by Samuel Woolley (2020, p. 13) in his 2020 book, *The Reality Game*, envisioning the potential near-future of democratic politics. In this impending reality, "political extremists, and all manner of predators can construct worlds in this social VR system where they can indoctrinate the young girl and others like her. They constantly barrage these kids, and even their parents and grandparents, with subtle political advertisements of dubious provenance and fake stories" (Woolley, 2020, p. 14). According to this narrative, people will soon live fully immersed in digital worlds where deepfakes, artificial intelligence (AI), and VR could make it impossible to distinguish truths from falsehoods.

When probing into discourses around fake news and post-truth, such dystopian portrayals of soon-to-be democratic ruins are prevalent. Indeed, calls for picturing a future of democratic decay are plentiful: "Imagine a world that considers knowledge to be 'elitist'" (Lewandowsky et al., 2017, p. 353); "imagine what elections will be like when we're no longer able to trust video and audio" (Cassauwers, 2019); "imagine the potential for deep disruption to our democracy" (Chesney & Citron, 2019b). Democracy is, these voices tell us, heading towards a cataclysmic breakdown, in which nothing can be trusted and/ or people reject truth. We will soon face a "future in which all information has become untrustworthy because the environment in which it exists has become so corrupted" (Schick, 2020, p. 189). While this crisis has yet to reach its most critical state, it is often claimed, we are already living through a "fake news epidemic" (McBrayer, 2020, p. 173).

Analogies and comparisons between the medical and political realms occupy a central role in contemporary democratic discourse. Naming the current situation an epidemic is far from accidental – it is a very particular discursive strategy that has continued to be used in post-truth worlds. This strategy was already prominent before COVID-19 but exploded in its wake (Simon & Camargo, 2021). Scholars, politicians, and journalists have all suggested that fake news is comparable to a dangerous, infectious *disease*, proliferating with alarming speed from body to body through inter personal contact. False information is said to be "spreading and replicating like a virus" (Parsons, 2017), representing a new form of "epidemic" (Amrita, 2017) or "infodemic" (Tentolouris et al., 2021), causing the "equivalent of a public-health crisis" (Steinmetz, 2018).

As an almost logical consequence of these medical metaphors, scholars and public intellectuals often argue that there is an urgent need to study the "epidemiology of fake news" (Kucharski, 2016, p. 525) and develop a proper "diagnosis" (Suiter, 2016, p. 26). Societies must detect "fake news pathogens" (Rubin, 2018) and test out "possible cures" (Corner, 2017, p. 1104). Hopefully, it is often claimed within these discourses, this could provide the first steps towards finding an "antidote" (Eysenbach, 2020, p. 4) or learning "'to control 'R_0' value – or the number of other people an infected person can transmit the misinformation virus to" (van der Linden, 2023, p. 102). The aim is to "curb its transmission" (Andrews, 2019) by boosting "people's immunity to fake news" (Svoboda, 2022), thus "inoculating them" (Zhang et al., 2022). Taking this metaphor further, some even equate fake news to a modern-day version of the "plague" (Amrita, 2017; Stelter, 2016), being "alarmingly resistant to treatment" (d'Ancona, 2017, p. 67). It behaves like "living, mutating organisms" (Korsunska, 2019, p. 162) and can even "evolve and update itself" (Li cited in Temming, 2018).

One proposed solution to this global post-truth crisis is to apply inoculation theory directly to the problem, thinking of government interventions as medicine for those "who have already been 'afflicted' with the informational virus" (van der Linden et al., 2020, p. 3). Politicians need to vaccinate entire populations *before* they get infected, launching " 'whole of nation' efforts, which are intended to inoculate their entire societies against information threats" (Singer & Brooking, 2019, p. 263). Another idea is to create democratic consent mechanisms like those found in medical research. In medicine, Professor of Philosophy Will Fish (2017) argues, "consenting to something – freely choosing it – is something that can only occur when certain conditions are met… Perhaps it's time we started to look at something similar for politics" (p. 212).

Medical analogies are not mere metaphors or representations, and their use are – as stated above – far from accidental. Instead, they constitute the discursive backbone of the democratic imaginary currently conjured up in scholarly, journalistic, and political discourses, highlighting the networked structure of present-day false information. Often, the medical vocabulary invoked to capture fake news and the post-truth era present these phenomena as simultaneously cultural and larger than life. On the one hand, fake news is caused by specific "bad actors" spreading chaos and destruction in societies from within. In this sense, it has a deeply human and cultural cause, namely malicious individuals and groups who distort reality for personal, economic, or political gains. Yet, on the other hand, post-truth and fake news are also claimed to be biological, intravenous, viral, and infectious – they are, in other words, constructed as being larger than life, beyond the cultural and human domain. This uncanny blend of culturalism and naturalism, portraying post-truth as both human and more than human, is one of the guiding tensions in post-truth worlds. Despite the seeming contradiction between the two, they often coexist quite neatly within these worlds, allowing for a continuous displacement of cause and effects. At certain times, particular groups, institutions, or fields can be blamed for this viral disease (drawing on a culturalist register), while, at others, blame can be given to fake news or post-truth in themselves, as if these could be understood apart from their specific human contexts and mobilizations (drawing on a naturalist register). In this context, particularly naturalist interpretations have dominated: fake news is often portrayed as having a self-sustained purpose or biological "will" of its own, like strains of bacteria or viruses.

Looking beyond the medical vocabulary, fake news is also described as equal to a form of *noise* or *fire*. From this perspective, it is seen as "noise pollution that makes it almost impossible to separate signal from noise" (Rosenbaum, 2017) or as a "conflagration threatening society" (Golson, 2021). In either capacity, fake news seems to transcend human notions of purpose or justice in its destructive path. This makes it emerge as a (supposedly) universally agreed-upon negative phenomenon, going beyond political orientation, geographical borders, class, gender, or race – like noise on a telephone line, a raging inferno, or smallpox, cholera, and plagues of the past: "This is not a battle between liberals and conservatives. It is a battle between two ways of perceiving the world, two fundamentally different approaches to reality" (d'Ancona, 2017, p. 5).

By framing fake news as an increase of noise in society or the spreading of disease between host bodies, the term becomes seemingly disembodied from political questions. As formulated by Professor Brian Hughes, it becomes "a profound challenge that transcends ideology, striking at the core of representative democracy: a sober, informed electorate" (Hughes, 2016). Despite political differences, it is claimed, political actors must join forces to stop fake news, as they should in the case of a burning city or a plague. Setting aside everyday disagreements and grudges, we all must work together and take part in the fight between what is good, rational, and true, and what is evil, infectious, and irrational. We must "vaccinate our society against this disease so as to maintain our democratic values" as argued by the European Union's Digital Commissioner Mariya Gabriel (cited in Stupp, 2017). If not, the world will soon find itself in a dystopian epoch with complete disregard for expertise and facts. In this binary scheme, siding with fake news is comparable to siding with the plague or cancer. This would not only be an act of cruelty against humanity, but also inexplicable and inhumane. Indeed, while fake news might not kill tens of millions of people, as did plagues of prior centuries, the current "information strain" is claimed to be spreading at an equal speed, potentially killing off *the* most significant human development since the last plague wreaked havoc on Earth: modern-day democracy.

One of the implications of the medicalized, biologized, and naturalized vocabulary is that contemporary discourses of post-truth become highly depoliticized. In presenting fake news as if it were a natural and larger-than-life phenomenon – a process and development with its own internal dynamics and motions – it moves to the realm beyond human dispute and conflict. Indeed, it seems that the question no longer becomes whether post-truth and fake news is a problem or not, but how we can collectively combat and solve it. The language of noise, fire, and disease thus serves to not only highlight the spread and dissemination of fake news, but also to point towards specific solutions or cures to the current crisis. This includes containment through content moderation, treatment through legal vaccination, or immunization through citizen media literacy. As highlighted by the applied mathematicians Brody and Meier (2018), "to combat the domination of noise [*fake news*], concerted efforts have to be made because noise will not disappear spontaneously. This has important implications for policy makers" (p. 2). In this line of reasoning, *noise* not only becomes a descriptive comparison but a benchmark for policy responses.

In sum, the vocabulary of plagues, viruses, disease, fire, and noise clearly serve as important metaphorical devices in post-truth worlds. Yet, they tell us little about the exact structure, content, or impact of fake news and post-truth, including the internal relations between these phenomena. Indeed, within the post-truth worlds examined in this book, the exact connection between fake news and post-truth often remains ambiguous. While some authors indicate that eradicating fake news would largely be synonymous with resolving the post-truth crisis, others argue that "fake news is more of a symptom... rather than a cause" (Ball, 2017). In the following sections, we will dive deeper into these conceptual and political issues.

Post-truth: the rise of an "alternative reality"

In 2016, post-truth went from living a life at the margins of political grammars in the US, Europe, and beyond to moving to its center. "Whoever wins the US presidential election," political commentator Matthew Norman declared in *The Independent*, "we've entered a post-truth world – there's no going back now" (Norman, 2016). Trump, Le Pen, Bolsonaro, Orbán, Modi, Brexit, populism, anti-immigration, vaccine hesitancy, climate change denial: all these phenomena have been said to signal an almost cataclysmic political shift, independent of any specific election outcome, event, or political context. This shift not only captures a series of individual societal developments, it is argued, but a completely new political landscape or reality. According to numerous commentators, 2016 thus marked the beginning of a new and never-before-seen era:

To everything there is a season: 1968 marked the revolution in personal freedom and the yearning for social progress; 1989 will be remembered for the collapse of totalitarianism; and 2016 was the year that definitively launched the era of "Post-Truth."

(d'Ancona, 2017, p. 7)

Within this narrative, liberal democracies have entered a new epoch that is as different from the past as the post-Cold War period was from the Cold War. Unlike previous times of democratic turmoil, this new world is distinct insofar as it affects not only the surface of democracy but its very foundation. Indeed, the otherwise stable anchors of democracy – namely truth, rationality, and facts – that citizens have clung to under political upheavals in the past are simply losing their grip: "Facts hold a sacred place in Western liberal democracies. Whenever democracy seems to be going awry, when voters are manipulated or politicians are ducking questions, we turn to facts for salvation. But they seem to be losing their ability to support consensus... The sense is widespread: We have entered an age of post-truth politics" (Davies, 2016).

Despite the sudden rise of post-truth in 2016, the first recorded use of the term was in 1992 (Oxford Dictionaries, 2016). The term was further popularized in a 2004 book by Ralph Keyes, named *The Post-Truth Era: Dishonesty and Deception in Contemporary Life.* To Keyes, US society had steadily entered a post-truth era in which lies and half-truths had come to dominate everyday life and the political landscape. The main driver of this development, he argued, was that it had become much easier and more rewarding to get away with misbehavior. According to Keyes (2004), several factors underpinned the culture or era of falsehoods, including the rise of celebrity fandom, valuing pseudo-authenticity and entertainment over integrity, academic "post-modernism," which relativizes all notions of truth, and so-called "techno-aided deception" (p. 197), enabling lying without consequences because of online anonymity. In addition to these factors, Keyes (2004) argued that "[d]ecades of official lies about Vietnam, Watergate, Irangate, and Iraq (to name just a few such events) have left us morally numb" (p. 11).

If we fast-forward to today, we find many of Keyes's arguments still in use, including the idea that the post-truth era is not only an era of lies, but also a new *epistemic culture* in which societal understanding of lies has fundamentally changed. According to the Oxford Dictionaries, which named "post-truth" the word of the year in 2016, post-truth refers to "circumstances in which objective facts are less influential in shaping public opinion than appeals to emotion and personal belief" (Oxford Dictionaries, 2016). Within this definition, we find several components of post-truth discourses more generally. This includes a binary relationship between "objective facts" and "emotions and personal belief." It also contains the notion of "public opinion," which is said to be undergoing more or less radical changes.

Channeling many of these assumptions, Professor Peter Dahlgren defines post-truth as "an emerging new epistemic regime, where emotional response prevails over factual evidence and reasoned analysis. Accuracy and transparency give way to algorithmic analyses of what people prefer to hear" (Dahlgren, 2018, p. 25). Not unlike the Oxford Dictionaries, we can once again see a binary distinction between "factual evidence" and "emotional response." The latter is said to increasingly dominate and threaten democracy. Additionally, we find the democratic masses (here referenced as "the people") who now only hear what they want to hear. To Dahlgren (2018), this development is connected to the rise of digital media, supporting political "echo-chambers" (p. 25), causing not only new circumstances, but also a completely new "epistemic regime." From this perspective, the post-truth era "should not be confused with classic deception or even lies" (Dahlgren, 2018, p. 25), as it represents a much deeper structural phenomenon.

In line with Dahlgren, Chesney and Citron (2019a) argue that society has descended "into a post-truth world, in which citizens retreat to their private information bubbles and regard as fact only that which flatters their own belief" (p. 155). Once again, rather than being limited to large quantities of false information in society, the post-truth era represents a completely new culture or world of its own: a "political subordination of reality" (McIntyre, 2018, XIV). From this line of thinking, "it would be naïve to think that fact-checking can somehow contain the problem of fake news" (Hannan, 2018, p. 224). Due to digital technologies, it is argued, "even in cases where fake news is quickly debunked, it has usually already been disseminated around the world several times" (Maddalena & Gili, 2020, p. 5).

Indeed, as large parts of the democratic populace have supposedly traversed beyond the realm of reality – living in isolated worlds or realities in which the universality of facts have come into question – fact-checking is no longer powerful in itself. In order to save democracy, there is instead a need to combat misinformation and fake news by getting to the root of the problem and "explain what is driving the fake news" in the first place (Hannan, 2018). Otherwise, there is little hope of getting back those who have become either indifferent or even resilient to truth.

Despite portraying fake news as a largely depoliticized issue, post-truth discourses have been tightly bound up with issues of politics, democracy, and participation. Indeed, it is often the supposed destruction of democratic practices that commentators lament. They do so in large part because they see democracy as connected to the production, use, and appropriation of truth itself. This also means that any attack on truth, rationality, and reason is automatically an attack on the Enlightenment foundations of democracy: "you *do* have to choose. Are you content for the central value of the Enlightenment, of free societies and of democratic discourse, to be trashed by charlatans – or not? … . The truth is out there, if only we demand it" (d'Ancona, 2017, p. 5, original emphasis).

Portraying truth as something that is "out there" is the other side of the often medicalized and naturalized language pointed to earlier: just as post-truth is seen as a biological or environmental threat, truth is also seen as having a necessary, essential, and universal content. Unsurprisingly, such ideas of truth can be found throughout contemporary post-truth discourses. If we only "flatten the curve" of fake news, remove the noise, and end the post-truth malaise, truth can once again flourish freely, as nature intended.

Fake news

In contemporary debates, post-truth and fake news are largely represented as pieces of the same puzzle. Not unlike post-truth, fake news is not new to the English vocabulary (Tandoc, Lim, & Ling, 2018), dating back even further than post-truth (McNair, 2018). Nonetheless, public use of the term has risen significantly in recent years (Farkas & Schou, 2018). This is reflected in English dictionaries that only recently added the term, if at all (Deeb, 2019; Steinmetz, 2017). Paradoxically, the Oxford English Dictionary initially remained hesitant to adopt "fake news," claiming that the term's meaning was "still evolving" (Steinmetz, 2017), while Merriam Webster also hesitated, yet claiming it was due its meaning being "self-explanatory" (Merriam-Webster, n.d.)

The Oxford English Dictionary (n.d.) defines fake news as "news that conveys or incorporates false, fabricated, or deliberately misleading information, or that is characterized as or accused of doing so." This resembles the definition given by Cambridge Dictionary (n.d) describing fake news as "false stories that appear to be news, spread on the internet or using other media, usually created to influence political views or as a joke."

While these definitions overlap, they also diverge on several details, particularly on whether fake news *appears* to be news (as proposed by the Cambridge Dictionary) or whether it actually *is* a form of news (as defined by the Oxford English Dictionary). This discrepancy is also found in scholarly definitions, with Mourão and Robertson (2019, p. 1080) describing it as manipulation "packaged like news" and Allcott and Gentzkow (2017, p. 213) defining it as "news articles that are intentionally and verifiably false."

While this epistemological incongruity might seem miniscule, it highlights a fundamental difficulty haunting much of the current political landscape: namely, pinning down the boundaries between what counts as fake and what does not. In part, this has to do with the notion of "news," which comes with a whole set of difficulties of its own, referring to "both a phenomenon out there in the world and a report of that phenomenon" (Zelizer, 2005, p. 68). Thus, when scholars define fake news as falsehoods "disguising themselves as real news" (Tandoc, 2021, p. 111), the question becomes: what is meant by "real" news?

Another set of tensions contained in contemporary discourses has to do with the *purpose* of fake news. In the Cambridge Dictionary's definition, fake news is said to predominantly serve as jokes or political manipulation. In contrast to this kind of vocabulary, Craig Silverman (2017), editor at *Buzzfeed*, argues that fake news comprises only "false information that was created for financial gain," excluding political manipulation (and non-commercial jokes, it seems). The same applies to *The Guardian* commentator, Ella Hunt (2016), who states that "[s]trictly speaking, fake news is completely made up and designed to deceive readers to maximize traffic and profit." From a slightly different perspective, Brian McNair (2018) defines fake news as "[i]ntentional disinformation (invention or falsification of known facts) for political and/or commercial purposes, presented as real news" (p. 46), explicitly excluding satire, parody and conspiracy theories (p. 45). Finally, others define the term much more broadly as "information that is inconsistent with factual reality" (Brody & Meier, 2018, p. 2) or "a wide spectrum of misinformation ranging from disinformation and false information to biased/slanted news" (Feingold et al., 2017, p. 35).

All of this points to a third set of tensions, namely as to the intentionality of fake news. While most definitions emphasize a strong deliberateness or purposefulness in the production of fake news, others do not. The question that seems to be at the core of this tension is this: does the production of fake news have to be an intentional act – done with the purpose of forging half-baked truths – or can it also include non-intentional dissemination of lies unknown to whoever happens to spread it? Similarly, it often remains ambiguous who is to blame for disseminating fake news. When described as noise, fire, or a disease, fake news seems to have little human agency involved, yet others point to specific bad actors as culprits.

These kinds of discrepancies and ambiguities continue to feature in the post-truth worlds unpacked here. They highlight why the "ontology of fakeness" is not necessarily set in stone and that the discourses are part of creating the very worlds they are trying to describe. When investigating contemporary definitions of fake news, we often encounter an array of other concepts with their own conceptual histories and meanings. This includes ideas such as deception, manipulation, propaganda, falsification, misinformation, disinformation, gaslighting, the Big lie, bias, and hoax. In this sense, fake news often acts as an umbrella term for a range of other phenomena linked to ideas of persuasion and deceit. Yet, as scholars and journalists diverge considerably on what to include and exclude, the exact meaning of fake news remains highly ambiguous. This ambiguity has often been a theme in itself. Professor Tandoc and colleagues hint at this blurriness in a review of 34 academic articles on the topic: "A careful reading of each article identified six ways that previous studies have operationalized fake news: satire, parody, fabrication, manipulation, propaganda, and advertising" (Tandoc et al., 2018, p. 142).

Adding to this internal conceptual ambiguity, the connection between fake news and ideas of a post-truth era are also difficult to pin down. While some argue that it is the quantity of fake news, not least as brought about by digital media, that has triggered the post-truth era, others suggest this era to be indicative of more wide-ranging structural changes. In the first camp, it is argued that "[t]he existence of fake content in social life and media is not a new phenomenon; however, its escalation is. Information can now propagate at a speed and breadth never seen before due to the affordances of social media" (Webb & Jirotka, 2017, p. 415), making democracy flooded by a "daily tsunami of information" (Dahlgren, 2018, p. 22). Meanwhile, others argue that "the spread of disinformation is [only] a symptom of wider phenomena that affect societies facing rapid change" (European Commission, 2018, p. 4).

What we may begin to see from these descriptions, then, is how fake news and post-truth serve important, yet also ambiguous, functions within an increasingly dominant discourse in and around the current state of democracy. In these new post-truth worlds, one of the major questions has been (and continues to be) the causes of its emergence. Why is it, contemporary voices ask, that we have entered a new age of post-truth politics? Who or what is to blame for the hollowing out of democracy? And why has fake news suddenly started to circulate at such rapid speed? In response to these questions, a series of different "villains" have been proposed as causes and carriers of the current democratic predicament. It is these we turn to next.

Who is to blame? Villain 1: social media

When it comes to discourses of post-truth and fake news, the rise and consequences of digital media are impossible to avoid. Once hailed as a powerful democratizing force – uniting the world through global connectedness, participation, and freedom – the internet has increasingly turned into something much more sinister. Just like previous technological revolutions, the adoption of digital tools has supposedly ushered in societal upheaval as well as a point of no return:

> The technology of any age in history shapes the culture of the time. With the advent of agriculture and farming tools, humans developed stationary civilizations and abandoned thousands of years of itinerancy... So too did the wires and tubes that make up the internet reshape our society and our behavior. The anonymity of the internet made people bold and free, and also able to distance themselves from the impacts of their words.
>
> (Donovan et al., 2022, pp. 15–16)

In this narrative, the free information flows and open debates of digital media came with a hidden cost: rampant misinformation and deception. Social media – originally celebrated as an empowering force for circumventing hegemonic power (Castells, 2012) – now represent democracy's greatest threat: "popular platforms such as Twitter and Facebook are powerhouses that enable misinformation to spread on a massive scale" (Webb & Jirotka, 2017, p. 414). Indeed, in these narratives, it is often stated that "bots, fake accounts, and easily exploited social media algorithms provides a technical infrastructure for packaging the lie and delivering it to your inbox" (Howard, 2020, p. 17).

This portrayal of social media platforms as vehicles of post-truth stands in sharp contrast to how they were perceived just a decade earlier. In 2012, *Buzzfeed* journalist John Herrman argued that the digital architecture of platforms, such as Twitter, allowed social media to function as a "Truth Machine," excelling at "vetting ascertainable facts" (Herrman, 2012). From this perspective, false information online could easily be resisted and counteracted by social media users. By collaboratively fact-checking stories, users would work against the dissemination of fake information by systematically spreading corrections and proper evidence. Boler and Nemorin expressed a similar optimism in 2013, arguing that social media could empower citizens living under authoritarian rule: "the proliferating use of social media and communication technologies for purposes of dissent from official government and/or corporate-interest propaganda offers genuine cause for hope" (Boler & Nemorin, 2013, p. 411). This optimism relays the self-portrayals of social media companies, describing their aim as giving "people the power to share and making the world more open and connected," as formulated by Meta CEO Mark Zuckerburg (cited in Hoffmann, Proferes, & Zimmer, 2018, p. 205). Fast-forward a few years and new forms of state-funded social media propaganda "effectively sways voters, suppresses rivals, sows confusion, defames opposition, and spreads fake news" (Boler & Davis, 2018, p. 75). It thus seems that gloom and despair have replaced prior optimism within a relatively short timeframe.

Many of the features of digital media that were once seen as democratizing are now cast as dedemocratizing. While decentralized production of content was highlighted as a means of public deliberation, many now focus on how it "leaves us open to lines of deliberate attack from those trying to deceive or discourage us: we believe we're in groups of like-minded people, and this leaves us open to be exploited by malicious actors" (Ball, 2017). Katharine Viner, editor-in-chief of *The Guardian*, articulates this supposedly causal relationship between digital media and post-truth with even greater strength, arguing that "technology *disrupted the truth*… ushering in an era when everyone has their own facts" (Viner, 2016, added emphasis).

As information travels through networks of users, there is a high risk of deception, as users perceive content not as deriving "from a fake news or hyper-partisan site," but as "information from their friends or relative" (Ball, 2017). This also means that *trust* starts to interfere with or combat *truth*: when users receive content from people they trust, they forget to assess its inherent accuracy. With this, the risk of rampant misinformation increases dramatically, according to a range of scholars and journalists (see, e.g., Howard, 2020; Vosoughi et al., 2018). In this way, "misinformation and biases infect social media, both intentionally and accidentally" (Ciampaglia & Menczer, 2018).

These discussions are often connected to concerns and ideas about echo chambers, filter bubbles, bots, and deepfakes. While the overlapping notions of echo chambers and filter bubbles pre-date pervasive debates around fake news and post-truth (Crawford, 2009; Pariser, 2011), they have increasingly served as explanatory devices for the current democratic crisis. Indeed, prominent voices have suggested that these interconnected phenomena are key villains of the post-truth era: "social media has allowed people to choose their favored 'echo chamber' in which most available information conforms to pre-existing attitudes and biases" (Lewandowsky, Ecker, & Cook, 2017, p. 359). Millions of people have become vulnerable to fake news, increasingly "trapped in a filter bubble composed of content shared by their contacts and selected by the social media's algorithms" (Kalpokas, 2018, p. 13).

Adding to these discourses of echo chambers and filter bubbles are so-called social bots, which are software-driven accounts that initiate or drive the dissemination of malicious content (Bump, 2017). In this context, there are diverging opinions on what exactly constitutes a social bot. Bots are varyingly described as "programmes performing repetitive functions" (Vasu, Ang, Teo, Jayakumar & Rahman, 2018, p. 11), "fake online personas through which a small group of operatives can create an illusion of a widespread opinion" (Lewandowsky, Ecker, & Cook, 2017, p. 354) or "artificially-intelligent digital 'robots'" (Boler & Davis, 2018, p. 75). That being the case, there is widespread concern that social media not only create or amplify problematic forms of social behavior (predicating the sharing of information on relations of trust rather than relations of truth), but also create opportunities for semi-autonomous forms of misinformation.

Finally, so-called deepfakes have become the latest fear in connection to social media, often envisioned as providing "fake news on steroids or an upcoming infodemic (or infocalypse)" (Kalpokas & Kalpokiene, 2022, p. 4). Deepfakes encompass digitally manipulated videos that can convincingly alter a person's actions or words. While this technology is still in its infancy, it already serves as a powerful vehicle of dystopian speculation (Chesney & Citron, 2019a). Indeed, it is often argued that "in our broken information ecosystem… AI and deepfakes are the latest evolving threat" (Schick, 2020).

From these descriptions, we can begin to see how digital and social media – understood variously as technological infrastructures, means of social behavior, or semi-autonomous entities with agency of their own – have come to constitute democratic villains in contemporary post-truth worlds. They have been used as explanatory devices in search of the foundations for the current situation. In so being, they have not been alone.

Villain 2: journalism

A second villain that has featured prominently in post-truth worlds is journalism, understood both as a field of professional practice and a set of channels of mass communication. Not unlike social media, we find a series of different portrayals of this supposed villain. The rise of post-truth and fake news has been explained as the simultaneous result of journalism's declining role in society, its declining standards of content, its increasing plurality, and its changing business models. In such descriptions, there is little agreement on the relationship between journalism, post-truth, and fake news and what is deemed cause and effect. What is common between these narratives is a longing or nostalgia for a time in which journalism represented one of society's pillars of truth: "For all its shortcomings, mainstream journalism has served as an essential institution of democratic public spheres and its decline – without any suitable alternative in sight – is profoundly worrisome" (Dahlgren, 2018, p. 25).

One of the more pervasive arguments currently being levelled is that the rise of fake news is a more or less direct attribute of the decline of (mainstream) journalism as a professional practice, authoritative gatekeeper, and institutional field. According to Professor Michael A. Peters, this is caused by increased privatization, pace, and fragmentation, accompanied by decreased depth in journalism: "Post-truth politics," he writes,

> is a development of an increasingly privatized and fragmented public news that began with the "sound bite" and "photo opportunity" to bypass public discussion in the regime of the 24-h news cycle, where news channels take on the mantle of party ideologies often deliberately distorting the truth.
>
> (Peters, 2017, p. 564)

In this sense, the problems currently facing democracies are not about fake news *per se*, it is claimed, but about the quality and integrity of the journalistic field: "We have a bad news problem, not a fake news problem," as stated by founder of fact-checking website *Snopes*, David Mikkelson (2016).

Others, like Professor Richard Sambrook (2018), writing for *The Conversation*, have argued that the problem is not necessarily one of quality or standards, but of trust, transparency, and accountability. "Many will shrug and say the media has brought it on itself through cynical tabloid journalism, phone hacking and more," Sambrook suggests, "But this too misunderstands that different news organisations work to very different ends. The Financial Times is in a different business to The Sun – or the BBC to The Daily Mail." From this perspective, the rise of fake news largely becomes an effect of declining journalistic standards, rather than a cause.

Adding to this line of argument, the decline of journalism – and the fake news created in its wake – has also been linked to external factors, particularly the rise of digital media. As digital media have come to dominate the public sphere, journalistic business models have been left in ruins, leaving the scene wide open for fake news to take hold, as proposed by Professor Philip Howard in the book *Lie Machines*:

Journalism, especially print media, has been transformed since the arrival of online media and platforms such as Google and Facebook. The most professional news outlets in every country now must compete with content producers – domestic and international – who produce junk news that is sensational, conspiratorial, extremist, and inflammatory commentary packaged as news. Changes in online ad markets and the mechanics of ad placement have encouraged the growth of junk news.

(Howard, 2020, p. 138)

There is often a sense that traditional news media are being swallowed up by the upsurge of a new and constantly evolving media landscape. Similar to fake news itself, the rise of digital media is often presented as almost having a life or agency of its own. Invoking Greek mythology, Professor Jayson Harsin thus argues that "[t]he news 'apparatus' is today a many-headed hydra (for each newspaper that dies, 2,000 new blogs, Facebook, and Twitter feeds are born!), with literally millions of channels, websites, social media feeds" (Harsin, 2015, p. 329).

Quite a few commentators have argued that it is precisely the barrage of new platforms, together with a loss of funding and staff at traditional media companies, that has contributed to a lowering of trust in journalism and the journalistic field. Writing for Columbia Journalism Review, Philip Eil (2018) captures this sense of withering trust by suggesting that, at least in a US context, "The general public doesn't care as much about press freedom and the First Amendment as we hope. They don't know as much about the basic principles of journalism as we assume. And they sure as hell don't trust journalism as much as we would like." In this line of argument, journalism represents the embodiment of free democratic speech, making declining trust in journalistic institutions equivalent to declining support for freedom of expression. Just as democracy and truth are often equated in post-truth discourses, so too is journalism intrinsically coupled with truth, free speech, and democracy.

Writing for *The Guardian*, James Ball (2018) exemplifies the connection between journalism, truth, and democracy by arguing that declining trust in journalism automatically leads to uninformed masses: "when people turn off mainstream news through fear of 'hidden agendas,' they become increasingly vulnerable to polarising and extremist messages from other sources." This lack of trust in mainstream media, what could be called a *de-sacralization* of the journalistic field, pushes citizens in the direction of polarization and alternative epistemic realities: "people increasingly see news as just another form of media, which they can choose to dip into or not. If it's depressing, or doesn't fit their interests, then why not just turn off?" (Ball, 2018). A decline in trust and the rise of fake news seem to be locked together in a spiraling feedback loop, although the exact causal relationship remains uncertain. Indeed, "[t]he declining trust in mainstream media could be both a cause and a consequence of fake news gaining more traction" (Allcott & Gentzkow, 2017, p. 215).

What we can begin to see, then, is that journalism has often been cast as both a victim and a villain in post-truth discourses. On the one hand, the journalistic field is articulated as a producer of the current post-truth moment, due in large part to its internal fragmentation, commercialization, and increased pace of constant news, as well as the withering away of ethical standards. On the other hand, journalism is also portrayed as caught up in the very thing it has been deemed to be a producer of. It is the victim of an avalanche of low quality content. The rise of digital media, the vaporization of sustainable business models, plummeting societal trust, and a lack of public authority has meant, according to many commentators, that the foundation of journalism is waning away. It is precisely due to these shifts that it has become possible for fake news to flourish largely uncontested. Despite ambivalence within post-truth discourses as to how much journalism should be cast as a villain or victim of post-truth – suffering a frontal attack or a self-inflicted wound – a tight coupling between journalism, truth, and democracy prevails. As a result, the declining societal role of journalism – described throughout post-truth worlds – automatically becomes a declining role of truth as well as democracy itself.

Villain 3: the masses

A final villain in our small gallery of post-truth wrongdoers is the democratic people or masses themselves. Indeed, as we have already touched upon above, there is no shortage of voices arguing that citizens and (perhaps) even entire populations are currently trapped in epistemic worlds or alternative realities, more or less completely disconnected from "proper" truth and rationality. This kind of rhetoric, linking the post-truth moment with either the coming of new secluded spaces or downright unintelligent masses, is not uncommon, as exemplified by *Huffington Post* commentator Matt Masur (2016): "The most important thing in a functional society is a well-informed public. What we have now is not only uninformed but misinformed masses. That's something that should scare us all."

Society is not only changing at the top of the food chain – where politicians and public figures spread lies and falsehoods – pressure against truth is also building rapidly from below. Lewandowsky, Ecker, and Cook (2017, p. 360) voice this idea very clearly, linking misguided and isolated publics with the rise of post-truth and fake news:

> We are now facing a situation in which a large share of the populace is living in an epistemic space that has abandoned conventional criteria of evidence, internal consistency, and fact-seeking. It follows that the current state of public discourse can no longer be examined through the lens of misinformation that can be debunked but as an alternative reality that is shared by millions.

Millions of people have supposedly become completely disconnected from truth, trapped in secluded epistemic worlds. This dystopian diagnosis of democratic masses having abandoned conventional criteria of evidence and rationality has also partially been relayed by Higgins (2016, p. 6), writing for *Nature*: "the public hears what it wants to hear, because many people get their news exclusively from sources whose bias they agree with." Other analysts reach similar conclusions, though from somewhat different angles. Some argue that the problem with misinformed citizens is not necessarily that they have a "biased" selection of sources or actively abandon "proper" forms of truth telling. Instead, it is the media landscape itself that makes selection impossible: "citizens are encircled by millions of channels, newspapers, websites, blogs and social media feeds creating an information – or misinformation – overload" (Taş, 2018, p. 3).

Drawing on an evolutionary register, Professor of Philosphy Justin McBrayer (2020) similarly argues that the human species simply cannot cognitively handle the current media environment, since "humans are naturally good at solving Stone Age problems" (p. 66). From a slightly different perspective, Maddalena and Gili (2020) argue that it is not simply our media, but also our societies that have become too complex for people to grasp. As a result, "the ability of mere individuals to understand the social world has decreased because they do not have the tools to comprehend what is happening around them" (Maddalena & Gili, 2020, p. 5).

From these diverging narratives, we can see that the exact reasoning for why citizens have ended up being indifferent to the power of facts and evidence differs quite substantially. The main conclusion, however, remains the same: millions of citizens have become gullible, easy to deceive, and indifferent to truth, living in their own secluded epistemic bubbles.

These arguments are to some extent not new, as political philosophers and commentators have lamented the inability of the public to process information for centuries. American intellectual Walter Lippmann presented in his 1925 book *The Phantom Public* – a follow-up to his famous *Public Opinion* – a bleak view on the role of the public in modern democratic societies. Within the first few pages of *The Phantom Public*, Lippmann (2010) compares the modern citizen to a "deaf spectator in the back row" (p. 25), a bewildered "puppy trying to lick three bones at once" (p. 28) and a "fat man … [trying] to be a ballet dancer" (p. 32). This sets the scene for his wider argument that modern citizens are more or less incapable of participating in democratic politics in the way envisioned in theories of democratic governance. According to Lippmann (2010), the citizen of the (then) contemporary United States is simply too preoccupied with "earning a living, rearing children and enjoying his [sic] life … to keep himself informed about the progress of his swarming confusion of problems" (p. 28). Modern life is too time-consuming to stay informed about societal matters, and even if citizens *do* have time, they only have "casual interest in facts and but a poor appetite for theory" (p. 28). To Lippmann

(2010), the result of this civic indifference is that, even though democratic ideals of informed citizens might claim otherwise, governance is in practice always carried out by "politicians, officeholders and influential men who make settlements with other politicians, officeholders and influential men" (p. 32). Due to this discrepancy between democratic ideals and the "actual" workings of this particular system, Lippmann proposed that democracy is in an undesirable state in which its system of governance is based on a "mere phantom ... an abstraction" (p. 40). Instead of pretending to involve the masses, democracies should acknowledge that people are largely indifferent and misguided and let the "knowledgeable men" decide the best course of action.

We can speculate whether current post-truth worlds do not, in their own way, invoke a *phantom*: namely in the form of Lippmann himself. Indeed, it seems that citizens are often portrayed precisely along the same lines as in 1925. In this "neo-Lippmannian discourse" it is not only the business of everyday life or disinterest that keeps citizens from being informed, but the supposed construction of whole new alternative realities of disinformation and fake news. The phantom public, it would seem, has migrated into a whole new world that is more or less completely secluded from the world of facts.

Democratic eschatology

This chapter has taken a first stab at unpacking and understanding the discursive rise of contemporary post-truth worlds. It has sought to examine how and in what ways issues of post-truth and fake news are currently being articulated, problematized, and understood across dominant narratives of our time. Doing so, it has showcased how a wide number of actors – from the fields of politics, science, and journalism – currently make sense of the state and future of democracy. In this still developing political terrain, fake news and post-truth are seen as a pandemic, undermining, and systematically challenging the very firmament of civilization. These are diseases or plagues that will kill the democratic tradition from within – noise that might drown out the signal of truth. What lies at the center of these contemporary narratives often amounts to a kind of democratic eschatology: that is, a series of discourses that are premised on foreseeing and predicting a future involving an almost inevitable decline and fall of democracy, including its ultimate disappearance and destruction. This democratic eschatology is, as demonstrated in this chapter, bound up with certain understandings and articulations of the relationship between democracy, rationality, and truth. While it often remains an implicit premise, post-truth worlds tend to strongly equate democracy with truth-telling, reason, and rationality. Democracy is seen as a necessary condition for the possibility of truth and vice versa. Thus, the contemporary mutations of truth – into fake, alternative, or deceptive forms – represents an external, existential threat that cuts to the very heart of this form of co-habitation.

These democratic eschatologies are histories with multiple subjects. Indeed, as shown in this chapter, it often remains uncertain exactly *who* or *what* is to blame for this ongoing crisis of truth and democracy. Although there are plenty of potential villains, there still seems to be no firm answer to the altogether enigmatic question: who did it? Our investigation of the supposed villains of contemporary post-truth worlds is, however, still incomplete. We have shown how digital media, journalism, and the masses have all been accused of being drivers of false information. Yet, we have yet to dive into the socio-political events that have been deemed the symbols or epitomes of post-truth. This is precisely what we will do in the next chapter.

References

Allcott, H., & Gentzkow, M. (2017). Social Media and Fake News in the 2016 Election. *Journal of Economic Perspectives, 31*(2), 211–236. www.doi.org/10.1257/jep.31.2.211

Amrita, M. (2017, 12 December). Understanding the Plague of Fake News and How to Combat it. *Medium*. https://medium.com/melissa-persauds-portfolio/understanding-the-plague-of-fake-news-and-how-to-combat-it-862d4920e61b

Andrews, E.L. (2019, 9 October). How Fake News Spreads Like a Real Virus. *Stanford Engineering*. https://engineering.stanford.edu/magazine/article/how-fake-news-spreads-real-virus

Ball, J. (2017). *Post-Truth: How Bullshit Conquered the World*. London: Biteback Publishing.

Ball, J. (2018, 22 January). Distrust of Social Media is Dragging Traditional Journalism Down. *The Guardian*. www.theguardian.com/commentisfree/2018/jan/22/distrust-social-media-traditional-journalism-fake-news

Boler, M., & Davis, E. (2018). The Affective Politics of the "Post-Truth" Era: Feeling Rules and Networked Subjects. *Emotion, Space and Society, 27*, 75–85. https://doi.org/10.1016/j.emospa.2018.03.002

Boler, M., & Nemorin, S. (2013). Dissent, Truthiness, and Skepticism in the Global Media Landscape: Twenty-First Century Propaganda in Times of War. In J. Auerbach & R. Castronovo (Eds.), *The Oxford Handbook of Propaganda Studies* (pp. 395–417). Oxford: Oxford University Press.

Brody, D.C., & Meier, D.M. (2018). How to model fake news, *Arxiv*, 1–17. https://arxiv.org/pdf/1809.00964.pdf

Bump, P. (2017, 12 June). Welcome to the Era of the 'Bot' as Political Boogeyman. *The Washington Post*. www.washingtonpost.com/news/politics/wp/2017/06/12/welcome-to-the-era-of-the-bot-as-political-boogeyman/

Cambridge Dictionary (n.d.). *Fake News*. Accessed 24 April 2023. https://dictionary.cambridge.org/dictionary/english/fake-news

Cassauwers, T. (2019, 15 April). Can Artificial Intelligence Help End Fake News? *Horizon – The EU Research and Innovation Magazine*. https://ec.europa.eu/research-and-innovation/en/horizon-magazine/can-artificial-intelligence-help-end-fake-news

Castells, M. (2012). *Networks of Outrage and Hope: Social Movements in the Internet Age*. Cambridge: Polity Press.

Chesney, R., & Citron, C. (2019a). Deepfakes and the New Disinformation War: The Coming Age of Post-Truth Geopolitics. *Foreign Affairs*, *98*(1), 147–155. www.foreign affairs.com/articles/world/2018-12-11/deepfakes-and-new-disinformation-war

Chesney, R., & Citron, D.K. (2019b). 21st Century-Style Truth Decay: Deep Fakes and The Challenge for Privacy, Free Expression, and National Security. *Maryland Law Review*, *78*(4), 882–891. www.washingtontimes.com/news/2019/jan/29/dan-coats-gina-

Ciampaglia, G. L., & Menczer, F. (2018, 20 June). Misinformation and Biases Infect Social Media, Both Intentionally and Accidentally. *The Conversation*. https://theconve rsation.com/misinformation-and-biases-infect-social-media-both-intentionally-and-accidentally-97148

Corner, J. (2017). Fake News, Post-Truth and Media–Political Change. *Media, Culture and Society*, *39*(7), 1100–1107. https://doi.org/10.1177/0163443717726743

Crawford, K. (2009). Following You: Disciplines of Listening in Social Media. *Continuum*, *23*(4), 525–535. https://doi.org/10.1080/10304310903003270

d'Ancona, M. (2017). *Post-Truth: The New War on Truth and How to Fight Back*. London: Ebury Press.

Dahlgren, P. (2018). Media, Knowledge and Trust: The Deepening Epistemic Crisis of Democracy. *Javnost – The Public*, *25*(1–2), 20–27. https://doi.org/10.1080/13183 222.2018.1418819

Davies, W. (2016, 24 August). The Age of Post-Truth Politics. *The New York Times*. www. nytimes.com/2016/08/24/opinion/campaign-stops/the-age-of-post-truth-politics.html

Deeb, A. V. (2019). "Fake News" Has Been Added to the Oxford English Dictionary. *Mashable Middle East*. https://me.mashable.com/culture/7507/fake-news-has-been-added-to-the-oxford-english-dictionary

Donovan, J., Dreyfuss, E., & Friedberg, B. (2022). *Meme Wars: The Untold Story of the Online Battles Upending Democracy in America*. New York: Bloomsbury Academic.

Eil, P. (2018, 11 April). 5 Ways Journalists Can Regain Trust from Readers. *Columbia Journalism Review*. www.cjr.org/analysis/trust-journalism.php

European Commission. (2018, 26 April). Tackling Online Disinformation: A European Approach. https://ec.europa.eu/digital-single-market/en/news/communication-tackl ing-online-disinformation-european-approach

Eysenbach, G. (2020). How to Fight an Infodemic: The Four Pillars of Infodemic Management. *Journal of Medical Internet Research*, *22*(6). https://doi.org/ 10.2196/21820

Farkas, J., & Schou, J. (2018). Fake News as a Floating Signifier: Hegemony, Antagonism and the Politics of Falsehood. *Javnost – The Public*, *25*(3), 298–314. https://doi.org/ 10.1080/13183222.2018.1463047

Feingold, R., Herman, L., Finkel, J., Jiang, S., Luo, M., Mears, R., ... Torres-Echeverry, N. (2017). Fake News and Misinformation: The Roles of the Nation's Digital Newsstands, Facebook, Google, Twitter and Reddit. *Stanford Law School* (*10*). https://law.stanford. edu/publications/fake-news-and-misinformation-the-roles-of-the-nations-digital-new sstands-facebook-google-twitter-and-reddit/

Fish, W. (2017). "Post-Truth" Politics and Illusory Democracy. *Psychotherapy and Politics International*, *14*(3), 211–213. https://doi.org/10.1002/ppi.1387

Golson, P. (2021, 5 May). The Disinformation Wildfire. *Brunswick*. www.brunswickgr oup.com/disinformation-wildfire-i18810/

Hannan, J. (2018). Trolling Ourselves to Death? Social Media and Post-Truth Politics. *European Journal of Communication, 33*(2), 214–226. https://doi.org/10.1177/02673 23118760323

Harsin, J. (2015). Regimes of Posttruth, Postpolitics, and Attention Economies. *Communication, Culture and Critique, 8*(2), 327–333. https://doi.org/10.1111/ cccr.12097

Herrman, J. (2012, 30 October). Twitter is a Truth Machine. *Buzzfeed News*. www.buzzf eednews.com/article/jwherrman/twitter-is-a-truth-machine

Higgins, K. (2016). Post-Truth: A Guide for the Perplexed. *Nature, 540*(7631), 9. https:// doi.org/10.1038/540009a

Hoffmann, A.L., Proferes, N., & Zimmer, M. (2018). "Making the World More Open and Connected": Mark Zuckerberg and the Discursive Construction of Facebook and its Users. *New Media & Society, 20*(1), 199–218. https://doi.org/10.1177/146144481 6660784

Howard, P.N. (2020). *Lie Machines: How to Save Democracy from Troll Armies, Deceitful Robots, Junk News Operations, and Political Operatives*. New: Haven: Yale University Press.

Hughes, B. (2016, 16 November). How to Fix the Fake News Problem. *CNN*. https:// edition.cnn.com/2016/11/16/opinions/how-to-fix-the-fake-news-problem-hughes/ index.html

Hunt, E. (2016, 17 December). What is Fake News? How to Spot it and What You Can Do To Stop it. *The Guardian*. www.theguardian.com/media/2016/dec/18/what-is-fake-news-pizzagate

Kalpokas, I. (2018). On Guilt and Post-Truth Escapism. *Philosophy & Social Criticism, 44*(10), 1127–1147. https://doi.org/10.1177/0191453718794752

Kalpokas, I., & Kalpokiene, J. (2022). *Deepfakes: A Realistic Assessment of Potentials, Risks, and Policy Regulation*. Cham: Springer.

Keyes, R. (2004). *The Post-Truth Era: Dishonesty and Deception in Contemporary Life*. New York: St. Martin's Press.

Korsunska, A. (2019). The Spread and Mutation of Science Misinformation. In N.G. Taylor, C. Christian-Lamb, M.H. Martin, & B. Nardi (Eds.), *Information in Contemporary Society*. https://doi.org/10.1007/978-3-030-15742-5_15

Kucharski, A. (2016). Post-Truth: Study Epidemiology of Fake News. *Nature, 540*(7634), 525–525. https://doi.org/10.1038/540525a

Lewandowsky, S., Ecker, U.K.H., & Cook, J. (2017). Beyond Misinformation: Understanding and Coping with the "Post-Truth" Era. *Journal of Applied Research in Memory and Cognition, 6*(4), 353–369. https://doi.org/10.1016/j.jarmac.2017.07.008

Lippmann, W. (2010). Excerpt from *The Phantom Public*. In J. Gribsrud, H. Moe, A. Molander, & G. Murdock (Eds.), *The Idea of the Public Sphere* (pp. 25–42), Lanham: Lexington Books.

Maddalena, G., & Gili, G. (2020). *The History and Theory of Post-Truth Communication*. Cham: Palgrave Macmillan.

Masur, M. (2016, 15 November). Bernie Sanders Could Replace President Trump with Little-Known Loophole. *The Huffington Post*. www.huffingtonpost.com/entry/bernie-sanders-could-replace-president-trump-with-little_us_5829f25fe4b02b1f5257a6b7

McBrayer, J.P. (2020). *Beyond Fake News: Finding the Truth in a World of Misinformation*. London: Routledge.

McIntyre, L. (2018). *Post-Truth*. Cambridge, MA: MIT Press.

McNair, B. (2018). *Fake News: Falsehood, Fabrication and Fantasy in Journalism*. London: Routledge.

Merriam-Webster. (n.d.). Words We're Watching: The Real Story of "Fake News." Accessed 24 April 2023. www.merriam-webster.com/words-at-play/the-real-story-of-fake-news

Mikkelson, D. (2016, 17 November). We Have a Bad News Problem, Not a Fake News Problem. *Snopes*. www.snopes.com/news/2016/11/17/we-have-a-bad-news-problem-not-a-fake-news-problem/

Mourão, R.R., & Robertson, C.T. (2019). Fake News as Discursive Integration: An Analysis of Sites That Publish False, Misleading, Hyperpartisan and Sensational Information. *Journalism Studies*, *20*(14), 2077–2095. https://doi.org/10.1080/1461670X.2019.1566871

Norman, M. (2016, 8 November). Whoever Wins the US Presidential Election, We've Entered a Post-Truth World: There's No Going Back Now. *The Independent*. www.independent.co.uk/voices/us-election-2016-donald-trump-hillary-clinton-who-wins-post-truth-world-no-going-back-a7404826.html

Oxford Dictionaries (2016). Word of the Year: Post-Truth. Accessed 24 2023. https://languages.oup.com/word-of-the-year/2016/

Oxford English Dictionary. (n.d.). *fake, n.2 and adj*. Oxford English Dictionary. Accessed 24 April 2023. www.oed.com/viewdictionaryentry/Entry/67776

Pariser, E. (2011). *The Filter Bubble: How the New Personalized Web is Changing What We Read and How We Think*. New York: Penguin Books.

Parsons, J. (2017, 23 January). How to Stop "Fake News": Psychologists Believe We Can Be "Inoculated" Against Misinformation. *The Daily Mirror*. www.mirror.co.uk/science/how-stop-fake-news-psychologists-9675939

Peters, M.A. (2017). Education in a Post-Truth World. *Educational Philosophy and Theory*, *49*(6), 563–566. https://doi.org/10.1080/00131857.2016.1264114

Rosenbaum, S. (2017, 18 November). Finding News in the Noise. *Huffington Post*. www.huffingtonpost.com/entry/finding-news-in-the-noise_us_5a105154e4b0e30a95850747

Rubin, V.L. (2018). The Disinformation Triangle: The Epidemiology of "Fake News." In *The Information without Borders Conference 2018*. http://victoriarubin.fims.uwo.ca/2018/01/11/keynote-speech-information-without-borders-conference-2018/

Sambrook, R. (2018, 1 June). Fake News Week: Three Stories that Reveal the Extreme Pressure Journalism is Now Under. *The Conversation*. https://theconversation.com/fake-news-week-three-stories-that-reveal-the-extreme-pressure-journalism-is-now-under-97568

Schick, N. (2020). *Deep Fakes and the Infocalypse: What You Urgently Need To Know*. London: Monoray.

Silverman, C. (2017). What Do We Mean When We Say Fake News? *The Fake Newsletter*. Accessed 24 April 2023. https://us2.campaign-archive.com/?u=657b595bbd3c63e045787f019&id=e0b2b9eaf0&e=30348b6327

Simon, F.M., & Camargo, C.Q. (2021). Autopsy of a Metaphor: The Origins, Use and Blind Spots of the 'Infodemic.' *New Media and Society*. https://doi.org/10.1177/14614448211031908

Singer, P. W., & Brooking, E.T. (2019). *LikeWar: The Weaponization of Social Media*. Boston: Mariner Books.

Steinmetz, K. (2017, 27 September). The Dictionary is Adding an Entry for "Fake News." *Time Magazine.* http://time.com/4959488/donald-trump-fake-news-meaning/

Steinmetz, K. (2018, 9 August). How Your Brain Tricks You Into Believing Fake News. *Time Magazine.* http://time.com/5362183/the-real-fake-news-crisis/

Stelter, B. (2016, 1 November). The Plague of Fake News is Getting Worse: Here's How to Protect Yourself. *CNN.* https://money.cnn.com/2016/10/30/media/facebook-fake-news-plague/

Stupp, C. (2017, 13 November). Gabriel Leading Commission Effort Against Fake News 'Disease.' *EURACTIV.* www.euractiv.com/section/digital-single-market/news/gabriel-leading-commission-effort-against-fake-news-disease/

Suiter, J. (2016). Post-Truth Politics. *Political Insight, 7*(3), 25–27. https://doi.org/10.1177/2041905816680417

Svoboda, E. (2022, 18 August). Vaccinating People Against Fake News. *Open Mind Magazine.* www.openmindmag.org/articles/vaccinating-people-against-fake-news

Tandoc, E.C. (2021). Fake News. In H. Tumber & S. Waisbord (Eds.), *The Routledge Companion to Media Disinformation and Populism* (pp. 110–117). London: Routledge.

Tandoc, E.C., Lim, Z.W., & Ling, R. (2018). Defining "Fake News": A Typology of Scholarly Definitions. *Digital Journalism, 6*(2), 137–153. https://doi.org/10.1080/21670811.2017.1360143

Taş, H. (2018). The 15 July Abortive Coup and Post-Truth Politics in Turkey. *Southeast European and Black Sea Studies, 18*(1), 1–19, https://doi.org/10.1080/14683857.2018.1452374

Temming, M. (2018, 27 September). Scientists Enlist Computers to Hunt Down Fake News. *Science News Explores.* www.snexplores.org/article/scientists-enlist-computers-hunt-down-fake-news

Tentolouris, A., Ntanasis-Stathopoulos, I., Vlachakis, P.K., Tsilimigras, D.I., Gavriatopoulou, M., & Dimopoulos, M.A. (2021). COVID-19: Time to Flatten the Infodemic Curve. *Clinical and Experimental Medicine, 21*(2), 161–165. https://doi.org/10.1007/s10238-020-00680-x

Vasu, N., Ang, B., Teo, T-A., Jayakumar, S., & Rahman, M.D.B.A. (2018, 19 January). *Fake News: National Security in the Post-Truth Era.* S. Rajaratnam School of International Studies, Nanyang Technological University website: www.rsis.edu.sg/wp-content/uploads/2018/01/PR180313_Fake-News_WEB.pdf

Viner, K. (2016, 12 July). How Technology Disrupted the Truth. *The Guardian.* www.theguardian.com/media/2016/jul/12/how-technology-disrupted-the-truth?

Vosoughi, S., Roy, D., & Aral, S. (2018). The Spread of True and False News Online. *Science, 359*(March), 1146–1151. https://doi.org/10.1126/science.aap9559

van der Linden, S. (2023). *Foolproof: Why Misinformation Infects Our Minds and How to Build Immunity.* London: 4th Estate.

van der Linden, S., Roozenbeek, J., & Compton, J. (2020). Inoculating Against Fake News About COVID-19. *Frontiers in Psychology, 11,* 1–7. https://doi.org/10.3389/fpsyg.2020.566790

Webb, H., & Jirotka, M. (2017). Nuance, Societal Dynamics, and Responsibility in Addressing Misinformation in the Post-Truth Era: Commentary on Lewandowsky, Ecker, and Cook. *Journal of Applied Research in Memory and Cognition, 6*(4), 414–417. https://doi.org/10.1016/j.jarmac.2017.10.001

Woolley, S. (2020). *The Reality Game: How the Next Wave of Technology Will Break the Truth.* New York: PublicAffairs.

Zelizer, B. (2005). Definitions of Journalism. In G. Overholser & K.H. Jamieson (Eds.), *The Institutions of American Democracy: The Press* (pp. 66–80). Oxford: Oxford University Press.

Zhang, L., Iyendo, T.O., Apuke, O.D., & Gever, C.V. (2022). Experimenting the Effect of using Visual Multimedia Intervention to Inculcate Social Media Literacy Skills to Tackle Fake News. *Journal of Information Science.* Advance online publication. https://doi.org/10.1177/01655515221131797

5 Crises upon crises

Post-truth – and the supposedly unstoppable barrage of misinformation, fake news, and alternative facts that has started to flood in its wake – has been deemed a major crisis for human civilization, signaling a deep-seated rupture within the very fabric of liberal democracies. Indeed, as shown throughout the previous chapters, a whole plethora of voices have explicitly articulated post-truth as a crisis event, whether this be labeled as an "epistemic crisis" (Hoggan-Kloubert & Hoggan, 2023), "infodemic crisis" (WHO, 2021), "information crisis" (LSE Commission on Truth Trust and Technology, 2018), "fake news crisis" (Nelson & Taneja, 2018, p. 3720) or "infocalypse" (Schick, 2020). Indeed, in this way, post-truth worlds often center on the idea that the very constitution of democracy is under siege. Unless wide-ranging measures are taken, the crisis cannot be avoided or rectified. The demise of truth – it is often claimed – signals the potential doom for society as we have come to know it.

With this chapter, we wish to go beyond the ways in which post-truth, misinformation, and fake news are articulated as a crisis *in and of themselves*. Doing so, we are interested in interrogating how these issues have been discursively entangled with a number of other (seemingly disconnected) crisis events over the past few years. More specifically, with this chapter we zoom in on three contemporary crisis moments, all of which have been articulated as symbols, causes, or proofs of a post-truth era. First, we dive into the rise and fall of Donald Trump as 45th president of the United States, culminating in the storm of the US Capitol Building in 2021. Second, we look closer at the COVID-19 pandemic in 2020 and the so-called infodemic that accompanied it. Third, we take a brief glimpse at the Russian invasion of Ukraine in 2022 and the ensuing struggles over information.

Our concern throughout these three cases is to understand how and in what ways issues of fake news, misinformation, and post-truth have been articulated and brought to the foreground in each crisis situation. By analyzing these seemingly disparate crisis moments, we wish to empirically dissect and understand how truth, politics, and democracy have been mobilized and interwoven within different domains. Although Trump's presidency, the COVID-19 pandemic,

DOI: 10.4324/9781003434870-7

and Russia's invasion of Ukraine span widely different geographies, scales, and issues, we nonetheless maintain that there is an analytical merit in exploring how and in what ways issues of post-truth and fake news have been discursively articulated within and around them. Why so? Because it seems to us that, despite the radical differences across the three cases explored here, there has nonetheless been a number of discursive similarities between them, not least in relation to how issues of fake news and misinformation have been articulated. To our mind, this is important to unpack as it can tell us something deeper about how fake news, disinformation, and post-truth – as phenomena, signifiers, and constructed threats – have become interweaved with diverse political struggles, visions, and solutions as to how democracy is and ought to be. How can it be, we ask in an open-ended manner, that across a number of different crises, we nonetheless seem to encounter the same ideas and discussions?

It is important to stress from the outset of this chapter that the events analyzed here are, of course, not exhaustive of how fake news has become coupled to different geo-political events. Other crises, from climate change to racial injustice, could also be highlighted. It is also important to stress that we by no means claim to provide fully-fledged analyses of any of the cases explored here. More than anything, the chapter provides a series of empirical glimpses that can and must be supplemented with other full-scale analyses of the myriad of geo-political, economic, and social issues that are so pertinent to each. Yet, by examining these three geo-political events, it is still our claim that we can begin to explore the ways in which post-truth worlds have coincided with and been strategically employed within seemingly disparate crisis moments. By understanding the latter, we can gain a deeper understanding of the former.

Some remarks on discourses and crisis

From a post-foundationalist and discursive perspective, crises are of particular significance (Nabers, 2017, 2019). Whenever a discrete set of events are labeled as a crisis, a whole discursive repertoire is also invoked. Stated somewhat simplified: a crisis signals that the current state of affairs – that is, the specific way in which the world has been formed up until a certain point – cannot go on. The crisis upsets and, in a sense, dislocates *the status quo*. Something is experienced as being out of joint. Not only that, a crisis forces us to explicitly articulate and name the meaning of the social world we currently inhabit. Crises call forth explanations. They urge us to take a stance and make sense of what is going on. Yet, these is nothing inevitably about how crises develop and take shape. When we state that a crisis "urges" or "forces" us to provide explanations of the social world, we do not mean this in any deterministic way. We are instead pointing to how the standardized and sedimented grammar of crises often entails such dispositions: whenever we are calling something a crisis, we have already acknowledged that something is dislocated. By naming and elaborating on that which has been dislocated, we begin to provide explanations for how the social world is currently ordered.

By dislocating existing discursive structures – however sedimented and seemingly neutral these may have seemed – crises invoke not only a rupture in the existing, but also a possibility for doing things otherwise. The crisis puts on display that the current way of ordering the world is not inevitable: it is the product of contingent decisions and can, in this precise sense, potentially be articulated in new ways. Accordingly, the discursive construction of crises often connects a diagnosis of the present with new articulations of how the future could and ought to be.

In the context of the North Atlantic Financial Crisis and the Eurozone crisis, Bob Jessop (2015) notes how moments of crisis not only give way to competing attempts to define, interpret, and hegemonize supposed causes (*why did it happen?*). Crises also give rise to political struggles to hegemonize the potential responses and future pathways *(what, if anything, is to be done?)*. In this sense, crises can be as much path-breaking as path-shaping processes. Yet, neither of these processes are ever self-evident or given. What is claimed to be either cause or solution will depend on the specific historical and political relations of the particular time.

As David Runciman (2016) succinctly notes, the concept of crisis is in and of itself deeply ambiguous, historical and – as a consequence – difficult to define:

> There are a number of fundamental difficulties involved in defining the scope of crises. These difficulties derive both from the ambiguity inherent in the term, and also from its current overuse to describe a wide variety of different political, social and cultural phenomena. These factors are related: crisis is a difficult concept to pin down not just in spite of its growing ubiquity as a label for all sorts of different kinds of events, but, in part, because of its growing ubiquity.
>
> (p. 3)

In our present era, crisis narratives have become increasingly prevalent, making the very meaning of crisis increasingly broad and fluid. Some scholars describe this as the rise of a "crisis society" (Heide & Simonsson, 2019; Rasmussen, 2021) – that is, a society in which the normative logic and political form of the crisis have started to become generalized or even permanent. What we take from these insights is that the very act of labeling a distinct set of events as a crisis is in itself deeply political. It is an act that has performative effects – it makes a difference. Doing so can, for example, be used to legitimize distinct forms of legislation, policing, and state violence that might otherwise not have been imaginable, e.g., by invoking a *state of exception* (Agamben, 2005) and martial law as a supposedly necessary response to the crisis itself.

Furthermore, even if a consensus can be established as to the causes of any particular crisis, this does not necessarily mean that there is going to be any agreement on the solutions. Indeed, in some situations, the hegemonic solution might even be to do nothing at all: that is, wander on as if nothing had happened. For a number of critical voices, this was precisely what took place in the aftermath of the financial crisis of 2007, as the neoliberal credos that had been a mainspring in the production of the meltdown seemed to go on unfettered. This led to, what the British sociologist, Colin Crouch (2011), has dubbed the strange non-death of neoliberalism. In this way, there is nothing to suggest that the invocation of a crisis will necessarily or by default (re-)politicize otherwise sedimented structures. Though crises may unearth the contingency of any given hegemonic order – thus displaying that things could indeed by otherwise – this need not be the case. Crises may just as well be discursively mobilized as a catalyst for further entrenching the already existing hegemony, turning potential *re*politicization into further *de*politicization – that is, a neutralization and naturalization of the present.

It is precisely in their capacity to condense and bring discursive struggles that might otherwise seem hidden to the foreground that we find crises important to study. It is through the oftentimes dense web of re- and depoliticization they are spun into that we find them analytically productive. And it is precisely for this reason that we wish to examine three contemporary crisis moments and use these as analytical prisms through which to further explore how fake news has become intertwined with wider ideas, visions, and solutions for what democracy is and ought to be in the 21st century.

Before diving in, a few more disclaimers are in order. As already stated, we do not pretend to provide a full-fleshed analysis of the crisis moments examined here. Moreover, the point of this chapter is not to claim that any of the crisis moments can be reduced to questions of truth, misinformation, and fake news. More modestly, our argument is that the issues of fake news and post-truth have become embedded in these different crisis moments, which, in turn, have become folded into broader discourses around fake news and post-truth. By understanding how and in what ways this has taken place, we might gain deeper insights into both visions and solutions currently presented for the future of democracy.

In a more theoretical register, we also want to make clear that the concept of crisis has a long philosophical and political history that we do not seek to fully unpack in this chapter. The history of the crisis concept is both multilayered and contested. We are well aware that there are entire academic fields dedicated to understanding not only the historical antecedents and development of crises, but also how to do crisis communication and management (see, e.g., Eastham et al., 1970; Heide & Simonsson, 2019; Koselleck, 2000; Nesbitt, 2017). In this chapter, we do not wish to gloss over these fields, yet neither do we pretend to take the full analytical force of these into account. Instead, deploying the post-foundationalist inventory we presented in Chapter 3, we wish to understand the strange morphing of post-truth worlds as they become intertwined and entangled with contemporary crisis narratives.

Crisis moment I: the rise and legacy of Trumpism (2016–)

It is difficult, if not impossible, to write about the post-truth era without bringing up Trump's name. Wherever one encounters issues of fake news and post-truth, references to Donald Trump are plenty.

The story is well known and perhaps even slightly worn out. Donald Trump became the 45th president of the United States in 2016, following a campaign shrouded in controversy and spectacle. During his presidency, his cabinet continuously spread lies, half-baked truths, and deception in seemingly all areas of political intervention. When voted out of the Oval Office in 2020, Trump repeatedly made unsubstantiated claims about voter fraud, urging his followers to "Stop the Steal." This culminated in an attack on the Capitol Building on 6 January 2021, where Trump supporters tried to violently stop the normal transition of power.

The rise and legacy of Donald Trump has, from the very beginning, been steeped in crisis narratives. Prominent journalists and scholars have argued that Trump's presidency and struggle to maintain power represents a major crisis for US democracy. As journalist, Susan B. Glasser (2021), writes in *The New Yorker*: "The Trump Administration is over; the Trump crisis is not." Professor Emeritus of Political Science, William Crotty (2021) similarly argues that "the presidential election of 2020 represented a crisis point in American history. Nothing less than the future of America's democracy was at stake" (p. 1).

Other voices have argued that Trump's presidency represents more of a symptom or an outcome of one or more existing crises. As political scientists, John Sides, Michael Tesler, and Lynn Vavreck (2018), write in their book, *Identity Crisis*, Trump's rise to power has been "symptomatic of a broader American identity crisis" (p. 10). In a similar vein, the editorial team at *The Guardian* (2021) argues that the *real* crisis is "America's growing polarisation – of which the president is a symptom as well as a cause." Writing for CNBC, journalists Emma Newburger and Tucker Higgins (2018), point to the 2007–2008 financial crisis as key to explaining Trump's rise to power, since this crisis "made Americans more comfortable expressing views that were anti-immigration." The exact role of Trump in creating or sustaining one of more democratic crises has thus often been marked by ambivalence and disagreement, though Trump's connection to crisis narratives has been persistent.

Similar to this ambiguous-yet-persistent link between Trump and crises, Trump has also continuously been linked to the notion of a post-truth era in different and sometimes contradictory ways. While some scholars, journalists, and politicians have argued that Trump fueled or even sparked the rise of a post-truth era, others have simply seen him as further evidence of this era's existence. Indeed, not unlike the villains of the previous chapter, Trump has been cast as both a cause and effect of fake news and post-truth. Opting for the latter interpretation, the editor-in-chief of *American Scientist*, Jamie Vernon, suggested in

2017 that the election of Trump proved the existence of latent post-truth tendencies: "this election confirms we have entered a post-truth era, in which facts are considered subjective and any information that conflicts with one's personal opinion is justifiably questionable" (Vernon, 2017). Other voices have attributed a more direct agency to Trump, suggesting that he not only confirmed the post-truth era, but was a mainspring in its production. As argued by Professor Timothy Snyder (2021): "Post-truth is pre-fascism, and Trump has been our post-truth president... Thanks to technological capacity and personal talent, Donald Trump lied at a pace perhaps unmatched by any other leader in history."

In this narrative, Trump becomes more than simply a politician. He becomes an epistemic game-changer or force that is changing the conditions of democracy, truth, and politics – the beginning of an "American Abyss" (Snyder, 2021). Drawing on the medical vocabulary of post-truth worlds, Trump has often been displayed as patient zero in a still-developing post-truth epidemic, or even the malicious doctor who released the pathogen.

While Trump epitomizes a profound epistemological shift for many, others suggest that he has merely been the latest instalment in a much longer political development. Writing for *Washington Monthly*, Nancy LeTourneau argued in 2018 that the "road Republicans took to becoming both post-truth and post-policy began long before Trump was elected president" (LeTourneau, 2018). Similarly, Ralph Keyes – the author who originally popularized the notion of post-truth – presents post-truth politics as the result of decades of "lies about Vietnam, Watergate, Irangate, and Iraq" (2004, p. 11).

Despite these different historical perspectives, the rise of President Trump is widely said to signal a fundamental transformation of the political landscape and democracy. To some, this is intimately connected to the rise of social media, which only recently became powerful political instruments. Trump is said to be the first major "post-truth politician" (Freedland, 2016), as he uses social media to fuel a new "'post-truth' era in American politics" by bypassing "traditional fact checkers" (Alaimo, 2016).

The idea of Trump as a post-truth politician builds on one of the most pervasive arguments about the post-truth era: namely that it is not simply about new quantities or forms of lies, but about a completely new epistemic culture or world. In post-truth politics, the very relationship between facts and fiction, once firmly cemented at the base of democracy, has supposedly shifted. In these discourses, Trump often comes to exemplify and embody a profound crisis caused by epistemic transformations that are claimed to have changed the very meaning of true and false. The post-truth era and its "parallel realities" become more or less synonymous with what has been labeled "Trumpism ... a forceful, if dark, salvo against a reason that, by taking refuge in the discourse of facts, had abandoned the obligation to justify its moral worth to a significant subset of those it sought to govern" (Jasanoff & Simmet, 2017, p. 762). Like fake news, commentators argue that Trumpism has obtained an "infectious quality"

(D'Antonio, 2018), taking on a performative life of its own that will "outlive Trump" (Tanenhaus, 2018).

Fake news as a floating signifier

We should, of course, not underestimate the very real power that Trump himself has had in creating and contesting the boundaries of both crisis narratives and post-truth discourses. Indeed, far from being just a privileged enemy to whom prerogative labels have been put, Trump has continuously sought to intervene and redraw the contours of what constitutes both a crisis and fake news: from arguing, only days after announcing his candidacy for president in 2015, that "our country is in a major crisis of incompetent leadership" (Trump, 2015) to lamenting Democrat claims of a "constitutional crisis" in 2019 as "pathetically untrue" (Trump, 2019). Trump has also (in-)famously made fake news a staple rhetorical tool to attack his perceived political opponents, particularly legacy news institutions.

Trump had not even been in office for a single day before he declared that he had "a running war with the media" (Rucker, Greg, & Miller, 2017). As part of his presidential campaign, Trump often claimed that fake news was nothing less than a political fiction or hoax intended to attack and delegitimize his candidature. On 11 January 2017, he wrote on Twitter: "FAKE NEWS – A TOTAL POLITICAL WITCH HUNT!" (Trump, 2017a). Soon after, Trump turned the table on its head and began what would become a highly systematic use of the term against media companies that had previously accused Trump and his supporters of spreading fake news. Companies such as CNN, *The New York Times,* and *Buzzfeed News*, all of which had brought stories linking fake news to the American right and Donald Trump (Oremus, 2016), were labeled as nothing more than "fake news media." Trump even went as far as to claim that he himself had invented the term "fake" to capture the dishonesty of traditional media (Salmon, 2017).

Fake news became a mainstay in Trump's political vocabulary, systematically used to try to discredit established news outlets. From the perspective of Trump, fake news is a symptom of a fundamental democratic problem, namely that mainstream media companies are inherently biased and deliberately attempting to promote liberal agendas, instead of representing "the people." This discourse is not new, as right-wing media platforms have long claimed that mainstream media are corrupt, liberally biased, systematic liars in need of replacement (Berry & Sobieraj, 2014). Two platforms promoting this kind of discourse are *Breitbart News* and *InfoWars*, both of which hosted exclusive interviews with Donald Trump during the 2016 American elections. Within this discourse, mainstream media and their "endless propaganda" are said to be soon replaced due to digital media, allowing Americans to communicate and become "aware that we don't need the mainstream media to define what reality is for us after all" (Snyder,

2014). In this sense, the notion of fake news became a potent signifier within an, in many ways, established discourse: "Don't believe the main stream (fake news) media. The White House is running VERY WELL. I inherited a MESS and am in the process of fixing it" (Trump, 2017b). Trump's intervention within post-truth worlds – his attempt to recast symbolic systems and reverse relations in the field – did not mark the emergence of fake news altogether. Indeed, prior to this point, the term was already in wide circulation. What Trump did, it seems to us, was to systematically re-use, co-opt, and appropriate an existing idea to his strategic advantage.

One way to understand Trump's persistent rhetorical use of fake news is through the notion of the *floating signifier,* as developed by Ernesto Laclau (2005). At its core, a floating signifier is a concept, word, or name (i.e., signifier), which is used within a number of different competing discourses. Its meaning has not yet been completely hegemonized but is instead floating between opposing political projects that all try to assert dominance over how it is to be understood. Fake news, in our view, has become such a concept, as different actors – including, but certainly not limited to Donald Trump – seek to infuse fake news with particular sets of meanings, so as to critique and politically attack perceived opponents or enemies.[1]

It is important to stress that by designating fake news as a floating signifier, we do not simply mean to say that the concept is vague. Rather, we seek to capture how fake news obtains conflicting meanings across different discourses and geo-political contexts. If we take, for example, Trump's rhetorical use of the term, fake news cannot generally be said to be vague, since Trump persistently uses it to lament the supposed "liberal bias" of established media in the US. In this sense, fake news has quite a clear meaning when viewed in isolation. Its meaning only begins to "float" when compared across multiple hegemonic projects. As soon we do so, the floating character of fake news immediately stands out.

To give a few examples, in 2017, Syrian President Bashar al-Assad dismissed a report from Amnesty International about torture in Syrian prisons by stating: "We are living in a fake news era. Everybody knows this. So we don't have to depend on this" (Isikoff, 2017). That same year, the French far-right party, Front National, created a "fake news alert team" to let followers know "whenever members of the team believed that France 2 journalists put out fake news" (Reporters Without Borders, 2017). In 2018, Russian officials dismissed evidence of chemical attacks in Syria as nothing but "fake news" and "unsubstantiated lies" (Milbank, 2018). In 2019, China's ambassadors to both the UK and Australia called evidence of Chinese persecution of Uighur Muslims "utterly fake news" (Karp, 2019) and "pure fabrication" (BBC News, 2019). That same year, North Korean officials stated that they "increasingly often see misrepresentation of information in the news environment" and "must counter the dissemination of such fake news" (BBC Monitoring, 2019). In 2020, Brazilian President

Jair Bolsonaro accused a journalist of spreading fake news (Santana, 2020), while Hungarian President Viktor Orbán accused European Union politicians of doing the same (Makszimov, 2020). Finally, at an aggregate level, "the number of journalists jailed around the world set yet another record in 2022" (Getz, 2022) not least due to the rise of so-called anti-fake news laws used to prosecute critical journalists (as we will return to in the next chapter).

Across these diverse cases, we can begin to see how, rather than simply being vague or ambiguous (i.e., a term in need of a clearer definition), the meaning of fake news has become fundamentally political. As a floating signifier, fake news has become central to political struggles across the world, as different actors try to obtain dominance over who gets to act as a truth-teller or knowledge gate-keeper in contemporary societies. This development has also been dubbed the "weaponization" (Egelhofer et al., 2020, p. 1325) or "politicization" (Brummette et al., 2018, p. 497) of fake news.

To return to Donald Trump and the US, we can see how Trump's persistent use of fake news to discredit journalists has been part of a larger politiciza-tion of fake news across the globe. We can also see how Trump's presidency has become intertwined with broader crisis narratives about politics, democ-racy, and, importantly, fake news. On the one hand, scholars, journalists, and public intellectuals have articulated the rise of Trump as the product, symbol, beginning, or proof of one of more existing crises, whether this be an identity crisis, polarization crisis, financial crisis, or post-truth crisis. On the other hand, Trump himself has actively intervened in these discourses, continuously appro-priating the notion of crisis to frame himself as fighting for "the people" against a "corrupt elite" and to attack established media as nothing but "fake news."

Taken together, Trump has in many ways become a master signifier within both contemporary crisis narratives and post-truth discourses. By this, we do *not* mean that Donald Trump is somehow unreal or that the effects of his presi-dency can be reduced to linguistic games. Nor do we imply that Trump and his allies have not been a driving force behind very real forms of deception and lies. Trump's presidency has had very real consequences, affecting people's lives through heightened vulnerability, state violence, climate destruction, oppression, and inequality. All of this should not be neglected. What we are trying to say, somewhat more modestly, is that the idea, image, and name Trump has simul-taneously taken on a performative life of its own, extending far beyond the geo-graphical boundaries of the US and his time in office. Trump's legacy has come to serve as a strong marker within post-truth discourses, representing not only a particular moment in US politics, but a wider crisis of democracy.

Crisis moment II: COVID-19 (2019–)

In late 2019 and early 2020, COVID-19 rapidly took center stage in world pol-itics, as the then new and unknown coronavirus spread from one country to the next. The outbreak was quickly designated as a "global emergency" by the World Health Organization (BBC News, 2020a) and "a public health crisis without precedent in living memory" by The Organization for Economic Cooperation and Development (OECD, see Gurría, 2020).

In being designated as a crisis, human health was not the only concern. As the United Nations (2021) stated: "The COVID-19 pandemic is more than a health crisis; it is an economic crisis, a humanitarian crisis, a security crisis, and a human rights crisis." The International Monetary Fund (IMF) similarly highlighted how "many countries now face multiple crises – a health crisis, a financial crisis, and a collapse in commodity prices." Other international organizations and leaders designated the disease as a "global crisis in education" (UNESCO, 2022) and "a crisis of international solidarity and cooperation" (Daccord cited in ODI, n.d.).

Due to the multitude of crisis narratives, researchers Paul Frosh and Myria Georgiou (2022) have argued that COVID-19 can be seen as a form of *meta-crisis*, "a crisis-event which makes visible modernity's general historical character as a perpetual crisis-condition" (Frosh & Georgiou, 2022, p. 240). From this position, rather than solely delineating a momentary state of emergency, COVID-19 brings to the forefront ingrained systemic flaws, inequalities, injustices, and fears within contemporary societies: "It is a crisis of the universality of risk, its inequitable distribution globally and locally, and of our capacities to reflect upon and develop a politics capable of addressing it" (Ibid.). With this in mind, we can begin to zoom in on the, for our purposes, most interesting crisis designations of all during COVID-19, namely that of the "infodemic crisis" (WHO, 2021).

In addition to being delineated as a health crisis, social crisis, and economic crisis, COVID-19 was also quickly dubbed an *infodemic*, As described by the World Health Organization (WHO), human civilization faced an "overabundance of information – some accurate and some not – that makes it hard for people to find trustworthy sources and reliable guidance when they need it" (WHO, 2020). According to Tedros Ghebreyesus, Director of the WHO, decisive action against fake news was urgently needed or else "we are headed down a dark path that leads nowhere but division and disharmony" (Ghebreyesus, 2020). The infodemic was almost from the very beginning being designated as part of the disease. Already in February 2020, Luigi Di Maio, Italy's Minister of Foreign Affairs, proclaimed that "an 'infodemic' of misleading news abroad was damaging Italy's economy and reputation" (BBC News, 2020b). Italy was one of the first European countries to experience a major outbreak of the novel virus; yet in these early days, it seems that political focus in the country was as much about damage control in terms of the country's image as it was about containing the virus. In these endeavors, the notion of the infodemic was central. Thus, from being a marginal concept, the "infodemic" quickly became a buzzword across politics, journalism, and scholarship (Simon & Camargo, 2021). As had been the case with "post-truth" in 2016, a range of prominent voices quickly adopted the term to lament the present state of affairs and call for legislative and techno-logical solutions to save democracy and (in the end) civilization.

Alongside the notion of the infodemic also came a further popularization of the already prevalent medical analogies for misinformation and fake news (explored in the previous chapter). As stated by Secretary-General of the United Nations, António Guterres (2020):

> As the world fights the deadly COVID-19 pandemic – the most challen-ging crisis we have faced since the Second World War – we are also seeing another epidemic – a dangerous epidemic of misinformation. Around the world, people are scared. They want to know what to do and where to turn for advice. This is a time for science and solidarity. Yet the global "misinfo-demic" is spreading.... . Wild conspiracy theories are infecting the Internet.

Just like a disease, bad information is infecting people. The COVID-19 epi-demic, the argument went, is causing an infodemic, which, in turn, is causing a *misinfo demic*. This raises the question, however, whether infodemics are always bad or whether they only *become* bad, if they mutate into misinformed variants. In academic, journalistic, and political discourse surrounding the COVID-19 infodemic, the answer seemed clear: infodemics are inherently bad and need to be eradicated (Simon & Camargo, 2021).

In academic publications, medical researchers describe the COVID-19 infodemic as a "disease infecting our information culture" (Solomon et al., 2020, p. 1806) with "deadly and contagious impact" (Gisondi et al., 2022, p. 2). According to them, 2020 marked nothing less than "the *year of online disinformation*" (Gisondi et al., 2022, p. 2, original emphasis). In an article for *The New York Times*, journalist Matt Richtel synonymizes the infodemic with falsehoods, functioning identically to COVID-19: "like a virus itself, [false ideas] can be easily transmitted from person to person, carried by both the unwit-ting and the devious and spreading almost invisibly through a vast virtual world" (Richtel, 2020).

Within these descriptions, falsehoods are often articulated as being on par with or even worse than COVID-19 itself. Fake news is "more pandemic than the virus" (Patel et al., 2020), "spreads faster and more easily" (Ghebreyesus, 2020) and "tends to be more dangerous sometimes as much as the virus itself" (Motsoaledi cited in SABC News, 2020). As a result, governments need to act fast. Humankind is facing not only a sudden health crisis, but also sudden truth crisis, according to these discourses.

In addition to threatening individual health, the infodemic is often described as threatening the collective health of democracies. Although misinformation has historically accompanied epidemics, this line of argument goes, social media is now making the COVID-19 infodemic spread on a never-before-seen scale, harming not only individuals but democracy as a whole (Naughton, 2020).

As argued by Orso et al. (2020): "social media… has dramatically increased the degree of credibility of personal opinions (beliefs, considerations, etc.) and allowed them to spread more rapidly. All of this is the opposite of democracy: opinion, contrary to facts, is always of the most influential people" (pp. 327–328).

To solve the infodemic, medical metaphors shape the proposed policy responses and solutions. The WHO (n.d.) urges citizens to "flatten the infodemic curve" and study "infodemiology." Professor of Sociology at Oxford University, Melinda Mills (2020), argues that "beyond monitoring and silencing these groups, our strongest weapon is to inoculate the general public against the infodemic by empowering them to spot and report misinformation." Professor of Psychology at Cambridge University, Sander van der Linden and colleagues, similarly call for "inoculating against fake news about COVID-19" (van der Linden et al., 2020). Other proposed solutions include the digital equivalent of social distancing, as argued by professor and journalist, John Naughton: "distancing was just about the only thing that worked with the 1918 Spanish flu epidemic. And in the online world, maybe we need something analogous" (Naughton, 2020).

From these solutions, we can see how medical metaphors not only shape the ways in which fake news is described as a crisis, but also how they carve out and limit our potential ways forward. The medical vocabulary guides not only how fake news and misinformation – in this case, as channeled through the notion of the infodemic – are articulated as a form of crisis, but also how they are presented as a *solvable* crisis. Since fake news and misinformation are similar to a virus in every way, shape, and form, governments, citizens, and scientists can draw from the lessons of medicine to fight it. If everyone acts fast and think like doctors, this line of reasoning goes, the crisis might be stopped.

As the above examples showcase, the infodemic metaphor is not only described as revolving around the COVID-19 pandemic, but also the overall state of democracy. Thus, contrary to past diseases, a number of voices claim, it is now personal opinions about COVID-19 that overshadow facts. This state of affairs represents nothing less than "the opposite of democracy." In this way, we can begin to see how the health crisis of COVID-19 is in many ways articulated as being almost inseparable from a broader democratic truth crisis. This also means that solving one has to involve the other. Only by curbing the infodemic can we also curb the pandemic. Similarly, so the argument goes, only by mitigating a democratic truth crisis can we curb a health crisis.

Taken together, we can begin to see how the COVID-19 pandemic, despite being a distinctly new phenomenon in 2019 and 2020, was articulated through many of the same narratives that were already dominant in public discourse before the pandemic: humanity is facing a barrage of false information, spreading like viruses and threatening to kill democracy as we know it. If we are to stop this impending catastrophe, dire actions have to be taken swiftly.

To our mind, what all of this highlights is how already existing discourses are selectively mobilized within an – at that point in time – emerging meta-crisis, revolving around the spread of COVID-19. Ideas that had already been established, regarding the decline of democracy in the face of misinformation, are once again activated and brought to the foreground. Yet, more than simply rehashing old ideas, new elements are simultaneously added: on a concrete level, we see how a new concept starts to gain traction, most prominently the notion of the infodemic. In what can only be described as a peculiar twist of events, it seems that this concept provided a compelling bridge from the already established medicalized vocabulary surrounding fake news and the new situation brought forth by COVID-19. Let us not forget that already in 2017 and 2018, a number of voices had described fake news and misinformation as a virus – spreading and infecting people's minds and democracy as a whole.

Seen in this light, it is hardly surprising that many of the ideas captured in already existing post-truth worlds were so quick to be adopted in new crisis narratives – for they already shared a common medicalized set of concepts. Nor is it surprising that the supposed infodemic crisis of COVID-19 was simultaneously presented as completely new and more of the same. It was presented as a novel threat in the sense of being linked to a never-before-seen pathogen (SARS-CoV-2) and a previously obscure term (the infodemic). Yet, it was also a continuation of the exact same threat that had previously been labeled under different names, such as the post-truth era, post-factual society, or misinformation age. In a very real sense, it became increasingly more difficult during COVID-19 to separate the extent to which fake news and misinformation are described as a crisis *in and of themselves* and the extent to which they are described as a product of a specific crisis moment, namely the emergence of COVID-19. This showcases how post-truth worlds have gradually been intermingled with a range of other pressing issues of our time.

Crisis moment III: the Russian invasion (2022–)

For many people in the Western world (and Europe in particular), 24 February 2022 marks a significant day. It marks the day Ukraine was invaded by Russia early in the morning, once again igniting the war that was already started in 2014 with Russia's annexation of Crimea. The invasion had been brewing for months, as Russia had been building up military capacity near the Ukrainian borders. Since then, the war has not only meant the forced displacement of millions of Ukrainians, but also the devastation of major Ukrainian cities and civilian lives through the continuous deployment of Russian airstrikes, military, and bombings.

The invasion was almost immediately labeled as a major geo-political crisis and was almost universally condemned. On the day of the invasion, the OECD released a public statement condemning Russia's actions, seeing them "as a clear violation of international law and a serious threat to the rules-based international order" (OECD, 2022a). A range of other international organizations and nation-states followed suit. In conjunction with a report, *Assessing the Impact of Russia's War against Ukraine on Eastern Partner Countries*, the OECD (2023) would later state: "Russia's war against Ukraine is causing a humanitarian, social, and economic crisis for the Ukrainian people. The consequences of this full-scale military invasion are disrupting the global supply of commodities, sharply increasing food and energy prices, and threating the recovery from the COVID-19 pandemic." The International Monetary Fund (IMF) also pointed to the close connections between the crisis on the ground in Ukraine and its effect on the global economy, stating that "[b]eyond the suffering and humanitarian crisis from Russia's invasion of Ukraine, the entire global economy will feel the effects of slower growth and faster inflation" (Kammer et al., 2022). A year into the conflict, *The New York Times* described the war as jeopardizing not only Ukraine and surrounding countries, but also "the security structure that has helped keep the peace on the continent since World War II" (Nagourney et al., 2023).

Amongst analysts and politicians, crisis narratives have thus been intimately linked to the invasion from the beginning. The invasion has first of all, as recounted above, been named a *humanitarian and social crisis* for the Ukrainian people (Fassihi, 2022). Second, as Russia's delivery of oil and gas to EU member states was significantly reduced following sanctions, the invasion also came be to known as an *energy crisis* (Lawson, 2023). In many European countries, energy prices soared in 2022 and there was suddenly widespread fear that major power-outs would roam the continent. Third, the invasion has also been dubbed a *refugee crisis*, as millions of Ukrainians have been displaced during the war (D'Agata & Redman, 2023).

In addition to being described as an energy crisis, humanitarian crisis, and refugee crisis, the war has also been described as an *information crisis* or *information war*, both by analysts and by governments on both sides (Bolin & Ståhlberg, 2023). At the onset of the war, the Russian government claimed to be fighting against an "unprecedented – not even campaign – but information war that has been unleashed against our country" (Peskov cited in SBS News, 2022). This, the Russian government claimed at the time, legitimized the implementation of further legal restrictions on free speech domestically (Jack, 2022). By tightening Russia's existing "anti-fake news law" (which we will return to in the next chapter), the Russian government intensified what *The Economist* (2023) would later call an escalating "war on truth."

A number of public actors have voiced the ways in which disinformation and fake news are integral to the war (Bond, 2023; Sardarizadeh & Robinson, 2022). In November 2022, the OECD released a report, describing how "[s]ystematic information manipulation and disinformation have been applied by the Russian government as an operational tool in its assault on Ukraine" (OECD, 2022b, p. 1). As outlined in the report, the use of misinformation is not in itself new, but the scale and breadth enabled by social media and algorithms are. This development hits fragile democracies the hardest, but "has destructive implications for all democracies" (Ibid. p. 2). *The Economist* presented similar arguments in April 2022, arguing that the war is not the first war in which social media plays a significant role in mediating conflict, but that it provides one of the most prominent examples of precisely this development.

In the European Union, leading politicians also designated the situation as an information war, responding to Russia's invasion by implementing not only trade sanctions, but also a union-wide ban on two Russian state-sponsored media outlets, RT and Sputnik. In defense of this decision, Josep Borrell, High Representative of the European Union for Foreign Affairs and Security Policy, argued that media bans are necessary to protect democracy from the existential threat of Russian disinformation:

> They [RT and Sputnik] are not independent media, they are assets, they are weapons, in the Kremlin's manipulation ecosystem... If the information is bad, democracy is bad. If the information is systematically contaminated by lies and twisted, citizens can't have a clear understanding of reality and their political judgment is similarly twisted.
>
> (Borrell cited in Petrequin, 2022)

Democracy is facing a barrage of bad information, Borrell argued, threatening to destroy the very foundation of the European Union. Yet, more so than that, Borrell suggested that this information crisis legitimizes measures, which some might see or criticize as being undemocratic. Given the circumstances – so the argument went – such measures are crucial for saving democracy. Borrell elaborated on this position a year later (we quote at length):

> This war is not only conducted on the battlefield by the soldiers. It is also waged in the information space, trying to win the hearts and minds of people. And you will tell me: "nothing new on that, Goebbels already invented [that] during the Second World War – to lie and to spread disinformation is nothing new." Well, what is new today is the intensity, the will and the instruments. Goebbels had no internet, and no social media instruments. But, today, people that behave like Goebbels – telling a lie 1,000 times – have a powerful capacity of multiplication at the speed of light and reaching everyone everywhere. ... If the information is toxic, democracy cannot work. If information is manipulated, people don't have a clear idea of what is going on. So, their choices are biased, and the information is the oil of the engine of democracy.

We have to take care of the quality of information because [it] is the sap, the blood, the oil, the thing that makes democracy work.

(Borrell, 2023)

Good information, Borrell argued, is the oil, the sap, or even the blood that makes democracy function. Like a delicate engine, democracy will no longer operate if the oil gets tainted. While disinformation is nothing new, the internet has made it possible for information to get corrupted at a never-before-seen scale and speed. This has made it possible for "people that behave like Goebbels" to make democracy's oil "toxic," potentially destroying the machine from within. Due to this existential threat, the European Union must act and take new and harsh measures.

Borrell's speech exemplifies how existing discourses around fake news, post-truth, and disinformation as a crisis *in and of themselves* are often weaved seamlessly into disparate crisis moments, in this case the war in Ukraine. Many aspects of Borrell's speech from 2023 could just as well have been said before the Russian invasion in 2022. For example, Borrell's argument that "If the information is toxic, democracy cannot work" bears strong resemblance to Macron's arguments in 2018 that "without reason, without truths there is no real democracy." Similarly, Borrell and Macron's arguments also overlap on the need for decisive action to protect democracy from toxic and corrupt information. So once again, we are seeing how already existing ideas are being appropriated and mobilized into new contexts.

The Russian invasion of Ukraine is a complex and (as of the time of writing) still developing war. As such, we do not in any way pretend that the empirical glimpses provided above do justice to this immense tragedy. The war deserves much more in-depth sociological and structural analysis, including of the myriad of ways in which social media and emergent technologies have been put to use in order to circulate discourses in and around the war. Moreover, detailed and careful analysis of the many distinct events of disinformation occurring during the war must be carried out. However, even though we do not pretend to say anything final about the invasion, it does seem to us that, not unlike the COVID-19 pandemic, we are once again seeing how already established discourses around issues of misinformation and fake news are being put to use. In so being, they are both reproduced and recast, as new arguments and nuances are continuously being added. Additionally, solutions proposed before the war – revolving around the policing and removal of bad information (as we will unfold in the next chapter) – are given new life, as fake news as a crisis *in and of itself* becomes inseparable from fake news as a biproduct of specific crisis moments.

Closing thoughts: truth in the midst of crisis

Crises are important events, not least from a discursive perspective that is concerned with how we collectively interpret, form, and give meaning to the world. Whether they be economic, health-related, military, or any combination of these, crises brings to the foreground normative assumptions that are otherwise often kept implicit in our day-to-day life. They not only reveal ruptures in the world as we know it, showcasing that what we thought was stable can indeed be reversed and undone. In the very act of doing so, they also tend to showcase the contingency of our collective worlds, displaying that things could indeed be otherwise. From a post-foundationalist perspective, crises are overflowing with discursive signification. They constitute discursive battlegrounds in which the stakes are both about defining what is currently taking place and what is to be done, if anything.

With this chapter, we have dived deeper into the construction of contemporary post-truth worlds by focusing on a select number of contemporary crisis moments. We have shown how, although the three crisis moments examined here have been widely different, they have nonetheless been entangled with notions of post-truth, fake news, and misinformation in similar ways. Taken together, the three crisis moments briefly discussed in this chapter all highlight how fake news is often at one and the same time portrayed as a crisis *in and of itself* – caused by technology, bad journalism, and misinformed masses – and a byproduct of specific geo-political crises, whether this be Russia's invasion of Ukraine, the COVID-19 pandemic, or the rise of Donald Trump. To our mind, this two-sidedness is key to understanding both fake news' continued importance on political agendas worldwide as well as the difficulty of pinning down exactly what fake news is and what causes it. As a signifier, it seamlessly moves within and between different crises as well as between political projects. By unpacking its meaning within specific crisis narratives, we can begin to understand its political significance as both a problem and a potential prompt for new political interventions.

As stated at the beginning of the chapter, the very act of labeling a particular set of events as a crisis is in itself deeply political. It is a way of problematizing particular relations and giving meaning to the world: it is in other words a discursive strategy. When actors do so, they almost always – willingly or not – begin to activate a distinct set of repertoires linked to the idea of crisis as such. Labeling something as a crisis is contingent. It is a political struggle in its own right whether a particular set of events should be labeled as a crisis or not. Our point in this chapter, then, is not to overtake the idea that all events we have encountered here must *necessarily* be labeled as crises. Far from it. We have simply been interested in how these series of events, which have already been discursively configured as crises by actors in the world, intermingle, reproduce, and reuse many of the tropes explored throughout the book.

To our mind, the chapter sheds new light on post-truth worlds. It does so by showcasing how issues of fake news and misinformation are deeply integral to a series of different crisis moments dissected here. Despite major differences between the actual events, the ideas linked to truth and facts remain more or less the same. It is as if existing post-truth worlds, as discussed in Chapter 4, are being latched onto diverse crisis event. In this sense, we might begin to see how the supposed coming of post-truth worlds is not just deemed a crisis for the future of liberal democracy, but also mobilized within a series of other crisis moments. This is interesting to our minds, insofar as it demonstrates how discursive elements from post-truth worlds are highly malleable: these normative ideas can be selectively mobilized, reused, and appropriated in a number of different contexts. Post-truth worlds, it seems to us, are as much a discursive formation in their own right, as they are a reservoir of normative ideas that can be articulated in other seemingly different contexts. With this chapter, then, we can begin to see how post-truth worlds wander into and become entangled with different issues. We can see how ideas formed in one setting are translated and morphed into other contexts. If this is the case, then there is nothing to suggest that they are going away any time soon. This ties to the notion that these ideas not only serve the purpose of describing specific crisis events, but also of legitimizing new regulatory, technological, and economic restructurings proclaimed to be potential solutions to restoring democracy. This is precisely what we will turn to in the following chapter.

Note

1 For more extensive analyses of fake news as a floating signifier, see Farkas & Schou (2018) and Farkas (2023).

References

Agamben, G. (2005). *State of Exception*. Chicago: University of Chicago Press.
Alaimo, K. S. (2016, 16 November). Where Donald Trump got his real power. *CNN*. https://edition.cnn.com/2016/11/15/opinions/social-media-facebook-   twitter-trump-alaimo/index.html
BBC Monitoring. (2019, 9 October). North Korea's KCNA, Russian TASS News Agency Hope to Fight "Fake News." *BBC Monitoring*. https://monitoring.bbc.co.uk/product/c20157yl
BBC News. (2019, 25 November). China's UK Ambassador: Uighur Camps Leak is "Fake News." *BBC News*. www.bbc.com/news/av/world-asia-china-50550535
BBC News. (2020a, 31 January). Coronavirus Declared Global Health Emergency by WHO. *BBC News*. www.bbc.com/news/world-51318246
BBC News. (2020b, 27 February). Coronavirus in Europe: Epidemic or "Infodemic"? *BBC News*. www.bbc.com/news/world-europe-51658511
Berry, J.M., & Sobieraj, S. (2014). *The Outrage Industry: Political Opinion Media and the New Incivility*. Oxford: Oxford University Press.

Bolin, G., & Ståhlberg, P. (2023). *Managing Meaning in Ukraine: Information, Communication, and Narration since the Euromaidan Revolution.* Cambridge, MA: MIT Press.

Bond, S. (2023, 28 February). How Russia is Losing – and Winning – the Information War in Ukraine. *NPR.* www.npr.org/2023/02/28/1159712623/how-russia-is-losing-and-winning-the-information-war-in-ukraine

Borrell, J. (2023). *Disinformation: Opening speech by High Representative/Vice-President Josep Borrell at the EEAS Conference on Foreign Information Manipulation and Interference.* European External Action Service. www.eeas.europa.eu/eeas/disinfo rmation-opening-speech-high-representativevice-president-josep-borrell-eeas-confer ence_en

Brummette, J., DiStaso, M., Vafeiadis, M., & Messner, M. (2018). Read All About It: The Politicization of "Fake News" on Twitter. *Journalism and Mass Communication Quarterly, 95*(2), 497–517. https://doi.org/10.1177/1077699018769906

Crotty, W. (2021). Introduction. In W. Crotty (Ed.), *The Presidential Election of 2020: Donald Trump and the Crisis of Democracy.* Lanham: Lexington Books.

Crouch, C. (2011). *The Strange Non-Death of Neoliberalism.* Cambridge: Polity Press.

D'Agata, C., & Redman, J. (2023, 21 February). Russia's War on Ukraine Sparked the Biggest Refugee Crisis This Century. We Meet Some of the Families Torn Apart. *CBS News.* www.cbsnews.com/news/ukraine-russia-war-refugee-crisis-catching-up-with-families-torn-apart/

D'Antonio, M. (2018, 9 October). Trumpism is winning, and that's terrifying. *CNN.* https://edition.cnn.com/2018/10/08/opinions/brett-kavanaugh-victory-for-trumpism-dantonio/index.html

Eastham, K., Coates, D., & Allodi, F. (1970). The Concept of Crisis. *The Canadian Journal of Psychiatry, 15*(15), 463–472. https://doi.org/10.1177/070674377001500508

Egelhofer, J.L., Aaldering, L., Eberl, J., Galyga, S., & Lecheler, S. (2020). From novelty to normalization? How journalists use the term "fake news" in their reporting. *Journalism Studies, 21*(10), 1323–1343. https://doi.org/10.1080/1461670X.2020.1745667

Farkas, J. (2023). Fake News in Metajournalistic Discourse. *Journalism Studies, 24*(4), 423–441. https://doi.org/10.1080/1461670X.2023.2167106

Farkas, J., & Schou, J. (2018). Fake News as a Floating Signifier: Hegemony, Antagonism and the Politics of Falsehood. *Javnost – The Public, 25*(3), 298–314. https://doi.org/10.1080/13183222.2018.1463047

Fassihi, F. (2022, 24 March). The U.N. General Assembly Adopts a Strong Resolution Blaming Russia for Ukraine's Humanitarian Crisis. *The New York Times.* www.nyti mes.com/2022/03/24/world/europe/un-general-assembly-russia-ukraine.html?

Freedland, J. (2016, 13 May). Post-Truth Politicians Such as Donald Trump and Boris Johnson are no Joke. *The Guardian.* www.theguardian.com/commentisfree/2016/may/13/boris-johnson-donald-trump-post-truth-politician

Frosh, P., & Georgiou, M. (2022). Covid-19: The Cultural Constructions of a Global Crisis. *International Journal of Cultural Studies, 25*(3–4), 233–252. https://doi.org/10.1177/13678779221095106

Getz, A. (2022, 12 December). Number of Jailed Journalists Spikes to New Global Record. *Committee to Protect Journalists.* https://cpj.org/reports/2022/12/number-of-jailed-journalists-spikes-to-new-global-record/

Ghebreyesus, T.A. (2020, 15 February). *Munich Security Conference*. World Health Organization.   www.who.int/director-general/speeches/detail/munich-security-con ference

Gisondi, M.A., Barber, R., Faust, J.S., Raja, A., Strehlow, M.C., Westafer, L.M., & Gottlieb, M. (2022). A Deadly Infodemic: Social Media and the Power of COVID-19 Misinformation. *Journal of Medical Internet Research, 24*(2). https://doi.org/ 10.2196/35552

Glasser, S.B. (2021, 22 April). The Trump Administration Is Over, but the Trump Crisis Is Not. *The New Yorker*. www.newyorker.com/news/letter-from-bidens-washington/the-trump-administration-is-over-but-the-trump-crisis-is-not

Gurría, A. (2020, 2 March). Coronavirus (COVID-19): Joint Actions to Win the War. *OECD*.   www.oecd.org/about/secretary-general/Coronavirus-COVID-19-Joint-acti ons-to-win-the-war.pdf

Guterres, A. (2020, 14 April). "This is a Time for Science and Solidarity:" Secretary-General Message on COVID-19 and Misinformation. United Nations. www.unodc. org/romena/en/Stories/2020/April/this-is-a-time-for-science-and-solidarity_-secret ary-general-message-on-covid-19-and-misinformation.html

Heide, M., & Simonsson, C. (2019). *Internal Crisis Communication: Crisis Awareness, Leadership and Coworkership*. New York: Routledge.

Hoggan-Kloubert, T., & Hoggan, C. (2023). Post-Truth as an Epistemic Crisis: The Need for Rationality, Autonomy, and Pluralism. *Adult Education Quarterly, 73*(1), 3–20. https://doi.org/10.1177/07417136221080424

Isikoff, M. (2017, 10 February). Defiant Assad Tells Yahoo News Torture Report is "Fake News." *Yahoo! News*. https://news.yahoo.com/exclusive-defiant-assad-tells-yahoo-news-torture-report-is-fake-news-100042667.html

Jack, V. (2022, 22 March). Russia Expands Laws Criminalizing "Fake News." *Politico*. www.politico.eu/article/russia-expand-laws-criminalize-fake-news/

Jasanoff, S., & Simmet, H. R. (2017). No Funeral Bells: Public Reason in a "Post-Truth" Age. *Social Studies of Science, 47*(5), 751–770. https://doi.org/10.1177/030631271 7731936

Jessop, B. (2015). Crisis Construal in the North Atlantic Financial Crisis and the Eurozone Crisis. *Competition and Change, 19*(2), 95–112. https://doi.org/10.1177/102452941 5571866

Kammer, A., Azour, J., Selassie Abebe Aemro, Goldfajn, I., & Rhee, C.Y. (2022, 15 March). How War in Ukraine Is Reverberating Across World's Regions. *IMF*. www. imf.org/en/Blogs/Articles/2022/03/15/blog-how-war-in-ukraine-is-reverberating-acr oss-worlds-regions-031522

Karp, P. (2019, 19 December). China's Ambassador to Australia Says Reports of Detention of 1m Uighurs "Fake News." *The Guardian*. www.theguardian.com/world/ 2019/dec/19/chinas-ambassador-to-australia-says-reports-of-detention-of-1m-uigh urs-fake-news

Keyes, R. (2004). *The Post-Truth Era: Dishonesty and Deception in Contemporary Life*. New York: St. Martin's Press.

Koselleck, R. (2000). *Critique and Crisis: Enlightenment and the Pathogenesis of Modern Society*. Cambridge, MA: MIT Press.

Laclau, E. (2005). *On Populist Reason*. London: Verso.

Lawson, A. (2023, 21 February). Energy Crisis Stemming from Ukraine War "Cost £1k for every UK Adult." *The Guardian*. www.theguardian.com/business/2023/feb/21/ene rgy-crisis-ukraine-war-uk-cost-gas

LeTourneau, N. (2018, 18 September). A Culmination of the GOP's Post-Truth and Postpolicy Politics. *Washington Monthly*. https://washingtonmonthly.com/2018/09/18/ a-culmination-of-the-gops-post-truth-and-post-policy-politics/

LSE Commission on Truth Trust and Technology. (2018). *Tackling the Information Crisis: A Policy Framework for Media System Resilience*. www.lse.ac.uk/media-and-communicati ons/assets/documents/research/T3-Report-Tackling-the-Information-Crisis.pdf

Makszimov, V. (2020, 5 May). Hungarian PM Orbán Accuses EPP of Spreading Fake News. *Euractiv*. www.euractiv.com/section/future-eu/news/hungarian-pm-orban-accu ses-epp-of-spreading-fake-news/

Milbank, D. (2018, 16 April). Trump's "Fake News" Mantra Becomes an Effective Weapon – Against America. *The Washington Post*. www.washingtonpost.com/opini ons/trump-bulldozed-truth--and-not-just-in-washington/2018/04/16/0f65718c-41b2-11e8-8569-26fda6b404c7_story.html?

Mills, M. (2020, 11 November). We Must Prevent a Vaccine "Infodemic" from Fuelling the Covid Pandemic. *The Guardian*. www.theguardian.com/commentisfree/2020/nov/ 11/vaccine-infodemic-covid-pandemic-anti-vaxxers-campaigns-persuade

Nabers, D. (2017). Crisis as Dislocation in Global Politics. *Politics*, *37*(4), 418–431. https://doi.org/10.1177/0263395716661341

Nabers, D. (2019). Discursive Dislocation: Toward a Poststructuralist Theory of Crisis in Global Politics. *New Political Science*, *41*(2), 263–278. https://doi.org/10.1080/07393 148.2019.1596684

Nagourney, E., Bilefsky, D., & Pérez-Peña, R. (2023, 27 February). A Year of War in Ukraine: The Roots of the Crisis. *The New York Times*. www.nytimes.com/article/rus sia-ukraine-nato-europe.html

Naughton, J. (2020, 14 March). Fake News about Covid-19 Can be as Dangerous as the Virus. *The Guardian*. www.theguardian.com/commentisfree/2020/mar/14/fake-news-about-covid-19-can-be-as-dangerous-as-the-virus

Nelson, J.L., & Taneja, H. (2018). The Small, Disloyal Fake News Audience: The Role of Audience Availability in Fake News Consumption. *New Media and Society*, *20*(10), 3720–3737. https://doi.org/10.1177/1461444818758715

Nesbitt, N. (Ed.). (2017). *The Concept in Crisis: Reading Capital Today*. Durham: Duke University Press.

Newburger, E., & Higgins, T. (2018, 11 September). Secretive Cabals, Fear of Immigrants and the Tea Party: How the Financial Crisis Led to the Rise of Donald Trump. *CNBC*. www.cnbc.com/2018/09/10/how-the-financial-crisis-led-to-the-rise-of-donald-trump.html

ODI. (n.d.). Global Leaders Reimagine a World Beyond Coronavirus. *ODI*. Accessed 24 April 2023, from https://odi.org/en/delivering-the-global-reset/the-global-reset-dialogue/

OECD. (2022a, 24 February). Statement of OECD Council on the Russian aggression against Ukraine. *OECD*. www.oecd.org/newsroom/statement-of-oecd-council-on-the-russian-aggression-against-ukraine.htm

OECD. (2022b). *Disinformation and Russia's War of Aggression Against Ukraine: Threats and Governance Responses*. https://doi.org/10.1787/37186bde-en

OECD. (2023, 23 January). Assessing the Impact of Russia's War against Ukraine on Eastern Partner Countries. *OECD*. www.oecd-ilibrary.org/development/assessing-the-impact-of-russia-s-war-against-ukraine-on-eastern-partner-countries_946a936c-en

Oremus, W. (2016, 6 December). Stop Calling Everything "Fake News." *Slate*. https://slate.com/technology/2016/12/stop-calling-everything-fake-news.html

Orso, D., Federici, N., Copetti. Roberto, Vetrugno, L., & Tiziana, B. (2020). Infodemic and the Spread of Fake News in the COVID-19-Era. *European Journal of Emergency Medicine*, *27*(5), 327–328. https://doi.org/10.1097/MEJ.0000000000000713

Patel, M., Kute, V., & Agarwal, S. (2020). "Infodemic" of COVID 19: More Pandemic than the Virus. In *Indian Journal of Nephrology*, 30(3), 188–191. https://doi.org/10.4103/ijn.IJN_216_20

Petrequin, S. (2022, 8 March). EU Pledges to Fight Russia's "Information War" in Europe. *Associated Press News*. https://apnews.com/article/russia-ukraine-business-europe-media-european-union-95c44aeb2e4182227e40ae9fbe6b5841

Rasmussen, M.V. (2021). *Krisesamfundet*. Copenhagen: Informations Forlag.

Reporters Without Borders. (2017, 17 March). *Predators of Press Freedom use Fake News as a Censorship Tool*. https://rsf.org/en/news/predators-press-freedom-use-fake-news-censorship-tool

Richtel, M. (2020, 6 February). W.H.O. Fights a Pandemic Besides Coronavirus: An "Infodemic." *New York Times*. www.nytimes.com/2020/02/06/health/coronavirus-misinformation-social-media.html?searchResultPosition=1

Rucker, P., Greg, W., & Miller, G. (2017, 21 January). Trump Wages War Against the Media as Demonstrators Protest his Presidency. *The Washington Post*. www.washingtonpost.com/politics/trump-wages-war-against-the-media-as-demonstrators-protest-his-presidency/2017/01/21/705be9a2-e00c-11e6-ad42-f3375f271c9c_story.html

Runciman, D. (2016). What Time Frame Makes Sense for Thinking about Crises? In P. F. Kjaer & N. Olsen (Eds.), *Critical Theories of Crisis in Europe from Weimar to the Euro* (pp. 3–16). London: Rowman & Littlefield. www.rowmaninternational.com/media/1159/critical_theories.pdf

SABC News. (2020, 28 March). Government Warns Against Fake News. *SABC News*. www.sabcnews.com/sabcnews/government-warns-against-fake-news/

Salmon, N. (2017, 8 October). Donald Trump Takes Credit for Inventing the Word "Fake." *The Independent*. www.independent.co.uk/news/world/americas/donald-trump-takes-credit-for-inventing-the-word-fake-a7989221.html

Santana, B. (2020, 22 June). Jair Bolsonaro accused me of spreading "fake news." I Know Why He Targeted Me. *The Guardian*. www.theguardian.com/commentisfree/2020/jun/22/jair-bolsonaro-fake-news-accusation-marielle-franco

Sardarizadeh, S., & Robinson, O. (2022, 8 March). Ukraine Invasion: False Claims the War is a Hoax Go Viral. *BBC News*. www.bbc.com/news/60589965

SBS News. (2022, 6 March). Free Speech Restrictions, Jail Terms for Publishing "Fake News": Life in Russia as War in Ukraine Continues. *SBS News*.

Schick, N. (2020). *Deep Fakes and the Infocalypse: What You Urgently Need To Know*. London: Monoray.

Sides, J., Tesler, M., & Vavreck, L. (2018). *Identity Crisis: The 2016 Presidential Campaign and the Battle for the Meaning of America*. Princeton: Princeton University Press.

Simon, F.M., & Camargo, C.Q. (2021). Autopsy of a Metaphor: The Origins, Use and Blind Spots of the "Infodemic." *New Media and Society*. https://doi.org/10.1177/14614448211031908

Snyder, M. (2014, 20 May). Is the Mainstream Media Dying? Ratings at CNN, MSNBC and Fox News Have all been Plummeting in Recent Years. *InfoWars*. www.infowars.com/is-the-mainstream-media-dying/

Snyder, T. (2021, 9 January). The American Abyss. *The New York Times*. www.nytimes.com/2021/01/09/magazine/trump-coup.html

Solomon, D.H., Bucala, R., Kaplan, M.J., & Nigrovic, P.A. (2020). The "Infodemic" of COVID-19. *Arthritis and Rheumatology, 72*(11), 1806–1808. https://doi.org/10.1002/art.41468

Tanenhaus, S. (2018, 11 October). How Trumpism will Outlast Trump. *Time Magazine*. http://time.com/5421576/donald-trump-trumpism/

The Economist. (2022, 2 April). The Invasion of Ukraine is Not the First Social Media War, but it is the Most Viral. *The Economist*. www.economist.com/international/the-invasion-of-ukraine-is-not-the-first-social-media-war-but-it-is-the-most-viral/21808456

The Economist. (2023, 30 March). The Kremlin Escalates its War on Truth. *The Economist*. www.economist.com/europe/2023/03/30/the-kremlin-escalates-its-war-on-truth?

The Guardian. (2021, 12 January). The Guardian View on Democracy in America: the Threat is Real. *The Guardian*. www.theguardian.com/commentisfree/2021/jan/12/the-guardian-view-on-democracy-in-america-the-threat-is-real

Trump, D. (2015, 19 June). Our country is in a major crisis of incompetent leadership. We cannot continue to go on with these politicians who do nothing but talk. *Twitter*. https://twitter.com/realDonaldTrump/status/611994802289307648

Trump, D. (2017a, 11 January). FAKE NEWS: A TOTAL POLITICAL WITCH HUNT! *Twitter*. https://twitter.com/realdonaldtrump/status/818990655418617856

Trump, D. (2017b, 18 February). Don't believe the main stream (fake news) media. The White House is running VERY WELL. I inherited a MESS and am in the process of fixing it. *Twitter*. https://twitter.com/realDonaldTrump/status/832945737625387008

Trump, D. (2019). The Democrats new and pathetically untrue sound bite is that we are in a "Constitutional Crisis." They and their partner, the Fake News Media, are all told to say this as loud and as often as possible. They are a sad JOKE! We may have the strongest Economy in our history, best... *Twitter*. https://twitter.com/realDonaldTrump/status/1127688823264169984

UNESCO (2022, 6 April). UNESCO Responds to the Global Crisis in Education Due to COVID-19. *UNESCO*. www.unesco.org/en/articles/unesco-responds-global-crisis-education-due-covid-19

United Nations (2021). UN Response to COVID-19. *United Nations*. www.un.org/en/coronavirus/UN-response

van der Linden, S., Roozenbeek, J., & Compton, J. (2020). Inoculating Against Fake News About COVID-19. *Frontiers in Psychology, 11*, 1–7. https://doi.org/10.3389/fpsyg.2020.566790

Vernon, J.L. (2017). Science in the Post-Truth Era. *American Scientist, 105*, 2–4. www.americanscientist.org/article/science-in-the-post-truth-era

WHO (2020). Novel Coronavirus (2019-nCoV). www.who.int/docs/default-source/coronaviruse/situation-reports/20200202-sitrep-13-ncov-v3.pdf

WHO. (2021). *Tackling the Global Infodemic.* www.afro.who.int/sites/default/files/Progress%20report%2021/docs/WHO-AFRO_SPRP_COVID-19_2.5.pdf

WHO. (n.d.). Let's Flatten the Infodemic Curve. Accessed 24 April 2023, from www.who.int/news-room/spotlight/let-s-flatten-the-infodemic-curve World Health Organization. (2020).

6   Restoring democracy

If, indeed, we are currently witnessing a wide spread crisis of truth, democracy and politics, then what is to be done? This question has been central to contemporary post-truth worlds, as a host of those currently diagnosing the state of affairs have proposed a range of different solutions to our current predicament. Yet, to propose a solution to a problem is never a neutral affair; it involves imagining not only the current state of the world, but also other ways in which the world could and ought to be structured.

This chapter is dedicated to investigating and understanding these solutions, treatments, and cures currently proposed and implemented to solve the widely diagnosed post-truth condition. By analyzing both real and imagined solutions from lawmakers, scholars, journalists, and social media companies alike, the chapter dives into the different ways in which liberal democracies are said to be able to recover from rapid deterioration. Starting with responses from policymakers across the globe, the chapter showcases how post-truth discourses not only act as descriptive devices, framing contemporary democratic problems in specific ways, but also as vehicles for prescriptive statements – imagining the potential for other democratic futures. Indeed, in a quite radical manner, post-truth worlds should be seen as deeply material, containing actionable visions for how to restructure policies, norms, practices, and technology in order to save democracy from impending doom. From a discursive perspective, this is highly interesting, as the solutions currently articulated are a constitutive part of the post-truth worlds examined in this book. In this precise sense, post-truth worlds simultaneously contain normative visions for the past, present, and future of democracy as a political system. Unpacking these different paths, the chapter will highlight both the differences and similarities in contemporary responses. It will do so, in particular, to describe the converging normative ideals that structure contemporary solutions to the post-truth condition. Overall, the chapter lays the groundwork for the third and final part of the book in which we will not only problematize and critically question post-truth worlds and existing solutions, but also try to carve out other paths going forward. Against the existing hegemonic order, we will propose that other counter-hegemonic projects are still

DOI: 10.4324/9781003434870-8

possible – perhaps even necessary, if we are to reclaim democracy in a genuinely democratic fashion.

State responses to post-truth

Policymakers around the world have proposed a series of solutions to the post-truth crisis. Against the backdrop of the COVID-19 pandemic, a host of countries imposed free speech restrictions in the name of stopping fake news and related phenomena. According to Human Rights Watch (2021), at least 83 governments implemented emergency measures to restrict free speech and peaceful protests. This included new laws and decrees criminalizing supposedly fake news about government actions in a series of diverse countries, such as Hungary, Thailand, Ethiopia, and Bolivia (Facsar, 2020; Freedom House, 2020; Human Rights Watch, 2020; Rising, 2021). It also involved the reactivation of old laws, such as Brazil's national security law from 1983, implemented during the country's military dictatorship and used in 2021 to detain government critics (Savarese, 2021). These developments surfaced alongside the WHO urging governments to fight the infodemic and researchers recommending that governments "bring in legislation and enforce criminal prosecutions for spreading misinformation" (Mills et al., 2020, p. 26).

Yet, already before COVID-19, free speech restrictions had become a prominent state solution to fake news across the globe (Lim, 2020; Neo, 2020). In 2017, French President Emmanuel Macron announced that he would take drastic measures to combat falsehoods and their interference with democracy: "We are going to develop our legal means of protecting democracy against fake news," he said, adding that "[t]housands of propaganda accounts on social networks are spreading all over the world, in all languages, lies invented to tarnish political officials, personalities, public figures, journalists" (cited in McAuley, 2018). This announcement was met with fairly cold sentiments, with French journalist Pierre Haski arguing that "the state should not transform itself into a ministry of truth" (cited in Nugent, 2018). In 2018, Malaysia implemented an Anti-Fake News Act to criminalize "anything that is not substantive, and dangerous to the economy and security of the nation," as formulated by Abdul Rahman Dahlan, Minister of Economic Planning (cited in Reuters Staff, 2018). This law was later revoked after protests and a change of government in 2019 (Lim, 2020), only to re-emerge in a new guise in 2021 during the COVID-19 pandemic (Zsombor, 2021).

These examples show how political responses to fake news and post-truth have been widespread and continually changing. It would thus be impossible to present a complete overview of the many solutions currently articulated. Still, it is worthwhile to follow at least some of the tracks being pursued around the globe.

Starting with Europe, a controversial law came into effect in Germany on 1 January 2018, known as the *Network Enforcement Act* or *NetzDG*. This law makes it mandatory for social media platforms to remove hate speech within 24 hours. If they do not, they face fines of up to 50 million euros (Olterman, 2018). Even before its implementation, the policy faced criticism from citizen groups and social media companies, with Facebook stating that it was "not suitable to combat hate speech and false news" as it shifted the "responsibility for complex legal decisions from public authorities to private companies" (Dilworth, 2017). Reporters Without Borders called it "a model for non-democratic states to limit Internet debate" (cited in Reporters Without Borders, 2017).

Once put in place, the legislation faced additional criticism, with Human Rights Watch warning that it could lead to "unaccountable, overbroad censorship and should be promptly reversed... The law sets a dangerous precedent for other governments looking to restrict speech online by forcing companies to censor on the government's behalf" (Human Rights Watch, 2018). In response to this criticism, the German government announced that they would seek to revise the law (Thomasson, 2018). Nonetheless, according to the judicial think tank Justitia, NetzDG was used by political leaders in countries such as Singapore, the Philippines, Venezuela, Honduras, and Russia to legitimize the implementation of their anti-fake news laws (Mchangama & Fiss, 2019).

Apart from legislative means, European politicians have looked towards specialized task forces as a solution to the fake news crisis. In the Czech Republic, the government launched a dedicated unit, called the "fake news police" (Faiola, 2017), with the purpose of countering disinformation online (particularly from Russia). As described by a research fellow at the Prague Security Studies Institute, the unit acts as a means of "self-defense" against false information (Faiola, 2017), involving not censorship but publicized fact checking. In Italy, the government has pursued similar means, collaborating with Facebook to launch a fact-checking unit specializing in scanning "Facebook pages we suspect spread false and misleading information" (Serhan, 2018). The self-described goal of the unit is to identify false stories, disseminate corrections to falsehoods, and promote truthful stories with the help of Facebook, algorithmically boosting corrections and prohibiting falsehoods from spreading.

In the United Kingdom, a specialized security unit was created to defend and actively intervene in cases of fake news and disinformation (Walker, 2018). When launched, a representative of the prime minister stated that "[w]e are living in an era of fake news and competing narratives. The government will respond with more and better use of national security communications to tackle these interconnected, complex challenges. To do this, we will build on existing capabilities by creating a dedicated national security communications unit" (Walker, 2018). While these different units have been given high priority, several aspects of their operations remain in the dark, as details are sparse regarding their exact mandate, organization, and legal room for manoeuvring.

In addition to national initiatives, the European Union has taken several steps to fight fake news. In 2015, the EU launched a specialized unit, East StratCom, to counter the spread of fake news and propaganda from Russia. Its annual budget has been steadily rising from €1.1 million in 2018 to €4 million in 2020 (East Stratcom, 2021). In March 2018, the European Commission's High Level Expert Group on Fake News and Online Disinformation delivered a report, entitled "A multi-dimensional approach to disinformation" (European Commission, 2018a). The report not only presented a diagnosis of the current democratic conjuncture, but also provided concrete tools and measurements for overcoming contemporary problems. Against any temptation to counteract disinformation through censorship, the Expert Group called for a combination of "short-term responses to the most pressing problems, longer-term responses to increase societal resilience to disinformation, and a framework for ensuring that the effectiveness of these responses is continuously evaluated, while new evidence-based responses are developed" (2018a, p. 5). Based on the report, the European Commission requested, among other measures, that social media companies "decisively step up their efforts to tackle online disinformation" (European Commission, 2018b, p. 8).

Looking beyond Europe, we also find interventions on numerous fronts to counter fake news and post-truth. In Southeast Asia, a range of countries have implemented drastic measures (BBC News, 2018; Schultheis, 2018; Neo, 2020). Governments in Singapore, Vietnam, Malaysia, Thailand, Cambodia, and The Philippines have all implemented anti-fake news laws criminalizing the creation and/or spreading of fake news, with punishments ranging from fines to several years in prison (Human Rights Watch, 2021; Neo, 2020). Adding to such laws, the government of Papua New Guinea imposed a nationwide, one-month ban on Facebook in 2018 (Roy, 2018). Similarly, Indonesia temporarily limited access to social media platforms in 2019 to "avoid incitement and false news from spreading to the wider public" (Tehusijarana & Valentina, 2019).

In Africa, the governments of Benin, Burkina Faso, Côte d'Ivoire, Ethiopia, Kenya, Malawi, Niger, Nigeria, South Africa, Uganda, Tanzania, and Zimbabwe have all proposed or implemented laws in the name of stopping fake news (Cunliffe-Jones et al., 2021; Machivenyika, 2020; Olewe, 2018). As formulated by Tanzanian President, John Magufuli, the aim has been to "weed out" the fake news "disease" (cited in Olewe, 2018). Cunliffe-Jones and colleagues have shown how the number of laws aimed at preventing false information has risen from 17 in 2016 to 31 in 2020 across 10 African countries (Cunliffe-Jones et al., 2021). During COVID-19, the Zimbabwean government threatened with prison sentences of up to 20 years for the spreading of fake news (Machivenyika, 2020).

Finally, looking to South America, different forms of anti-fake news laws and decrees have been implemented in countries such as Venezuela, Nicaragua, and Bolivia (CPJ, 2020; Lubianco, 2020). Multiple others have been proposed in Chile, Brazil, Peru, Paraguay, and El Salvador (Grigori, 2018; Lubianco, 2020). In addition to these solutions, task forces have also been established, for example in Brazil, where the federal police set up a dedicated anti-fake news unit during the 2018 elections (FENAPEF, 2018), as well as in Argentina, where the government has created an Observatory of Disinformation and Symbolic Violence on Digital Media and Platforms to protect "citizens from false, malicious and fallacious news" (IAPA, 2020).

As can be seen from these many initiatives and legal measurements, the field of political innovation is continuously adapting, evolving, and changing in response to the threat of fake news and post-truth. This also makes it enormously difficult to pin down or map out the breadth and scope of current actions. Yet, despite these difficulties, it does seem fair to state that quite comprehensive and radical measures are being taken, not only to guard democracy against the supposed enemies of disinformation, but perhaps also to reform the very contents and structures of democracy itself. Following this line of inquiry, the next section takes a closer look at the underlying arguments proposed as to how and why democracy needs saving.

Back to truth

As described above, policymakers across the globe have come to focus their efforts to save democracy on new measures to stop or punish the producers of fake news. Whether in the form of legislation, bans, or task forces, the idea has been that fake news and disinformation must be stopped and that rather drastic measures are the way to do so. However, in attempting to combat these new democratic challenges, policymakers and state officials have not been alone. Instead, many different actors have joined the fight. They have often done so – as we will showcase in this section – in an attempt to once again affirm the authority of traditional truth-telling fields. Politics, journalism, and science in particular have been seen as watchdogs of truth, and it is only by once again securing the foundations for these fields, it is claimed, that democracy can begin to prosper.

In the world of politics, a wide range of politicians, scholars, and media professionals have called for the reclamation of the political system's truth-telling capacities. Turning to the inner workings of democracy itself, proponents claim that a proper and well-functioning democracy cannot function without truth and rationality – both among decision-makers and citizens. To once again return to Macron's speech before the US Congress, the founding idea is that "[w]ithout reason, without truth, there is no real democracy because democracy is about true choices and rational decisions" (Macron, 2018). With this in mind, re-establishing democracy is often taken to mean re-establishing the conditions in which reason, truth, and rational decisions can be made. Already in 2016, *The Economist* proposed this line of argumentation, suggesting that defending against lies, misinformation and, indeed, fake news requires an explicit movement in favor of truth. To counter the post-truth era, the magazine argued, "mainstream politicians need to find a language of rebuttal (being called "pro-truth" might be a start). Humility and the acknowledgment of past hubris would help. The truth has powerful forces on its side. Any politician who makes contradictory promises to different audiences will soon be exposed on Facebook or YouTube" (The Economist, 2016).

The idea of finding a new language to refute attacks on truth runs throughout many contemporary efforts to reinvigorate the political system. Often presented in tandem with technological and legal solutions, it is argued time and again that without truth and reason, politics will not (and cannot) work. Writing for the European Council on Foreign Relations, Sebastian Dullien and Jeremy Shapiro (2017) argue that "[i]t is time to recognize that the integrity of information about current events and persons of public interest is part of the critical infrastructure of liberal democracy. If that infrastructure is compromised, the stability of the political system (and of liberal democracy itself) is threatened." Re-establishing the authority of politics plays a key role in post-truth worlds. So does the truth-telling capacity of the scientific field. This has also been presented as key to solving our contemporary democratic situation. Science, it has been argued, is under dire attack and saving it will be crucial for democracy going forward. Not unlike the calls for bringing back truth within politics, a number of voices have called for the reaffirmation of scientific authority. As Professor Richard L. Hasen summarises in his book, *Cheap Speech*, there is an "essential need" for "inculcating respect for truth, science, and the rule of law" (Hasen, 2022, p. 162).

Writing for *American Scientist*, Jamie Vernon (2017, p. 2) channels a similar sentiment, arguing that the solution to the post-truth condition is to make sure "researchers and technologists have a seat at the table when important decisions are made." Resonating with these concerns, Jenny Rohn (2017) argues in *The Guardian* that "scientists can no longer go [at] it alone. We need new allies, and new strategies. Non-scientists who believe that science and the truth are concepts worth salvaging can actively help sell science too." What is being called for is, in a sense, new relational work that (re)connects the scientific world and its practitioners to politicians, journalists, and citizens who are also dedicated to a pro-truth movement.

Science has thus been cast as a remedy for the post-truth condition – one that is so important that it almost transcends democracy itself. From this position, scientific thought – understood variously as a particular method of questioning reality, a certain skeptical attitude, or a field of self-validating and self-falsifying knowledge – should not only hold a privileged position in democratic decision-making; more radically, it should also be the *prima facie* way of securing modern society. In this sense, it is sometimes claimed that science should be awarded primacy over even public opinion and politics. Scientific truth, expertise, and knowledge are, in these instances, seen as so foundational for societal survival that their role must be secured, even at the expense of popular sovereignty. Professor Leigh Ackland (2017) argues as follows:

An understanding of the nature of science is absolutely fundamental to combat post-truth, which is the antithesis of science. While it is not feasible to expect people to understand the details of scientific studies, it is crucial that the importance of evidence-based information that underpins scientific analyses is clear. Improved understanding of the principles of science could be achieved in a number of ways: by better school education, by scientists taking on leadership roles in society and connecting more effectively with people, by a greater advocacy for science and scientists and by the promotion of the fact that science is required for the survival of the planet in the future.

In this kind of rhetoric, what is at stake is not only democracy but rather the very survival of the planet. In this scenario, scientists are seen as the heroes of our time.

With these examples, we can begin to see how the scientific field has, in a similar gesture to the political world, sought to reclaim its position as truth tellers, both as authorities to the democratic masses and as actionable leaders, more or less independent of popular will. Like the political system, science too must reclaim its ability to speak against misinformation, lies, and fake news.

Completing this triptych, journalism has also been called upon as savior and watchdog of democracy, truth, and critical thinking. As Professor Brian McNair (2018) puts it, the waning away of journalistic elites is equal to the implosion of the liberal democratic world:

> If the crisis of trust in journalistic elites and the loss of authority of elites in other spheres such as politics and academia are not addressed in the coming years, it is quite possible that the entire structure of liberal democracy which has driven global evolution forward since 1945 will collapse in the face of rising authoritarianism and "post-truth" cultural movements such as that embodied by the alt-right in the United States or in Putin's Kremlin, or will be eroded to the point where it is unrecognisable as the generally progressive, if messy and imperfect polity we see (still).
>
> (McNair, 2018, p. 51)

Without journalistic elites, democracy risks collapsing into authoritarianism, it is argued. This bleak image often underpins calls for protecting established news institutions. Jeff Nesbit, in an article for *Time Magazine*, argues that "the only antidote to fake news is real news" (Nesbit, 2016). According to him, social media's measures against fake news have not been far-reaching enough. The reason for this, Nesbit argues, is that these tend to sidestep or even circumvent traditional gatekeepers of truth, namely journalists. "Facebook needs to embrace journalism as a full partner," Nesbit argues, "It *is* the real news expert. Facebook has dishonored this obvious truth for years" (Nesbit, 2016, added emphasis). Indeed, for the "fake news beast" to be "slain" – the "virulent poison that now presents an existential threat to democracy" (Nesbit, 2016) – real news must be brought in as the cure. This will help generate and accelerate the flow of capital itself, insofar as real news "has the potential to generate more revenue, over time, than any platform can ever make through the promotion of content from fake news sites" (Nesbit, 2016).

Legacy news institutions have played a key role in situating journalism as a cure against fake news and post-truth (Koliska et al., 2020; Lischka, 2021). In doing so, several scholars have argued that journalists contribute to moral panics around the topic (Bratich, 2020; Carlson, 2018; Morozov, 2017). As summarized by Carlson (2018), fake news has become an "ultimate other for traditional news organisations struggling to reassert control over the media environment amid declining public opinion" (p. 386). By equating truth and journalism, while also essentializing truth and democracy, established news media have positioned themselves as the bulwarks against impending democratic collapse.

This impetus to strengthen or elevate traditional news media and journalistic practices into a watchdog of truth – a cure for post-truth – comes in a number of different sizes and shapes. Some, like Walter Hussman Jr., writing for *The Wall Street Journal*, have argued that strengthening objectivity in journalism is fundamental for restoring "public trust in the Fourth Estate, which is essential to our democracy" (Hussman Jr., 2023). As is often the case with discourses around post-truth, however, others have argued for the opposite, namely that "truth-seeking news media must move beyond whatever 'objectivity' once meant to produce more trustworthy news" (Downie Jr., 2023; see also Farkas, 2023).

Antidotes and immunity

Survival, antidotes, disease, cures, and poison: the highly medicalized vocabulary surrounding post-truth worlds is not just limited to describing its supposedly viral nature and ability to spread or infect, but also frames a range of solutions proposed to solve the post-truth era. During COVID-19, The United Nations enlisted "digital first-responders" to try to contain the spread of misinformation (United Nations, 2020), while the European Union urged citizens to practice "information hygiene" and "build immunity to disinformation" (EEAS, 2021). Already before the pandemic, researchers from the University of Cambridge floated the idea of developing a so-called "fake news vaccine" (BBC News, 2017a). The way to do so, the researchers argued, would be to expose individuals to small doses of misinformation and fake news within a controlled environment, not unlike vaccines for biological viruses. This idea was further developed in the beginning of 2018 into an online game (Lewsey, 2018), described as an "experiment in providing 'general immunity' against the wide range of fake news that has infected public debate" (University of Cambridge, 2018). Players were invited to write fake news themselves through stolen identities: "If you know what it is like to walk in the shoes of someone who is actively trying to deceive you," the researcher in charge of the project argued, "it should increase your ability to spot and resist the techniques of deceit. We want to help grow 'mental antibodies' that can provide some immunity against the rapid spread of misinformation" (Sander van der Linden cited in Lewsey, 2018).

As shown in Chapters 4 and 5, the vocabulary of immunity, antidotes, and medicalized treatment extends far beyond the confines of these researchers. Often, in these discourses, the vocabulary of diseases and sickness seems to almost automatically be followed by a vocabulary of cures and antibodies. Yet, in the case of the fake news vaccine, we can begin to see how cure and treatment almost collapse. To save democracy from misinformation and fake news, individuals must be *exposed* to misinformation and fake news. Drawing on the medical notion of inoculation, protecting the community means exposing the community. Combating the enemy means internalizing and embodying the enemy's internal logics. To negate the thing that seeks to negate the community, the very negation must be internalized. This logic is, in many aspects, close to what Italian political philosopher Roberto Esposito (2011) captures by the idea of *immunitas*. According to Esposito, the idea of protecting the community by introducing the very thing that is to be negated – for example, countering violence with violence – has become increasingly widespread in the contemporary political order. The idea that fake news and post-truth in this way can be combated by introducing and internalizing fake news and post-truth also bears resemblance to Derrida's work on the *pharmakon*. Through a deconstructive reading of Plato's *Phaedrus*, Derrida (1981) showcases how the word *pharmakon* is highly ambivalent, referring simultaneously to poison, disease, and the false as well as the cure, remedy, and truth. Fake news and post-truth are, in a similar sense, articulated through this fundamental ambivalence: they are both the poison to be combated and the remedy for doing so.

This immunological scheme, collapsing poison and antidote, also comes to the foreground in calls for educational efforts against post-truth. In March 2018, the BBC launched an initiative "to help young people identify real news and filter out fake or false information" (BBC News, 2017b). According to James Harding, director of BBC News, the idea is to "go into schools to speak to young people and give them the equipment they need to distinguish between what's true and what's false." Resonating these concerns, a number of university and tech company projects have experimented with "pre-bunking" disinformation, that is exposing people to fictional manipulation to "boost their defenses" and "improve resiliency" (Klepper, 2022).

These examples show how the medicalized vocabulary of post-truth often intermingles with what may best be termed as the language of *the natural*. Appropriating terms from a quasi-biological or even zoological register, this type of solutionism views the fight against misinformation and fake news as a learning process – an almost evolutionary mechanism, pitting the most evolved parts of the species against those lagging behind. In a 2017 piece in *Forbes*,

Karl Moore and Liam Timmins (2017) write that "[e]xecutives, senior business people, and Boomers should realize that in a post-truth world, Millennials are in their natural habitat." Indeed, according to these authors, "millennials" (born in the 1980s and 1990s) have been trained their whole lives to not only navigate different media at once, but also distinguish between universal Truths (capital T) and subjective truths (small t), and fact from opinion. By both homogenizing and essentializing the traits and natural capacities of millennials, Moore and Timmins (2017) argue that "[t]heir minds have been trained to pull the most significance or useful interpretation from feeds of information. They know more than any-body that context is key." Resonating this sentiment, though this time focusing on Generation Z (born between the mid-1990s and early 2010s), Stef W. Kight (2020) of *Axios* writes that, "as the first generation to grow up with social media, Gen Z has an innate understanding of how to create and move online content, which makes them less susceptible to misinformation." Somewhat curiously – though quite telling for the heterogeneity of narratives in post-truth worlds – other voices have argued the opposite, stating that younger citizens are in fact to blame for the post-truth sickness, as the "social media generation may not be equipped – or sufficiently interested – to actually understand what news is, and how it differs from other kinds of information" (Richardson, 2017).

Only technology can save us now

While re-establishing the foundational position of truth, integrity, and expertise – whether through education, laws, task forces, games, or the strengthening of science, journalism and (truth-based) politics – has been a dominant trope, technologies also feature as prominent rescue vehicles. Indeed, *technological solutionism* – the idea that technologies can and will save us from problems that are, by and large, not technological (Morozov, 2013) – has in many ways become completely integral to the post-truth worlds (Creech, 2020).

Not unlike misinformation and the kind of immunological scheme attributed to it, technology is often portrayed in a double fashion as both a poison and a remedy: "Technology helped fake news. Now technology needs to stop it" (Cook, 2017). Writing for World Economic Forum, Arijit Goswami (2022) argues that, although disinformation produced through artificial intelligence (AI) represents the biggest threat to the stability of our societies, AI-driven solutions represent our biggest hope, at least for now: "Until humans learn to objectively evaluate online content, AI-based technologies have to be our ally in combatting disinfor-mation online" (Goswami, 2022). Channeling similar sentiments, Schick (2020) concludes in her book, *Deep Fakes and the Infocalypse*, that in order to "avoid a permanent 'fucked up dystopia'" (p. 189), we need new technologies "built by the 'good guys'" (p. 195).

Echoing technological solutionism, the European Commission (2018b) has argued that technological measures need to be taken in order to make "detection and analysis of online disinformation more accurate and timely" (p. 15). This includes the use of "artificial intelligence ... for verifying, identifying and tagging disinformation," "[c]ognitive algorithms that handle contextually-relevant information" and "[i]nnovative technologies, such as blockchain" that can "enable transparency and traceability, and promote trust in news displayed on the Internet" (p. 11). Lewandowsky, Ecker, and Cook (2017) propose a similar set of solutions, arguing against the use of "censorship or other undemocratic means" (p. 364), instead proposing what they call "technocognition" (p. 365). This encompasses "an inter-disciplinary approach to the design of information architectures that incorporates principles borrowed from behavioral economics to 'nudge' ... against the spread of misinformation" in order to "build bridges between the socially-defined epistemic islands that define the post-truth era" (p. 362). In this line of solutionism, it is not only fake news that needs to be corrected, but also the citizens currently living in alternative epistemic realities or worlds. Pennycook and colleagues (2020) propose a similar set of solutions, proposing "accuracy nudges that social media platforms could directly implement" (p. 778).

As an alternative to these more or less top-down approaches – focused on algorithmic nudging as a means of intervention – bottom-up approaches have also been proposed to solve the post-truth crisis, appealing to people's motivation for truth-seeking behavior. One such solution departs from the call by *The Economist* for politicians and citizens to openly declare themselves pro-truth through digital media. Founded by behavioral social scientists, the website protruthpledge.org encourages "politicians – and everyone else – to commit to truth-oriented behaviors and protect facts and civility" (Intentional Insights, n.d.). By signing the online pledge, users agree to make earnest efforts to (1) "share truth" by verifying facts and citing sources; (2) "honor truth" by acknowledging when people share true information and defend them when they are attacked for sharing truth; and (3) "encourage truth" by asking people to retract falsehoods and celebrate such retractions (Intentional Insights, n.d.). The pledge is available in several languages, including English, Spanish, Russian, and German. Tsipursky, Votta, and Mulick (2018) conducted a survey of people who signed the pledge, self-reporting their social media engagement before and after doing so. While acknowledging the obvious limitations of self-reported data, the authors conclude that pro-truth pledges can successfully "help address the epidemic of fake news sharing by private citizens" by appealing "to the identity of people" and enabling "positive reputational rewards for honesty" (Tsipursky et al., 2018, p. 28). At the time of writing – more than five years after its launch– fewer than 15,000 people have signed the pro-truth pledge.

Silicon valley strikes back

Social media companies play an important part in post-truth worlds, not only as discursive villains, but also as self-portrayed solutionists. Promises from companies like Meta (previously Facebook), Alphabet (previously Google), and X (previously Twitter), however, have largely come as reactions to mounting criticism (Carbone, 2018). In 2018, Facebook (now Meta) admitted that the British–American political consulting firm, Cambridge Analytica, used personal information about tens of millions of American Facebook users to target them with political ads during the 2016 US election (Facebook, 2018a). The company emphasized that Cambridge Analytica's actions were a "breach of trust," although it admitted that the data was obtained based on Facebook's own policies at the time (Facebook, 2018a). To make matters worse, it simultaneously became clear that the Internet Research Agency – a Russian firm with ties to the Kremlin – systematically infiltrated US election debates on social media using thousands of fake accounts and ads on platforms such as Facebook, Instagram, YouTube, and Twitter (Diresta et al., 2018). Meta CEO Mark Zuckerberg had initially called the notion of Russian interference a "pretty crazy idea" (cited in Solon, 2016), a decision he later described as one of his "greatest regrets in running the company" (cited in Smith, 2018).

In response to these scandals – intimately linking social media to fake news and post-truth – Meta, X, and Alphabet have all promised to implement far-reaching solutions to counter and even pre-emptively stop so-called bad actors: "It's an arms race and we need to constantly improve too. It's why we're investing heavily in more people and better technology to prevent bad actors misusing Facebook" (Facebook, 2018b). While emphasizing both human and technological solutions, most social media companies have particularly turned to the latter. Both Facebook and Twitter announced they were implementing new forms of AI and machine learning to stop misinformation (Biggs, 2021; Huddleston Jr., 2022; Facebook, 2018c). Drawing directly on the medical vocabulary of post-truth worlds, then CEO of Twitter, Jack Dorsey, presented Twitter's efforts using the analogy of a sick patient in need of both diagnosis and treatment:

> We aren't proud of how people have taken advantage of our service, or our inability to address it fast enough. If you want to improve something, you have to be able to measure it. The human body has a number of indicators of overall health, some very simple, like internal temperature. We know how to measure it, and we know some methods to bring it back in balance … . What we know is we must commit to a rigorous and independently vetted set of metrics to measure the health of public conversation on Twitter. And we must commit to sharing our results publicly to benefit all who serve the public conversation.
>
> (Dorsey, 2018)

In this line of argumentation, social media suffers from bad health – something that is essentially comparable to a fever. To treat this disease, an exact diagnosis is a crucial first step, requiring supposedly objective measurements and accurate equipment, not unlike a thermometer measuring the temperature of the human body. For Twitter, these measurements must be independent of human judgment, instead relying on the proclaimed neutrality of technology (in this case new forms of computational analysis). Further elaborating on the medical vocabulary, Twitter's response to fake news built directly on the notion that fake news is causing bad health on social media. The human body is thus a guiding metaphor not only for how technological solutions are described but also for their actual implementation.

In emphasizing the importance of countering the post-truth condition, social media companies present fake news as being simultaneously a product of so-called bad actors (a rather elusive group) and a depersonalized and depoliticized phenomenon that proliferates "in the wild." In both narratives, the causal relationship implied in the production of fake news remains ambiguous too. Echoing the almost larger-than-life characterization found in the medical post-truth vocabulary, Meta, for example, states that "[e]very day, our team fights the spread of false news" (Facebook, 2018d), making no explicit reference to the actual people creating such content. It simply spreads and exists out there. At other times, the company describes an "arms race" against "bad actors" (Zuckerberg, 2018) and "adversaries" (Zuckerberg, 2020).

While Meta, X, and Alphabet's solutions to this problem vary in scope, they are equally techno-centrist. Meta states that the company has implemented new forms of machine learning that not only diagnoses and contests fake news on its platforms, but also pre-emptively removes it *before* it becomes infectious:

> Over the past year, we've gotten increasingly better at finding and disabling fake accounts. We now block millions of fake accounts each day as people try to create them – and before they've done any harm. This is thanks to improvements in machine learning and artificial intelligence, which can proactively identify suspicious behavior at a scale that was not possible before.
>
> (Facebook, 2018c)

Preventing harm *before* it becomes harmful. Measuring health *before* it deteriorates. These are the kind of narratives often promoted and produced by social media companies and other tech giants. While the responses provided by these actors are situated in a widely different political context than when they rose to power in the early-to-mid 2000s, the same techno-centrism and optimism still seem to be at play. Although the public image of these companies has turned progressively more sour, it seems that they still view technological development as necessarily bound up with democracy. Better technology – more technology – will lay the foundation for a better democracy.

The effects of these solutions and their widespread techno-determinism are yet to materialize and be determined. Meta, X, and Alphabet have all stated that they are committed to cooperating transparently. The sincerity of this claim remains unclear, to say the least – especially since all these companies have been accused of misinforming the public and evading responsivity, both generally and in connection to specific cases, such as the infiltration of US elections by the Internet Research Agency. For example, a report commissioned by the US Senate concludes the following:

> Regrettably, it appears that the platforms [Twitter, Facebook, Instagram, and YouTube] may have misrepresented or evaded in some of their statements to Congress; one platform claimed that no specific groups were targeted (this is only true if speaking strictly of ads), while another dissembled about whether or not the Internet Research Agency created content to discourage voting (it did). It is unclear whether these answers were the result of faulty or lacking analysis, or a more deliberate evasion.
>
> (Diresta et al., 2018, p. 6)

One solution, many solutions

Taken together, we can begin to see a whole array of different forms of intervention and transformation, both implemented and imagined, being proposed to the diagnosed truth crisis. From legally removing the fake news infodemic to immunologically caring for the community, from developing machine learning for content removal to learning from those who have grown up in the natural habitat of fake news: a whole series of discursive worlds are starting to take form, dedicated to carving ways out of the current post-truth predicament.

While there is little consensus as to what will actually be most effective for saving democracy, the various solutions often share a common set of underlying premises. No matter how different the array of solutions might seem, some common assumptions have continued to inform them. Most, if not all, see the coming of fake news, post-truth, infodemics, and alternative facts as existential problems to be dealt with through different kinds of actions – either state-led, technology-premised, or market-oriented. Most, if not all, see democracy as being under siege, insofar as truth and reason have historically constituted the core critical infrastructure of liberal democracy. In this sense, there is an almost *necessary*, if not binding, relationship between truth, reason, and democracy. Some, but not all, see the current crisis as a defeat of existing systems of expertise, trust, and knowledge, located, not least, within the holy trinity of politics, science, and journalism. For these voices, saving democracy hinges on once again securing the integrity and authority of these three fields. Some, but once again not all, view the problem as one not of institutions but of individual capacities and resistances. In the virulent language of immunology, it is the individual that must become resilient to the ongoing barrage of fake news and misinformation. The conditions of possibility for democracy are, this line of reasoning suggests, marked by the degree to which an informed citizenry can exist. Such an informed citizenry means a citizenry that has the proper antibodies to withstand the disease of misinformation. Thus, although individual solutions may appear different, similar ideas about truth, reason, and democracy run as guiding threads throughout. In all the different pathways, misinformation and fake news are the problems to be overcome, and democracy is fundamentally tied to the ability to make rational decisions.

All discourses are not just marked by their presences but also by their absences – that is, the silences and things that are left unsaid. Across current debates and solutions, one of the things that remains glaringly absent is the role of popular sovereignty, political participation, and the people. It is striking how contemporary commentators tend to work with an almost completely rationalist and reason-based understanding of democracy. Not only has this meant an emphasis on rationality as a critical infrastructure of democracy, it has also implied a squandering of the democratic tradition – that is to say, the tradition of popular sovereignty and equality that runs throughout the history of democracy. In the following chapters, it is precisely this attempt to undo the democratic paradox that we will consider much more in-depth. We do so in order to offer an alternative view on our current political predicament – and perhaps other ways out.

References

Ackland, L. (2017, May/June). Post-Truth and the Rejection of Science. *Australasian Science*. www.australasianscience.com.au/article/issue-mayjune-2017/post-truth-and-rejection-science.html

BBC News (2017a, 23 January). Cambridge Scientists Consider Fake News "Vaccine." *BBC News*. www.bbc.com/news/uk-38714404

BBC News. (2017b, 6 December). BBC to Help Students Identify "Fake News." *BBC News*. www.bbc.com/news/entertainment-arts-42242630

BBC News. (2018, 15 November). Are These People Really a Threat to National Security? *BBC News*. www.bbc.com/news/video_and_audio/headlines/46213536/are-these-people-really-a-threat-to-thai-national-security

Biggs, T. (2021, 15 July). Twitter Expands Efforts in AI-Assisted War on COVID Fake News. *The Sydney Morning Herald*. www.smh.com.au/technology/twitter-s-expands-efforts-in-ai-assisted-war-on-covid-fake-news-20210714-p589oa.html

Bratich, J. (2020). Civil Society Must Be Defended: Misinformation, Moral Panics, and Wars of Restoration. *Communication, Culture & Critique, 13*(3), 311–322. https://doi.org/10.1093/ccc/tcz041

Carbone, C. (2018, 16 August). Fake News Backlash? Twitter CEO Rethinking How Platform Works, Wants to Reduce "Echo Chambers." *Fox News*. www.foxnews.com/tech/fake-news-backlash-twitter-ceo-rethinking-how-platform-works-wants-to-reduce-echo-chambers

Carlson, M. (2018). The Information Politics of Journalism in a Post-Truth Age. *Journalism Studies, 19*(13). https://doi.org/10.1080/1461670X.2018.1494513

Cook, J. (2017, 17 November). Technology Helped Fake News. Now Technology Needs to Stop it. *Bulletin of the Atomic Scientists.* https://thebulletin.org/2017/11/technology-helped-fake-news-now-technology-needs-to-stop-it/

CPJ. (2020, 9 April). Bolivia Enacts Decree Criminalizing "Disinformation" on COVID-19 Outbreak. *Committee to Protect Journalists.* https://cpj.org/2020/04/bolivia-enacts-decree-criminalizing-disinformation/

Creech, B. (2020). Fake News and the Discursive Construction of Technology Companies' Social Power. *Media, Culture & Society, 42*(6), 952–968. https://doi.org/10.1177/0163443719899801

Cunliffe-Jones, P., Diagne, A., Finlay, A., & Schiffrin, A. (2021). Bad Law – Legal And Regulatory Responses To Misinformation In Sub-Saharan Africa 2016–2020. In P. Cunliffe-Jones, A. Diagne, A. Finlay, & A. Schiffrin (Eds.), *Misinformation Policy in Sub-Saharan Africa: From Laws and Regulations to Media Literacy* (pp. 105–218). London: University of Westminster Press.

Derrida, J. (1981). *Dissemination* (B. Johnson, Trans.). Chicago: University of Chicago Press.

Dilworth, M. (2017, 30 May). Facebook Claims Germany's New Law to Tackle Fake News will Cause Tech Companies to Delete Legal Content. *The Independent.* www.independent.co.uk/news/business/news/facebook-germany-fake-news-law-tech-companies-delete-legal-content-social-media-hate-speech-fine-a7763081.html

Diresta, R., Shaffer, K., Ruppel, B., Matney, R., Fox, R., Albright, J., & Johnson, B. (2018). *The Tactics & Tropes of the Internet Research Agency.* New Knowledge. https://disinformationreport.blob.core.windows.net/disinformation-report/NewKn owledge-Disinformation-Report-Whitepaper.pdf

Dorsey, J. (2018, 1 March). If you want to improve something, you have to be able to measure it: The human body has a number of indicators of overall health, some very simple, like internal temperature – We know how to measure it, and we know some methods to bring it back in balance. *Twitter.* https://twitter.com/jack/status/9692342 83633115137

Downie Jr., L. (2023, 30 January). Newsrooms that Move Beyond "Objectivity" Can Build Trust. *The Washington Post.* www.washingtonpost.com/opinions/2023/01/30/newsrooms-news-reporting-objectivity-diversity/

Dullien, S., & Shapiro, J. (2017, 16 January). How to Avoid a Post-Truth World. European *Council of Foreign Relations.* www.ecfr.eu/article/commentary_how_to_avoid_a_post_truth_world

East Stratcom. (2021, 27 October). *Questions and Answers about the East StratCom Task Force.* The European External Action Service. www.eeas.europa.eu/eeas/questions-and-answers-about-east-stratcom-task-force_en

EEAS. (2021, 18 January). Building Immunity to Disinformation. www.eeas.europa.eu/eeas/building-immunity-disinformation_en

Esposito, R. (2011). *Immunitas: The Protection and Negation of Life.* Cambridge: Polity Press.

European Commission (2018a). *A Multi-Dimensional Approach to Disinformation.* https://doi.org/10.2759/0156

European Commission (2018b, 26 April). *Tackling Online Disinformation: A European Approach.* https://ec.europa.eu/digital-single-market/en/news/communication-tackl ing-online-disinformation-european-approach

Facebook (2018a, 21 March). Hard Questions: Update on Cambridge Analytica. *Facebook Newsroom.* https://newsroom.fb.com/news/2018/03/hard-questions-cambri dge-analytica/

Facebook (2018b, 31 July). Removing Bad Actors on Facebook. *Facebook Newsroom.* https://newsroom.fb.com/news/2018/07/removing-bad-actors-on-facebook/

Facebook (2018c, 10 May). Russian Ads Released by Congress. *Facebook Newsroom.* https://newsroom.fb.com/news/2018/05/russian-ads-released-by-congress/

Facebook (2018d, 19 October). The Hunt for False News. *Facebook Newsroom.* https:// newsroom.fb.com/news/2018/10/inside-feed-hunt-false-news-october-2018/

Facsar, F. (2020, 4 July). Hungary's COVID-19 Law Creates "Uncertainty" for Journalists. *Deutsche Welle.* www.dw.com/en/hungary-law-to-fight-coronavirus-creates-uncertai nty-for-journalists/a-53027631

Faiola, A. (2017, 22 January). As Cold War Turns to Information War, a New Fake News Police Combats Disinformation. *The Washington Post.* www.washingtonpost.com/ world/europe/as-cold-war-turns-to-information-war-a-new-fake-news-police/2017/ 01/18/9bf49ff6-d80e-11e6-a0e6-d502d6751bc8_story.html

Farkas, J. (2023). Fake News in Metajournalistic Discourse. *Journalism Studies.* Advance online publication. https://doi.org/10.1080/1461670X.2023.2167106

FENAPEF (2018, 9 January). Polícia Federal dará início nos próximos dias em Brasília às atividades de um grupo especial formado para combater notícias falsas durante o processo eleitoral. A medida tem o objetivo de identificar e punir autores de "fake news" contra ou a favor dos candidatos [The Brazilian Federal Police is putting together a special operations group in Brasilia to fight fake news during the national election. The initiative is aimed at identifying and persecuting those producing fake news in favor of or against candidates]. *Twitter.* https://twitter.com/fenapef/status/950741290790150145

Freedom House (2020, 14 May). Bolivia: Supreme Decree Threatens Freedom of Expression. *Freedom House.* https://freedomhouse.org/article/bolivia-supreme-dec ree-threatens-freedom-expression

Goswami, A. (2022, 20 July). Is AI the Only Antidote to Disinformation? *World Economic Forum.* www.weforum.org/agenda/2022/07/disinformation-ai-technology/

Grigori, P. (2018, 11 May). 20 projetos de lei no Congresso pretendem criminalizar fake news [20 bills in Congress aim to criminalize fake news]. *Pública.* https://apublica.org/ 2018/05/20-projetos-de-lei-no-congresso-pretendem-criminalizar-fake-news/

Hasen, R. L. (2022). *Cheap Speech: How Disinformation Poisons Our Politics – and How to Cure It.* New Haven: Yale University Press.

Huddleston Jr., T. (2022, 13 July). Meta has a New AI Tool to Fight Misinformation – and it's Using Wikipedia to Train Itself. *CNBC.* www.cnbc.com/2022/07/13/meta-wikipe dia-want-to-fight-misinformation-with-new-ai-tool-sphere.html

Human Rights Watch (2018, 14 February). Germany: Flawed Social Media Law. www. hrw.org/news/2018/02/14/germany-flawed-social-media-law

Human Rights Watch (2020, 6 May). Ethiopia: Free Speech at Risk Amid Covid-19. www.hrw.org/news/2020/05/06/ethiopia-free-speech-risk-amid-covid-19

Human Rights Watch. (2021, 11 February). Covid-19 Triggers Wave of Free Speech Abuse. www.hrw.org/news/2021/02/11/covid-19-triggers-wave-free-speech-abuse

Hussman Jr., W. (2023, 15 February). Bring Back Objective Journalism. *The Wall Street Journal.* www.wsj.com/articles/bring-back-objective-journalism-news-reporting-obje ctivity-public-opinion-trust-fourth-estate-reporters-media-newspaper-8a2c6ba

IAPA. (2020, 20 October). Legal Restrictions. *Inter American Press Association*. https://en.sipiapa.org/notas/1214190-legal-restrictions

Intentional Insights (n.d.), Pro-Truth Pledge. Accessed 24 April 2023. www.protruthpledge.org/

Kight, S. W. (2020, 15 September). Gen Z is eroding the power of misinformation. *Axios*. www.axios.com/2020/09/15/gen-z-is-eroding-the-power-of-misinformation

Klepper, D. (2022, 24 August). "Pre-bunking" shows promise in fight against misinformation. *AP News*. https://apnews.com/article/technology-misinformation-eastern-europe-902f436e3a6507e8b2a223e09a22e969

Koliska, M., Chadha, K., & Burns, A. (2020). Talking Back: Journalists Defending Attacks Against their Profession in the Trump Era. *Journalism Studies*, *21*(11), 1496–1513. https://doi.org/10.1080/1461670X.2020.1763190

Lewandowsky, S., Ecker, U.K.H., & Cook, J. (2017). Beyond misinformation: Understanding and coping with the "post-truth" era. *Journal of Applied Research in Memory and Cognition*, *6*(*4*), 353–369. https://doi.org/ 10.1016/j.jarmac.2017.07.008

Lewsey, F. (2018, 20 February). *Fake News "Vaccine": Online Game May "Inoculate" by Simulating Propaganda Tactics*. University of Cambridge. www.cam.ac.uk/research/news/fake-news-vaccine-online-game-may-inoculate-by-simulating-propaganda-tactics

Lim, G. (2020). *Securitize / Counter – Securitize: The Life and Death of Malaysia's Anti-Fake News Act*. Data & Society. https://datasociety.net/library/securitize-counter-securitize

Lischka, J. A. (2021). Fighting an Indestructible Monster: Journalism's Legitimacy Narratives During the Trump Era. *Journal of Language and Politics*, *20*(5), 803–823. https://doi.org/10.1075/jlp.21031.lis

Lubianco, J. (2020, 16 December). 11 Laws and Bills Against Disinformation in Latin America Carry Fines, Prison and Censorship. *LatAm Journalism Review*. https://latamjournalismreview.org/articles/laws-and-bills-against-disinformation-in-latin-america/

Machivenyika, F. (2020, 31 May). Spreading Fake Covid-19 News Attracts Jail Term. *The Herald*. www.herald.co.zw/spreading-fake-covid-19-news-attracts-jail-term/

Macron, E. (2018, 25 April). Address to the U.S. Congress. *CNN*. http://transcripts.cnn.com/TRANSCRIPTS/1804/25/ctw.01.html

McAuley, J. (2018, 10 January). France Weighs a Law to Rein in "Fake News," Raising Fears for Freedom of Speech. *The Washington Post*. www.washington post.com/world/europe/france-weighs-a-law-to-rein-in-fake-news-raising-fears-for-freedom-of-speech/2018/01/10/78256962-f558-11e7-9af7-a50bc3300042_story.html

Mchangama, J., & Fiss, J. (2019). *The Digital Berlin Wall: How Germany (Accidentally) Created a Prototype for Global Online Censorship*. Justitia. http://justitia-int.org/en/the-digital-berlin-wall-how-germany-created-a-prototype-for-global-online-censorship/

McNair, B. (2018). *Fake News: Falsehood, Fabrication and Fantasy in Journalism*. London: Routledge.

Mills, M., Rahal, C., Brazel, D., Yan, J., & Gieysztor, S. (2020). *COVID-19 Vaccine Deployment: Behaviour, Ethics, Misinformation and Policy Strategies*. London: The Royal Society. https://royalsociety.org/-/media/policy/projects/set-c/set-c-vaccine-deployment.pdf

Moore, K., & Timmins, L. (2017, 7 September). How Do We Navigate a "Post-Truth" World? Follow the Millennials, *Forbes*. www.forbes.com/sites/karlmoore/2017/09/07/how-do-we-navigate-a-post-truth-world-follow-the-millennials/

Morozov, E. (2013). *To Save Everything, Click Here: Technology, Solutionism, and the Urge to Fix Problems That Don't Exist*. London: Penguin Books.

Morozov, E. (2017). Moral Panic Over Fake News Hides the Real Enemy – the Digital Giants. *The Guardian*. www.theguardian.com/commentisfree/2017/jan/08/blaming-fake-news-not-the-answer-democracy-crisis

Neo, R. (2020). A Cudgel of Repression: Analysing State Instrumentalisation of the "Fake News" Label in Southeast Asia, *Journalism*, *23*(9), 1919–1938. https://doi.org/10.1177/1464884920984060

Nesbit, J. (2016, 16 December). The Only Antidote to the Poison of Fake News. *Time Magazine*. https://time.com/4605146/fake-news-antidote/

Nugent, C. (2018, 7 June). France is Voting on a Law Banning Fake News: Here's How it Could Work. *Time Magazine*. https://time.com/5304611/france-fake-news-law-macron/

Olewe, D. (2018, 16 May). Kenya, Uganda and Tanzania in "Anti-Fake News Campaign." *BBC News*. www.bbc.com/news/world-africa-44137769

Olterman, P. (2018, 5 January). Tough New German Law Puts Tech Firms and Free Speech in Spotlight. *The Guardian*. www.theguardian.com/world/2018/jan/05/tough-new-german-law-puts-tech-firms-and- free-speech-in-spotlight

Pennycook, G., McPhetres, J., Zhang, Y., Lu, J. G., & Rand, D. G. (2020). Fighting COVID-19 Misinformation on Social Media: Experimental Evidence for a Scalable Accuracy-Nudge Intervention. *Psychological Science*, *31*(7), 770–780. https://doi.org/10.1177/0956797620939054

Reporters Without Borders. (2017, 19 July). Russian Bill is Copy-and-Paste of Germany's Hate Speech Law. *Rsf.org*. https://rsf.org/en/news/russian-bill-copy-and-paste-germanys-hate-speech-law

Reuters Staff (2018, 5 March). Malaysia's Najib Pushes to Outlaw "Fake News" Before Election. *Reuters*. www.reuters.com/article/us-malaysia-politics-idUSKBN1GH1HV

Richardson, N. (2017). Fake News and Journalism Education. *Asia Pacific Media Educator*, *27*(1), 1–9. https://doi.org/10.1177/1326365X17702268

Rising, D. (2021, 30 July). Thai Media Restrictions Raise Freedom of Expression Concerns. *AP News*. https://apnews.com/article/business-health-media-coronavirus-pandemic-ebbe28f11fb5a2f12b6663522a148765

Rohn, J. (2017, 25 January). Scientists Can't Fight "Alternative Facts" Alone. *The Guardian*. www.theguardian.com/science/occams-corner/2017/jan/25/alternative-facts-experts-scientists-fight-alone-humanities

Roy, E.A. (2018, 29 May). Papua New Guinea Bans Facebook for a Month to Root Out "Fake Users." *The Guardian*. www.theguardian.com/world/2018/may/29/papua-new-guinea-facebook-ban-study-fake-users

Savarese, M. (2021, 20 March). Critics of Brazil's President Being Targeted by Security Law. *AP News*. https://apnews.com/article/brazil-coronavirus-pandemic-crime-jair-bolsonaro-national-security-26b64ed8319cbab9292abf627bbdd6be

Schick, N. (2020). *Deep Fakes and the Infocalypse: What You Urgently Need To Know*. London: Monoray.

Schultheis, E. (2018, 28 July). Cambodia Eviscerates its Free Press: And the Whole Region Suffers. *The Atlantic.* www.theatlantic.com/international/archive/2018/07/cambodia-southeast-asia-free-press/566018/

Serhan, Y. (2018, 24 February). Italy Scrambles to Fight Misinformation Ahead of its Elections. *The Atlantic.* www.theatlantic.com/international/archive/2018/02/europe-fake-news/551972/

Smith, D. (2018, 11 April). Mark Zuckerberg Vows to Fight Election Meddling in Marathon Senate Grilling. *The Guardian.* www.theguardian.com/technology/2018/apr/10/zuckerberg-facebook-testimony-latest-news-regulation-congress

Solon, O. (2016, 11 November). Facebook's Fake News: Mark Zuckerberg Rejects "Crazy Idea" That it Swayed Voters. *The Guardian.* www.theguardian.com/technology/2016/nov/10/facebook-fake-news-us-election-mark-zuckerberg-donald-trump

Tehusijarana, K.M., & Valentina, J. (2019, 22 May). Jakarta Riot: Government Temporarily Limits Access to Social Media, Messaging Apps. *The Jakarta Post.* www.thejakartapost.com/life/2019/05/22/jakarta-riot-government-temporarily-limits-access-to-social-media-messaging-apps.html

The Economist (2016, 10 September). Post-Truth Politics: Art of the Lie. *The Economist.* www.economist.com/leaders/2016/09/10/art-of-the-lie

Thomasson, E. (2018, 8 March). Germany Looks to Revise Social Media Law as Europe Watches. *Reuters.* www.reuters.com/article/us-germany-hatespeech/germany-looks-to-revise-social-media-law-as-europe-watches-idUSKCN1GK1BN

Tsipursky, G., Votta, F., & Mulick, J.A. (2018). A Psychological Approach to Promoting Truth in Politics: The Pro-Truth Pledge. *Journal of Social and Political Psychology,* 6(2), 271–290. https://doi.org/10.5964/jspp.v6i2.856

United Nations. (2020, 21 May). UN Launches New Initiative to Fight COVID-19 Misinformation Through "Digital First Responders." *UN News: Global Perspective Human Stories.* https://news.un.org/en/story/2020/05/1064622

University of Cambridge (2018, 20 February). Fake News "Vaccine": Online Game May "Inoculate" by Simulating Propaganda Tactics. www.cam.ac.uk/research/news/fake-news-vaccine-online-game-may-inoculate-by-simulating-propaganda-tactics

Vernon, J.L. (2017). Science in the Post-Truth Era. *American Scientist, 105,* 2–4. www.americanscientist.org/article/science-in-the-post-truth-era

Walker, P. (2018, 23 June). New National Security Unit Set up to Tackle Fake News in UK. *The Guardian.* www.theguardian.com/politics/2018/jan/23/new-national-security-unit-will-tackle-spread-of-fake-news-in-uk

Zsombor, P. (2021, 13 March). Malaysia Uses Emergency Powers to Impose "Fake News" Law. *Voice of America.* www.voanews.com/a/press-freedom_malaysia-uses-emergency-powers-impose-fake-news-law/6203266.html

Zuckerberg, M. (2018, 4 September). Protecting Democracy is an Arms Race. Here's How Facebook Can Help. *The Washington Post.* www.washingtonpost.com/opinions/mark-zuckerberg-protecting-democracy-is-an-arms-race-heres-how-facebook-can-help-win-it/2018/09/04/53b3c8ee-b083-11e8-9a6a-565d92a3585d_story.html?noredirect=on

Zuckerberg, M. (2020, 15 February). Learn Fast and Fix Things: Social Media and Democracy. Munich Security Conference. https://securityconference.org/en/medialibrary/asset/conversation-learn-fast-and-fix-things-social-media-and-democracy-20200215-1700/

Part III

Out of post-truth worlds

7   Post-truth and post-politics
Splitting the difference

In contemporary post-truth worlds, liberal democracy is often said to be experiencing a sudden rupture or crisis. This has rapidly derailed the otherwise stable political system into a state of uncertainty, unrest, and turbulence. Indeed, as we have shown so far in this book, the current crisis facing liberal democracies worldwide has been conceptualized as nothing less than a breaking of politics and truth. What is starting to come undone, according to increasingly pervasive crisis narratives, is the social and political contract at the heart of liberal democracies themselves: democracy *is* truth and without the latter the former cannot survive.

In these dominant discourses, we find a noticeable lack of historical context and nuance regarding the role and development of liberal democracies prior to the rise of the post-truth era. The prevalent story seems to be that democracy has remained a relatively stable, prosperous, and internally coherent form of governance until the villains of the post-truth era very recently derailed it. In this third part of the book, we want to complicate and critically challenge these narratives by situating our contemporary moment within a wider political and historical framework. If we wish to understand our current political predicament, we need to locate the emergence of post-truth worlds within a broader set of institutional, political, and social developments: we need to bring history back in.

Drawing on the historical accounts provided by critical political theorists – most notably Chantal Mouffe, Jacques Rancière, Wendy Brown, and Colin Crouch – this chapter dives into a range of institutional and political developments facing advanced liberal democracies since the 1970s and 1980s. By doing so, we outline how democracies have been subject to a series of fundamental political and economic changes that are prior to our contemporary post-truth worlds. This has had significant implications for how we understand and experience democracy as a political system today. Summarized in a somewhat simplified way, these developments have meant that market-oriented and competition-focused forms of politics have increasingly come to dominate policy agendas. Contrary to the political-economic settlement of the post-war years (premised on taming the

DOI: 10.4324/9781003434870-10

economy and building welfare institutions), past decades have witnessed the blossoming of a remarkably different form of politics. Social and economic collectivism has made way for forced individualism, welfare expansion has made way for austerity, and the voice of the democratic people has increasingly made way for the logics of the global market economy.

These major political transformations have been highly layered, continuously challenged, and contradictory, sometimes taking place in rapid bursts, other times through incremental and accumulative changes (Brenner, Peck, & Theodore, 2010). Even so, the overall result has been a gradual, convergent movement towards increasingly undemocratic, depoliticized, and (perhaps even) authoritarian states of democracy (Bruff, 2014). Through increasingly coercive forms of neoliberalization, liberal democracies have moved into what scholars have defined as *post-democratic* (Crouch, 2004, 2011; Rancière, 1999) or even *post-political* territory (Mouffe, 1993, 2005a, 2005b, 2018). As this chapter details, this entails a mode of democracy in which rationality has replaced popular sovereignty, consensus has replaced conflict, competition has replaced collectivism, and the needs of the capitalist market has replaced the will of the democratic people.

By relating post-truth worlds to these historical transformations of liberal democracies over the past half century, we will argue that the fundamental idea of a post-truth and post-factual era in many ways represents both a misguided product of and cure for post-political trends. As will become clear over the course of the chapter, the democratic ideas underlying post-truth worlds have largely relied on tropes found in existing post-political vocabularies. Thus, far from being a rupture in the fabric of democracy, discourses of post-truth expand upon and further entrench already prominent political-economic and institutional developments, prescribing more post-politics in an effort to solve a growing crisis of this very form of governance. What is troubling about this is not only that current solutions to the supposed post-truth crisis risk further hollowing out liberal democracies, but also that they might even push authoritarian and technocratic politics further. Rather than deepening democratic institutions, the current moment risks dismantling these even more, throwing liberal democracy further away from democratic ideals of collective decision-making, egalitarianism, and popular sovereignty. By beginning to open these discussions, this third part of the book shifts gears and approach. Instead of seeking to understand the internal logics of post-truth worlds, we now want to engage head on with the normative ideas they contain: we want to make them part of a much larger story of democratic change. In doing so, we also want to begin to question the viability and attraction of post-truth worlds as vehicles of description, diagnosis, and solution. Do we actually live in a post-truth era? Does this diagnosis really help us understand the present state of democracy? And does it in any meaningful way present a viable course for strengthening democracy in times of crisis?

Democracy as truth, the truth of democracy

In May 2018, *The Washington Post* ran an opinion piece by journalist Jennifer Rubin entitled "In a post-truth world, there is no democracy" (Rubin, 2018). This title was precise insofar as it captured one of the most pervasive assumptions within post-truth worlds. As shown in the previous chapters, neither Rubin nor *The Washington Post* have been alone in endorsing the idea that post-truth marks the end of democracy. One of the founding assumptions of contemporary post-truth worlds is that democracy always *has been* and always *must be* based on an unconditional, perhaps even "sacred" (Davies, 2016), relation to facts. It was precisely this sentiment that Macron (2018) expressed in his speech to the US Congress. According to Macron, "we are living in a time of anger and fear because of … current global threats. But these feelings do not build anything. You can play with fear and anger for a time. But they do not construct anything." One of the major threats pinpointed by Macron (alongside terrorism) was the "ever-growing virus of fake news, which exposes our people to irrational fear and imaginary risks" (Macron, 2018). As already recounted in the introduction to this book, Macron articulated the impact of this so-called "virus" as nothing less than an attack on the spirit of democracy and its rational underpinnings. This fundamental idea, claiming that *truth is democracy* and *democracy is truth*, has continued to be one of the most ubiquitous assumptions in post-truth worlds. Yet, when diving into the complex history of democratic development, we find that this simple narrative quickly becomes challenged on multiple fronts.

Democracy, political theorists and historians alike highlight, remains a complex and continuously developing set of institutions, practices, and ideals. Not only is its intellectual history deeply layered, stretching across numerous competing ideas about the "true" purpose of politics, the actual instantiations and manifestations of democracy are also multiple, developing, and contested (Held, 1989, 2006; Müller, 2011; Rosenfeld, 2019). To claim there is no "true" democracy, because the democratic tradition has always been divided and open to negotiations, can almost seem like a trivial point. Trivial as it may be, democratic debates continue to be saturated with claims to the contrary: that is, ideas about what democracy *must be* in order to properly function and deliver on its promises. Indeed, to claim that there is nothing necessary about democracy in the strictest sense of the term seems to invoke chills in large parts of the established public sphere. The notion that "you are either with us, or against us," as proclaimed by former US President, George W. Bush, also holds true for democracy. You are either with *us* (the democrats) or against us. That said, we should not be led astray by this fearmongering. Instead of posing the question through a binary distinction between being-with and being-against, we want to underline that there is no eternal ground or ultimate foundation from which democracy can be instituted once and for all. What democracy is and can be remains disputed (or, at the very least, in flux). Thus, while we are certainly wholeheartedly *for* democracy ourselves, we see no use in the idea that democracy only exists in the singular. This is a dangerous fiction, which does not help us get anywhere. We ought instead to historicize and question this fiction: under what conditions can democracies prosper? And what challenges does such conditions face?

According to a number of prominent critical scholars, such as Mouffe, Brown, Rancière, and Crouch, liberal democracies have gradually entered a new phase since the 1970s and 1980s. Not only did a series of profound political, economic, and technological restructurings take place in these decades, the very fabric of democracy itself was transformed. Chantal Mouffe has been one of the most prominent analysts and vocal opponents of these changes. Mouffe has developed her account of advanced liberal democracies (and their discontents) through a series of important publications since the 1980s, including *The Return of the Political* (Mouffe, 1993), *On the Political* (Mouffe, 2005a) and *The Democratic Paradox* (Mouffe, 2005b). In these works, she attempts to think through the democratic tradition in order to unpack and understand the current state of liberal democracies. Her starting point for doing so has, on the one hand, been an engagement with the history of political philosophy, while on the other hand, it has been a more normative engagement with promoting participatory, inclusive, and pluralist forms of democratic participation. According to Mouffe, it is precisely these latter aspects that are all too often denied or obscured within contemporary forms of politics and democracy. As she makes clear, it seems that democracy has to some extent become incapable of dealing with political issues and problems in a genuinely *political way*. Part of the reason for this political deficit has to do with the increasingly uncontested hegemony of liberalism, particularly in its contemporary neoliberal and globalized guise. To be sure, Mouffe underlines, the very idea of "liberalism" as a political-philosophical school of thought also remains multiple and cannot be reduced to a closed set of propositions. That being the case, it does seem possible, she maintains, to highlight, if not "a common essence" then "a multiplicity of ... . 'family resemblances'" (Mouffe, 2005a, p. 10). These resemblances revolve around two distinct understandings of politics, namely a *rationalist* and an *individualist* vision. In their most crass manifestations, these vectors have formed the basis of an aggregative model of democracy that "envisages politics as the establishment of a compromise between different competing forces in society" (Mouffe, 2005a, p. 12). This is a model in which "[i]ndividuals are portrayed as rational beings, driven by the maximization of their own interests and as acting in the political world in a basically instrumental way. It is the idea of the market applied to the domain of politics which apprehended with concepts borrowed from economics" (Mouffe, 2005a, p. 13). While some authors, such as Jürgen Habermas and John Rawls, have sought to overcome this rather limited conception of individual subjectivity and political participation, they still end up relying too narrowly on the idea that a universal consensus can and must be reached. In so doing, they propel the "central trait of most liberal thought ... . [namely] the rationalist belief in the availability of a universal consensus based on reason" (2005a, p. 11). For Mouffe, this kind of argumentation is problematic on ontological grounds. Indeed, for her, neither rationalism nor individualism is a good starting point for understanding what is specific to democracy. The problem is that they cannot grasp the nature of antagonism, exclusion, and political conflict. They are – in short – blind to how hegemonic struggles take place.

As we have already hinted at a number of times, Mouffe detects a series of important changes taking place in Western democracies from the 1970s up until today. According to her, what started to take place at that point in time was a shift in the internal constitution of liberal democracies. Up until then, liberal democracies had largely functioned as a compromise between two seemingly opposite political philosophical strands: namely the *liberal tradition* (as understood above) and the *democratic tradition*. Mouffe labels the tension between these two as the *democratic paradox*:

> with modern democracy, we are dealing with a new political form of society whose specificity comes from the articulation between two different traditions. On one side we have the liberal tradition constituted by the rule of law, the defence of human rights and the respect of individual liberty; on the other the democratic tradition whose main ideas are those of equality, identity between governing and governed and popular sovereignty. There is no necessary relation between these two distinct traditions but only a contingent historical articulation. Through such an articulation ... . liberalism was democratized and democracy liberalized. Let's not forget that, while we tend today to take the link between liberalism and democracy for granted, their union, far from being a smooth process, was the result of bitter struggles.
>
> (Mouffe, 2005b, pp. 2–3)

According to Mouffe, the tension-filled balance between the liberal and democratic traditions – their continuous struggle back and forth – has become increasingly undone since the 1980s. Indeed, for her, popular sovereignty has gradually been taken out of the equation. This has taken place, she argues, against the background of increasingly pervasive neoliberal policy agendas, emphasizing market-premised forms of political intervention over and above the voice of the democratic people. "What has happened under neo-liberal hegemony," Mouffe argues, "is that the liberal component has become so dominant that democratic values have been eviscerated. Several previous democratic advances have been dismantled, and under the motto of 'modernization,' core democratic values have been dismissed as 'archaic'" (2013, p. 124).

Contrary to the (often) utopian scholarly ideas found in the 1990s – proclaiming Western democracies to have reached a place that "constitutes a great progress in the evolution of humanity" (Mouffe, 2005a, p. 1) – Mouffe

argues that liberal democracies have actually progressively become *less* democratic. What consolidated in the 1990s, not least with Anthony Giddens and
the so-called Third Way in the United Kingdom, was a *post-political climate*
or *zeitgeist*. This was one in which the balance between the liberal and the
democratic tradition had not only tipped in favor of the former, but where real
political choices and conflicts were also increasingly replaced by either technocratic experts or consensus across the middle of the political spectrum. This
supposed pinnacle of humanity, Mouffe suggests, has been imagined to be a
time in which

> a world "without enemies" is now possible. Partisan conflicts are a thing of
> the past and consensus can now be obtained through dialogue. Thanks to
> globalization and the universalization of liberal democracy, we can expect
> a cosmopolitan future bringing peace, prosperity, and the implementation of
> human rights worldwide.
>
> (2005a, p. 1)

In this utopian future, it has even become possible to create a political "world
'beyond left and right,' 'beyond hegemony,' 'beyond sovereignty' and 'beyond
antagonism'" (2005a, p. 2).

According to Mouffe, the coming of this new rule by consensus – a form of
government that claims to move beyond dispute, disagreement, and entrenched
political divides – has had fatal consequences for democracy. Resonating this
sentiment, Wilson and Swyngedouw (2014, p. 3) somewhat ironically note that
the era of an "untroubled, undivided, cohesive and common-sense society"
envisioned by political elites is actually marked by deep political apathy and
electoral participation at an all-time low. For Mouffe, this has, on the one
hand, meant that "[t]he status quo has become naturalized and made into the
way 'things really are'" (Mouffe, 2005b, p. 5). This is captured by Margaret
Thatcher's famous "TINA" slogan: "there is no alternative." On the other hand,
it implies the consolidation of a "post-political trend ... . [that] deprives democratic citizens of an agonistic debate where they can make their voices heard and
choose between real alternatives" (2013, p. 119). Part of this latter development
consists in promoting increasingly technocratic modes of politics, building not
on the idea of partisan confrontation but on "neutral" and "rational" management of societal affairs. This also means, Mouffe suggests, that contrary to the
democratic tradition's emphasis on promoting differences of opinions and the
voice of the people, "political questions ... . [are] reduced to mere technical
issues to be dealt with by experts. No space ... [is] left for the citizens to have
a real choice between different political projects and their role ... [is] limited to
approving the 'rational' policies elaborated by those experts" (Mouffe, 2018,
p. 4). Taken together, these developments lead Mouffe to portray the current
state of democracy in a fairly bleak way:

the role of parliaments and institutions that allow citizens to influence political decisions has been drastically reduced. Elections no longer offer any opportunity to decide on real alternatives through the traditional "parties of government." The only thing that post-politics allows is a bipartisan alternation of power between centre-right and centre-left parties. All those who oppose the "consensus in the centre" and the dogma that there is no alternative to neoliberal globalization are presented as "extremists" or disqualified as "populists." Politics therefore has become a mere issue of managing the established order, a domain reserved for experts, and popular sovereignty has been declared obsolete.

(Mouffe, 2018, p. 17)

As Mouffe first pointed out two decades ago, the problem with these developments – which have only accelerated since then – is that they create a *democratic deficit* (Mouffe, 2005b). As popular sovereignty is taken away, new spaces start to open, paving the way for very grim forms of politics.

The neoliberal takeover

Mouffe attributes the gradual dismantling of liberal democracies with the increasingly widespread adoption of *neoliberal* policies and institutional developments. Indeed, for Mouffe, the unquestioned and unquestionable hegemony of competition-oriented and market-driven policies is precisely what has laid the foundation for the cancelation of politics *proper*. As is often noted, neoliberalism remains a notoriously contested concept, both by those using it to analyze contemporary politics and by those claiming it to be little less than a slur used by the Left. As Peck, Theodore, and Brenner noted in 2009, "[l]ong before the advent of the globalizing financial crisis of 2008–2009, neoliberalism had become a rascal concept. Largely a critic's term, it had been circulating, simultaneously, as an oppositional slogan, a zeitgeist signifier, and an analytical construct. Partly as a result of this contradictory pattern of usage and signification, the life of this keyword has always been controversial" (Peck, Theodore, & Brenner, 2009, p. 96). Our aim here is not to take stock of neoliberalism or its continued relevance in contemporary social scientific inquiry. Somewhat more modestly, we simply deploy it here, based on some of the scholars whose trail we follow, to hold together a series of developments with certain family resemblances taking place across liberal democracies since the 1970s and 1980s.

The emergence of neoliberal policies and rationales is often associated with a series of important events, most noticeably, the growing economic instability facing advanced capitalist states in the 1970s and 1980s. Contrary to the seemingly unstoppable growth of the post-war years, where expansive welfare regimes were erected alongside the deepening of democratic institutions, profound political, and economic dislocations characterized the early 1970s. As outlined by Brenner (2004), the post-war compromise was cast into disarray by a series of major shifts, including the breakdown of the Bretton Woods system, the 1973 oil crisis, the demise of Fordist mass production industries, the globalization of industries and the economic crises of Keynesian welfare states. As a response to these crisis tendencies, the 1970s and early 1980s also became the decade where three horsemen of neoliberalism took center stage: Margaret Thatcher in the United Kingdom, Ronald Reagan in the United States, and the so-called Chicago Boys in Chile after the 1973 coup. As Peck and Tickell (2007, p. 28) recount, "these vanguard regimes took momentous steps to construct, in the name of economic liberalization, a capital-centric order in which the impediments to accelerate finance-oriented accumulation were minimized or removed." A large part of this discourse was formulated around the idea of downsizing or even dismantling the proclaimed all too large and enveloping state apparatus. Through privatization, marketization, and deregulation (or rather *re*regulation), the purpose was to create an altogether new political regime and form of state.

Far from being a grand and calibrated machinery that reorganizes society in a linear and calculated way, the on-going turn towards neoliberal policies has been marked by deep contradictions, failures, experiments, and local dependencies (Brenner et al., 2010; Peck, 2013; Peck & Tickell, 2007). There is not one purified and total neoliberal system, nor some grand conspiracy to be unraveled. More simply, there is a series of ongoing political efforts to reform and refunctionalize existing institutions, policies, discourses, and ideas. As Brenner and colleagues (2010) make clear,

> neoliberal reform dynamics do not reflect the inexorable unfolding of a preconceived, preconstituted ideological blueprint, replicated in a "pure" form in one jurisdiction after another. Rather, they are forged in and through real-time, *in situ* forms of regulatory experimentation and institutional tinkering in which previous efforts to confront recurrent problems directly influence the ongoing search for alternative solutions.
>
> (p. 190, original emphasis)

An important aspect to be kept in mind is that, while both neoliberal proponents and scholars have claimed these policies to be about dismantling, withdrawing, or rolling back the state, actually existing neoliberalism has turned out to be messy and layered. Indeed, rather than simply removing existing institutions, processes of neoliberalization have often been marked by both continuities and discontinuities, forward- and backwards-rolling changes, incremental and radical. As Loïc Wacquant (2009), for example, has stressed time and again in his studies of the United States, neoliberalism has far from warranted the coming of small government. Instead, an expanding and increasingly interventionist set of policies has been put in place.

While much more could be said about these developments, one of the important points we want to take from these is that, as a mode of political-economic restructuring (characterized through layered, situated, and contradictory processes of change), neoliberalism has increasingly come to imply the hegemony of markets over democratic politics, capital over community, and competition over democratic participation. It has led to the rise of what Wendy Brown (2015) succinctly characterizes as a new form of reason, converting "the distinctly political character, meaning, and operation of democracy's constituent elements into economic ones" (p. 17). Not only does this mean that supposed "economic necessities" increasingly dictate political outcomes, but also that "the market becomes *the*, rather than *a* site of veridiction *and* becomes so for every arena and type of human activity.... from mothering to mating, from learning to criminality, from planning one's family to planning one's death" (Ibid., p. 67, original emphasis).

The capitalist market economy has very little use for the ideals found in the democratic tradition, namely questions of equality, inclusion, and popular sovereignty. It often thrives, at least in its contemporary finance-dominated and globalized guise, much better with technocratic measurements and undemocratic means of political intervention. Indeed, in what has fast become a growing body of literature, many scholars have argued that the last decades have paved the way for an increasingly more *authoritarian* form of neoliberalism (Bruff, 2014; Bruff & Tansel, 2018). Not least in the wake of the 2007–2008 financial crisis and the austerity politics that followed, authors such as Ian Bruff (2014) argue that policymakers have increasingly come to rely on coercive and legal mechanisms that are not susceptive to democratic scrutiny. This has implied a shift "*toward* constitutional and legal mechanisms and the move *away* from seeking consent for hegemonic projects" (Bruff, 2014, p. 116, original emphasis).

Politics *after* the demos

What starts to emerge from these accounts is an image of a liberal democratic tradition that has progressively become more divided or cut in two. The tension between the liberal and democratic traditions has shifted towards the former, meaning that political ideals of civic dispute, popular sovereignty, and egalitarian rule by the people have gradually been replaced by a focus on individual rights, economic consensus, and supposedly rational decision-making. This post-political condition dominating the contemporary political landscape across liberal democracies signals the emergence of an era in which genuinely political aspects of democracy have been withdrawn. In its place, an ideal of democracy based on expert-led truth, economic necessities, and (what is claimed to be) universal consensus has become hegemonic. Mouffe, Brown, Wacquant, Brenner, Peck, and Bruff have certainly not been alone in critically dissecting this increasingly pervasive hegemony of rationality and politics beyond conflict.

With the help of another figure from the academic Left, French political philosopher Jacques Rancière, we now want to move deeper into the post-political condition by attending to his analysis of democratic developments in the 20th century. This will allow us to bring to the fore the specificity of our post-political time – namely what it means to think and act within a democracy without the demos (people).

Like Mouffe, Rancière also seeks to capture the particular set of institutional logics that have become dominant across liberal democracies since the 1970s and 1980s. He does so in order to foreground what he terms the coming of an altogether new form of politics, namely *post-democracy*. In his 2005 book, *Hatred of Democracy*, Rancière (2014) provides a series of important reflections on these topics. What are, he asks, the minimum criteria or conditions for any system to be deemed democratic? If one were to compile a list of democratic features, what would it include? Rancière here lists the following: "short and non-renewable electoral mandates that cannot be held concurrently; a monopoly of people's representatives over the formulation of laws; a ban on State functionaries becoming the representatives of the people; a bare minimum of campaigns and campaign costs; and the monitoring of possible interference by economic powers in the electoral process" (2014, p. 72). Yet, as he quickly remarks, if one applies these very conditions to contemporary democracies, one will find a distinct lack of any of these traits:

> what we call democracy is a statist and governmental functioning that is exactly the contrary: eternally elected members holding concurrent or alternating municipal, regional, legislative and/or ministerial functions and whose essential link to the people is that of the representation of regional interests; governments which make laws themselves; representatives of the people that largely come from one administrative school; ministers or their collaborators who are also given posts in public or semipublic companies; fraudulent financing of parties through public works contracts; businesspeople who invest colossal sums in trying to win electoral mandates; owners of private media empires that use their public functions to monopolize the empire of the public media.
>
> (Rancière, 2014, pp. 72–73)

In short, there is very little to suggest that what we now call democracy shares anything with what we might associate, even in a commonsensical fashion, with democracy as an idealized system and mode of political rule. For Rancière, this almost complete discrepancy between idealized conditions of democracy and its actual manifestations reveals nothing less than the following: "We do not live in democracies ... . We live in States of oligarchic law" (2014, p. 73).

For some, this might be a hard pill to swallow. Indeed, as political economist Colin Crouch remarks, "no one can say that contemporary western societies are anti-democratic, like the world's many dictatorships" (2016, p. 71). "Elections, free debate, the rule of law all function," Crouch continues, "but somehow the dynamism of the political system is moving elsewhere" (Ibid.). It is precisely this movement of dynamism that Rancière (2014) wants to capture by invoking the term oligarchic law. It is a system that – on its surface – looks and behaves like a democracy, but which, when one probes deeper, reveals itself to be far from what it appears to be. What has emerged from this type of "peaceful oligarchic government" (2014, p. 74) is in many ways a paradoxical system. The current state of oligarchic law is, according to Rancière, internally divided into two conflicting sets of justificatory orders. On the one hand, democracy refers "to a principle of popular sovereignty" (2014, p. 76), that is to say the conflicting and resistance-filled political worlds of a (supposedly) sovereign people. This is similar to what Mouffe captures through the notion of the democratic tradition. Yet, on the other hand, not least since the decline and collapse of the Soviet Union and consolidation of the global market economy, a new "consensual vision" of democracy has started to become established "on the back of an oligarchic system" (2014, p. 78). This is, indeed, the kind of lopsided liberalism also brought to the foreground by Mouffe. For Rancière, the consensual setting has meant that "our basic reality does not leave us the choice to interpret it and merely requires responses adapted to the circumstances, responses which are generally the same, whatever our opinions and aspirations. This reality is called the economy; in other words, the unlimited power of wealth" (2014, p. 77). It is precisely these two opposing orders – preaching popular sovereignty and economic necessity at the same time – that leaves contemporary governments caught in a strange bind.

Rancière wants to capture this somewhat peculiar constellation of governed and governing, politicization and de-politicization, with the notion of post-democracy. In *Disagreement: Politics and Philosophy* from 1999 (originally published in 1995), this term denotes "the government practice and conceptual legitimization of a democracy *after* the demos, a democracy that has eliminated the appearance, miscount, and dispute of the people and is thereby reducible to the sole interplay of state mechanisms and combinations of social energies and interest" (1999, p. 102). This is, he suggests, the true meaning behind what is often captured by the term "consensus democracy" (p. 102). Consensus democracy is a state of affairs where the political order has shifted towards notions of hard economic necessities, implemented *for* the market *by* experts and elites. Popular sovereignty, dispute, and disagreement, meanwhile, seem to have all but vanished.

In our opinion, what is important about these remarks is that they move us some steps further in understanding the particularities of our current state of democracy. With Mouffe, we learned that consensus democracy and its implicit ideas of reason have been a way of cutting democracy in two, emphasizing its liberal tendencies over its egalitarian and popular sovereign ones. With Rancière, we can move even further, stating that consensus establishes more than just a post-political landscape. It amounts to nothing less than a specific "regime of the perceptible" (1999, p. 107).

In the theoretical language mobilized throughout this book, we can think of this regime as a particular way of grounding the world that simultaneously seeks to neutralize and depoliticize itself in the very process of doing so. This regime, Rancière maintains, is identified by a specific way of understanding the constitution of the social world in which

> parties are presupposed as already given, their community established and the count of their speech identical to their linguistic performance. What consensus thus presupposes is the disappearance of any gap between a party to a dispute and a part of society. It is the disappearance of the mechanisms of appearance, of the miscount and the dispute opened up by the name "people" and the vacuum of their freedom. It is, in a word, the disappearance of politics.
>
> (1999, p. 102)

The hegemony of the market

Following Mouffe, Rancière, Brown and others, we can begin to see how liberal democracies have been subject to a range of major transformations since the 1970s. All of these predate the proclaimed and supposedly sudden rise of a post-truth era. These insights complicate one of the dominant narratives contained within post-truth worlds, namely that democracy has remained a relatively stable system until a sudden rupture occurred. Instead of a sudden rupture, numerous scholars point to a gradual shift away from popular dispute and towards an increasingly consensus-oriented form of decision-making – subordinate to market logics. For Rancière, this amounts to nothing less than the disappearance of politics itself, as the potential for societal change based on the will of the people has diminished.

Rancière has not been alone in sharing this bleak analysis. Political economists like Colin Crouch and Wolfgang Streeck have also suggested that liberal democracies have increasingly become empty democratic shells. In *Buying Time*, Streeck (2014) updates some of the ideas proposed by Crouch (2004) in his work, *Post-Democracy*. While Crouch was (and continues to be) less bombastic than either Mouffe or Rancière about the changes taking place in liberal democracies, he also notes how the dynamism and political energy previously tied to political institutions and popular sovereignty have increasingly moved elsewhere – namely to political and economic elites. Streeck places this history in a wider perspective. Doing so, he notes how, contrary to increasing voter turnouts during the 1960s and 1970s (commonly referred to as the golden years of Fordist-Keynesianism), electoral participation has continually gone down in most Western democracies ever since. "The trend is universal," Streeck notes, "and there is no sign that it is about to change. More than one-half of national elections with the lowest post-war turnout took place after the year 2000" (2014, p. 54). This decline has only continued globally after Streeck's analysis (Schäfer & Schwander, 2019; Solijonov, 2016). To give some recent examples: in November 2019, Spain saw its lowest voter turnout in history, surpassing its previous all-time low from 2016 (Rodon, 2020). That same year, Japan saw its second-lowest turnout in history (Kyodo, 2019). In 2022, France recorded its lowest voter turnout ever in its first-round presidential election, while Italy also saw record low voter participation that year (Roméo, 2022). Though researchers disagree on the exact causes of the global decline of voting across liberal democracies (Karp & Milazzo, 2016), the trend is widespread and has been so for several decades (Solijonov, 2016). Concurrently, trust in political institutions has also declined in both Europe and the United States (Pew Research Center, 2023; Solijonov, 2016), with Gallup measuring record low levels of citizen trust in US institutions in 2022 (Halpert, 2022).

According to Streeck, the decline in voter turnout and general faith in the democratic system is particularly noticeable when looking at citizens at the bottom of the material and symbolic class system, as unemployment levels and welfare dependence are strongly correlated with negative voter turnout. For Streeck, this reveals nothing less than an internal collapse of the democratic order:

> Everything suggests that declining electoral participation in the capitalist democracies is a sign not of contentment but of resignation. The losers from the neoliberal turn cannot see what they might get from a change of government; the TINA ("There is no alternative") politics of "globalization" has long arrived at the bottom of society where voting no longer makes a difference in the eyes of those who would have most to gain from political change.
>
> (Streeck, 2014, p. 55)

This is a harrowing diagnosis. Yet, Streeck goes deeper, arguing that what is really at stake is the very relationship between *democracy* and *capitalism* (see also Streeck, 2016). To him, it is the connection between these two that has been transformed as part of the present political-economic conjuncture. The compromise set up the in post-war years – suggesting that "democracy was impossible without capitalism, … just as capitalism was claimed to be impossible without democracy" (2014, p. 57) – is far from being as straightforward as it might seem. Compared to previous epochs, this was in many ways a new formation that strayed away from the ideas of the interwar years. Here, capitalists and the bourgeoisie, on the one hand, detested the idea of a workers' government dispossessing them of their power, while the radical Left, on the other hand, seemed content with little less than a genuine "dictatorship of the proletariat." At the same time, rampant fascism did little to indicate that capitalism and democracy would become mutual conditions of possibility. Be that as it may, a compromise was indeed set up, and this was one founded on two "competing principles of distribution" (2014, p. 58). On the one hand, Streeck argues, this compromise was based on *market justice*, understood as the "distribution of the output of production according to the market evaluation of individual performance" (2014, p. 58). On the other hand, it built on *social justice*, a set of principles shaped by cultural norms, which "follows collective ideas of fairness, correctness and reciprocity, concedes demands for a minimum livelihood irrespective of economic performance or productivity, and recognizes civil and human rights to such things as health, social security, participation in the life of the community, employment protection and trade union organization" (Streeck, 2014, p. 58). In the post-war years, these two principles existed in a state of mutual tension. They correspond, in many ways, to the kind of tension already touched upon multiple times in this chapter: a tension between market forces and popular sovereignty, necessity and contingency, de-politicization and genuine moments of democratic politics.

For Streeck, it is precisely this tension that starts to come undone with the gradual ascendance of neoliberal policies in the 1970s and 1980s. This took place, he suggests, by gradually establishing the primacy of the market over politics through reforms of political-economic institutions. The aim was to earn the trust of capital itself "by giving credible guarantee at the level of policy and institutions that they [advanced capitalist states] will not intervene in 'the economy' – or that, if they do, it will only be to protect and enforce market justice" (Streeck, 2014, p. 62). The founding premise for doing so, Streeck argues, was to *neutralize* democracy. Indeed, for market justice to flourish, democracy had to be dismantled or, at least, configured in such a way that it left minimal options for political struggles and anti-capitalist sentiments. In this sense, the *sine qua non* for large-scale neoliberalization of large parts of the world was nothing less than a withdrawal of democracy. Politics had to move from the scene of popular sovereignty to the sealed-off worlds of technocracy and expert-led decision-making.

Post-truth and post-politics

What this chapter has presented so far is a relatively panoramic survey of different attempts by critical scholars to understand and grapple with the political and institutional changes that have been taking place in advanced liberal democracies since the 1970s and 1980s. Beyond intellectual differences – both substantial and minor – the discussed authors all point to a shift in liberal democratic states. This is a change that fundamentally shifts the normative matrix of justification and legitimation at the core of democratic institutions. Popular sovereignty, the democratic tradition, and social justice – all political registers broadly revolving around ideas of equality, fairness, participation, and the voice of the people – have been overtaken or become subordinate to oligarchy, (neo) liberalism, and market justice. Thus, the tension or compromise instilled in the post-war years between conflicting registers of justification has become partially undone or at least uneven. Unlike previous periods, a new consensual setting has emerged premised on the consolidation of the prospering of globalized capitalism, market-like structures, and decision-making power in the hands of the few. This is a consensus that openly favors supposedly objective and rational solutions formulated by economic experts and political elites as necessary and in many ways non-negotiable responses to societal problems. Yet, it is also a consensus that, while claiming to represent the voice of the people, works in ways largely detached from political struggle and popular will (see Gilens & Page, 2014).

In our opinion, one of the most striking aspects about contemporary post-truth worlds is how they make use of democratic ideas that perfectly fold into the existing orders of post-politics and post-democracy. As we noted above, the idea that "democracy is about true choices and rational decisions" (as proclaimed by Macron) has been pervasive in contemporary discourses. Facts, it has been claimed time and again, "are essential for the functioning of democracy" (Viner, 2016). Indeed, it is precisely from this underlying premise that several voices have claimed that, unless drastic measures are taken, we will soon be living in a "fucked-up dystopia" (Schick, 2020, p. 189). For many, the end of the factual will also be the end of the democratic. As Michiko Kakutani (2018, pp. 19–20) argues in her book, *The Death of Truth*:

> Truth is a cornerstone of our democracy. As the former acting attorney general Sally Yates has observed, truth is one of the things that separates us from an autocracy: "We can debate policies and issues, and we should. But those debates must be based on common facts rather than raw appeals to emotion and fear through polarizing rhetoric and fabrications. … Not only is there such a thing as objective truth, failing to tell the truth matters."

Resonating this sentiment, Errol Morris, writing for *Time Magazine*, declares truth to be beyond dispute, beyond conflict:

> The truth is not a liberal plot. Truth stands apart from any political party and any kind of partisanship. The fact that anyone would think differently is in and of itself a cause for alarm. How much do we want to give up on? The shape of the Earth? The heliocentric universe? The pythagorean [sic] theorem? The structure of DNA?
>
> (Morris, 2018).

From these statements, as well as the analysis presented previously in this book, we can begin to see how ideas of rationality, reason, and truth – understood as singular objects that can and should be grasped as such – serve as dominant normative claims in post-truth worlds. Indeed, as Professor John Keane (2018) emphasizes, many have been "convinced that the 'relativism' of the postmodernists unhelpfully adds to the confusion surrounding 'truth' based on 'evidence' and 'facts.' What is now urgently needed, they say, is the recovery of truth." Equating democracy with truth is, however, not the only way contemporary post-truth worlds value the liberal tradition over the democratic. These increasingly dominant discourses also – often aggressively – suggest that the democratic people are simply unfit to participate in politics in the current era, as "democracy is threatened because we have a significant number of ignorant and apathetic voters stuck in the same boat with a small and ever-more radicalized group of partisans" (McBrayer, 2020, p. 166). Part of the reason for this, as we showcased in Chapter 4, is that citizens supposedly have become relegated to an "epistemic space that has abandoned conventional criteria of evidence, internal consistency, and fact-seeking" (Lewandowsky, Ecker, & Cook, 2017, p. 360).

If we relate the dominant claims of post-truth worlds to the ideas of post-politics or post-democracy, we can begin to see their normative similarities. Rather than providing mere descriptions of contemporary democracy, post-truth worlds channel specific ideas about how democracy ought to function, which gives primacy to the liberal tradition over the democratic. Indeed, in many of their most substantive arguments, post-truth worlds directly overtake normative ideas associated with post-political and post-democratic trajectories. Like these, post-truth worlds presuppose that democracy is at its core bound to truth, evidence, and rational dialogue and that expert judgments and hard economic necessities have to rule over popular dispute for democracy to function. As a consequence, post-truth worlds tend to suggest that the crisis of democracy is not only sudden, but that it is first and foremost due to a waning capacity for engaging in consensus-based dialogue and respecting expert-led decision-making.

Building on the critical scholarship discussed in this chapter, we want to suggest that the current democratic crisis is in fact neither sudden nor linked to issues of factuality or reason alone. More fundamentally, what is at stake is a crisis of democracy caused by the increasingly pervasive dismantlement of proper democratic institutions, popular sovereignty, and political participation. Developments such as declining voter participation, declining trust in political institutions, and the election of populist leaders cannot simply be explained by irrationality and misinformation but has to be taken seriously as genuine demands for breaking with the status quo in post-political and post-democratic times. Not only do signs of liberal democratic decline and capitalist crisis predate post-truth discourses and social media by decades, but they also point towards deeper problems within the liberal democratic order stemming from the hegemony of market logics over all forms of political collaboration, participation, and dispute. By lamenting apathy or populism as simply the result of a post-truth era, scholars, journalists, and policymakers not only risk neglecting the democratic tradition, but also entrenching the very crisis they claim to be solving. The problem is not that truth is disappearing, but that democracy is.

Other scholars have presented similar arguments, proposing that the contemporary crisis of liberal democracies is not primarily one of fake news but of fake democracy. As Marcus Gilroy-Ware (2020) writes in the book, *After the Fact?*, "the problem is not so much fake news as *fake democracy*, in which everything has been put up for sale, any version of democracy has been hollowed out by corporate control over its institutions, and much of what those in power say is either spin or outright deceit" (p, 62, original emphasis). Writing for *openDemocracy*, Freedman and Fenton (2017) similarly conclude as follows:

> The central issue for us, however, is not that we are suddenly surrounded by "fake news" but that we have been living with fake democracy. A democratic facade that promises much but delivers little. It has promised popular rule and self-governance through market exchanges and constitutional guarantees but instead we have a shrink-wrapped democracy that celebrates only the most pallid forms of participation and engagement with all political nutrients removed. So we are now facing a new democratic fakery in which elite media institutions – from the BBC and the *New York Times* to Google and Facebook – are using the crisis posed by the growth of anti-establishment politics to argue that *only they* are capable of sustaining a consensual, rational and credible information ecology that can expose "fake news" and protect "established truths." The problem is that they intend to achieve this by relying on the same personnel, the same evangelical belief in algorithms and the same agendas that failed dismally in their democratic responsibilities … that are intimately connected to the neoliberal order.
>
> (Freedman & Fenton, 2017)

As Freedman and Fenton argue, the appropriation of post-political or fake democratic ideas is not only present in the normative underpinnings of contemporary post-truth discourses, but it has also seeped into the *solutions* currently implemented to solve the supposed lapse of reason. In the following chapter, it is precisely these solutions – both real and imagined – that we will discuss. We do so in order to argue that not only will these solutions most likely fail, they might even add to our predicament by using post-political measures to combat post-politics itself. The snake seems to be biting its own tail as the cure for a broken democracy consists of more of the same: limiting popular sovereignty and political dispute in order to secure rationality, market consensus, and reason.

References

Brenner, N. (2004). *New State Spaces Urban Governance and the Rescaling of Statehood.* Oxford: Oxford University Press.

Brenner, N., Peck, J., & Theodore, N. (2010). After Neoliberalization? *Globalizations*, *7*(3), 327–345. https://doi.org/10.1080/14747731003669669

Brown, W. (2015). *Undoing the Demos: Neoliberalism's Stealth Revolution*. New York: Zone Books.

Bruff, I. (2014). The Rise of Authoritarian Neoliberalism. *Rethinking Marxism*, *26*(1), 113–129. https://doi.org/10.1080/08935696.2013.843250

Bruff, I., & Tansel, C. B. (2018). Authoritarian Neoliberalism: Trajectories of Knowledge Production and Praxis. *Globalizations*, *16*(3), 233–244. https://doi.org/10.1080/14747731.2018.1502497

Crouch, C. (2004). *Post-Democracy*. Cambridge: Polity Press.

Crouch, C. (2011). *The Strange Non-Death of Neoliberalism*. Cambridge: Polity Press.

Crouch, C. (2016). The March Towards Post-Democracy, Ten Years On. *Political Quarterly*, *87*(1), 71–75. https://doi.org/10.1111/1467-923X.12210

Davies, W. (2016, 24 August). The Age of Post-Truth Politics. *The New York Times*. www.nytimes.com/2016/08/24/opinion/campaign-stops/the-age-of-post-truth-politics.html

Freedman, D., & Fenton, N. (2017, 23 October). Media and Twenty First Century Fake Democracy. *openDemocracy*. www.opendemocracy.net/en/media-and-twenty-first-century-fake-democracy/

Gilens, M., & Page, B. L. (2014). Testing Theories of American Politics: Elites, Interest Groups, and Average Citizens. *Perspectives on Politics*, *12*(3), 564–581. https://doi.org/10.1017/S1537592714001595

Gilroy-Ware, M. (2020). *After the Fact? The Truth About Fake News*. London: Repeater Books.

Halpert, M. (2022, 5 July). Trust In U.S. Institutions Hits Record Low, Poll Finds. *Forbes*. www.forbes.com/sites/madelinehalpert/2022/07/05/trust-in-us-institutions-hits-record-low-poll-finds/?sh=7927d453dbd5

Held, D. (1989). *Political Theory and the Modern State: Essays on State, Power and Democracy*. Cambridge: Polity Press.

Held, D. (2006). *Models of Democracy*. Stanford: Stanford University Press.

Kakutani, M. (2018). *The Death of Truth: Notes on Falsehood in the Age of Trump*. New York: Tim Duggans Books.

Karp, J. A., & Milazzo, C. (2016). Globalization and Voter Turnout in Times of Crisis. In J. Vowles & G. Xezonakis (Eds.), *Globalization and Domestic Politics: Parties, Elections, and Public Opinion Globalization and Domestic Politics: Parties, Elections, and Public Opinion* (pp. 190–208). Oxford: Oxford University Press. https://doi.org/10.1093/acprof:oso/9780198757986.003.0010

Keane, J. (2018, 23 March). Post-Truth Politics and Why the Antidote Isn't Simply "Fact-Checking" and Truth. *The Conversation*. https://theconversation.com/post-truth-politics-and-why-the-antidote-isnt-simply-fact-checking-and-truth-87364

Kyodo. (2019, 22 July). In Second-Lowest Figure Since End of WWII, Voter Turnout in Japan's Upper House Election Falls Below 50%. *The Japan Times*. www.japantimes.co.jp/news/2019/07/22/national/politics-diplomacy/second-lowest-figure-since-end-wwii-voter-turnout-japans-upper-house-election-falls-50/

Lewandowsky, S., Ecker, U.K.H., & Cook, J. (2017). Beyond Misinformation: Understanding and Coping with the "Post-Truth" Era. *Journal of Applied Research in Memory and Cognition*, *6*(4), 353–369. https://doi.org/10.1016/j.jarmac.2017.07.008

Macron, E. (2018, 25 April). Address to the U.S. Congress. *CNN*. http://transcripts.cnn. com/TRANSCRIPTS/1804/25/ctw.01.html

McBrayer, J. P. (2020). *Beyond Fake News: Finding the Truth in a World of Misinformation*. London: Routledge.

Mouffe, C. (1993). *The Return of the Political*. London: Verso.

Mouffe, C. (2005a). *On the Political*. London: Routledge.

Mouffe, C. (2005b). *The Democratic Paradox*. London: Verso.

Mouffe, C. (2013). *Agonistics: Thinking the World Politically*. London: Verso.

Mouffe, C. (2018). *For a Left Populism*. London: Verso.

Morris, E. (2018, 22 May). Why Donald Trump Can't Kill the Truth. *Time Magazine*. http://time.com/5287062/errol-morris-ashtray-donald-trump-lies-fake-news/

Müller, J.-W. (2011). *Contesting Democracy: Political Ideas in Twentieth-Century Europe*. New Haven: Yale University Press.

Peck, J. (2013). *Constructions of Neoliberal Reason*. Oxford: Oxford University Press.

Peck, J., Theodore, N., & Brenner, N. (2009). Postneoliberalism and its Malcontents. *Antipode*, *41*, 94–116. https://doi.org/10.1002/9781444397352.ch5

Peck, J., & Tickell, A. (2007). Conceptualizing Neoliberalism, Thinking Thatcherism. In H. Leitner, J. Peck, & E. S. Sheppard (Eds.), *Contesting Neoliberalism: Urban Frontiers* (pp. 26–50). New York: Guilford Press.

Pew Research Center. (2023, 17 May). *Public Trust in Government: 1958–2022*. Pewresearch.org. www.pewresearch.org/politics/2022/06/06/public-trust-in-government-1958-2022/

Rancière, J. (1999). *Disagreement: Politics and Philosophy*. Minneapolis: University of Minnesota Press.

Rancière, J. (2014). *Hatred of Democracy*. London: Verso.

Rodon, T. (2020). The Spanish Electoral Cycle of 2019: A Tale of Two Countries. *West European Politics*, *43*(7), 1490–1512. https://doi.org/10.1080/01402382.2020.1761689

Roméo, L. (2022, 15 June). Voter Turnout Issue Looms over French Legislative Elections after Record First-Round Abstention. *France 24*. www.france24.com/en/france/20220 615-voter-turnout-issue-looms-over-french-legislative-elections-after-record-first-round-abstention

Rosenfeld, S. (2019). *Democracy and Truth: A Short History*. Philadelphia: University of Pennsylvania Press.

Rubin, J. (2018, 1 May). In a Post-Truth World, There is No Democracy. *The Washington Post*. www.washingtonpost.com/blogs/right-turn/wp/2018/05/01/in-a-post-truth-world-there-is-no-democracy/

Schäfer, A., & Schwander, H. (2019). "Don't Play if You Can't Win": Does Economic Inequality Undermine Political Equality? *European Political Science Review*, *11*(3), 395–413. https://doi.org/10.1017/S1755773919000201

Schick, N. (2020). *Deep Fakes and the Infocalypse: What You Urgently Need To Know*. London: Monoray.

Solijonov, A. (2016). *Voter Turnout Trends around the World*. www.idea.int/sites/default/files/publications/voter-turnout-trends-around-the-world.pdf

Streeck, W. (2014). *Buying Time: The Delayed Crisis of Democratic Capitalism*. London: Verso.

Streeck, W. (2016). *How Will Capitalism End? Essays on a Failing System*. London: Verso.

Viner, K. (2016, 12 July). How Technology Disrupted the Truth. *The Guardian*. www.theg
uardian.com/media/2016/jul/12/how-technology-disrupted-the-truth?CMP=soc_568
Wacquant, L. (2009). *Punishing the Poor: The Neoliberal Government of Social
Insecurity*. Durham: Duke University Press.
Wilson, J., & Swyngedouw, E. (2014). Seeds of Dystopia: Post-Politics and the
Return of the Political. In J. Wilson & E. Swyngedouw (Eds.), *Post-Political and
its Discontents: Spaces of Depoliticisation, Spectres of Radical Politics* (pp. 1–24).
Edinburgh: Edinburgh University Press.

8 Ways out?

Truth, technology, and democracy

Post-truth discourses not only describe and articulate what is currently deemed wrong with democracy. They also contain concrete visions and solutions for how to fix the proclaimed crisis of truth. As detailed in Chapter 6, there have been solutions aplenty: while some have already been implemented, examined, and revised, others remain blueprints, ideas, and sketches. Rather than any direct process of implementation, we are dealing with a field of solutions that remains both chaotic and in flux. Each hastily suggested idea is often followed by a range of new ones, including calls for revisions, alternatives, or even repeals. In what can seem like a frantic race against time, politicians, journalists, scholars, and economic elites all scramble to come up with as many profound and radical fixes as possible. The speed and messiness of these processes are continuously legitimized by relying on some of the core tropes found in post-truth worlds – most notably that democracy's demise is inevitable unless truth is restored and reclaimed. By foretelling impending societal destruction, many of the solutions currently articulated focus on ends over means. They often place truth over and above some of the otherwise fundamental elements of democracy. If truth can once again become sacred, this line of argumentation seems to go, most means are justified, even the removal of power from the democratic people through legislation, policing, technological censorship, or strengthening of traditional truth-telling fields.

With this chapter, we seek to continue the critical dialogue opened in the previous one. Departing from our historical contextualization of post-truth worlds, this chapter presents a critical discussion of the solutions currently proposed to solve the proclaimed democratic crisis. What role do such solutions assign to the democratic people? What means do they articulate as justifiable to reestablish truth and consensus? And how can we, in such discussions, begin to see how the relation between truth, rationality, and popular sovereignty is being reconfigured?

Our main argument in this chapter is that current solutions to fake news, posttruth, and infodemics all too often end up being both implausible and questionable. Worse yet, they might even reproduce post-political ideas, deepening an

DOI: 10.4324/9781003434870-11

already severe lack of democratic participation. Interrogating four main sets of solutions, we argue that democracy seems to be caught in a strange bind. Having been fed post-political measures for the last 40+ years, scholars, journalists, politicians, and elites now all seem unable to escape its vocabulary. All too often, those wishing to defend democracy and politics from post-truth sentiments seem to simply want to strengthen post-political rule. If only the consensus-based and market-premised mode of governance established since the 1970s could be bolstered and protected from the "misinformed masses," then democracy would be safe again. If only truth could once again be reinstated as sacred, self-evident, and singular, then politics would once again become civil. Yet, the problem with these ideas is that they build on a democratic fiction: advanced liberal democracies have *not* suddenly entered a crisis due to a recent barrage of fake news. Instead, they have been under attack for decades by continual efforts to make democracies less democratic and more subordinate to global markets and supposed economic necessities. Indeed, part of the reason we are currently seeing the flourishing of populist movements, the longing for alternative facts, and other political registers, might very well be the deep democratic deficit that has expanded since the 1970s. Citizens are tired of the status quo and of being told to simply accept the outcome of global capitalism and consensus-based rule. Instead of decrying these developments as the result of fake news, it is high time we took them seriously.

Solutions and their discontents

As shown in Chapter 6, there has been and continues to be a whole range of both real and imagined solutions to the proclaimed post-truth crisis of democracy. Here, we want to reflect on and discuss four major strands within the current landscape of solutions. We do so, as hinted at above, to argue that the dominant ideas currently discussed do not get us where we want to go in terms of saving or reclaiming democracy. On the contrary, they might serve to further call into question our existing institutions and political practices.

Solution 1: moralizing, condemning

Post-truth worlds have often been underpinned by a series of strongly moralizing claims. Citizens are said to live in increasingly secluded epistemic spheres, disconnected from nothing less than reality itself. The dominant explanation is that people are increasingly deceived by social media and partisan news, simply no longer care about truth, or have become unable to grasp societies' complexity. These uneducated, disengaged, and ignorant masses are susceptible to being swayed by anti-democratic or even authoritarian currents, this line of reasoning goes. Accordingly, their voices can no longer be trusted. Fake news and post-truth constitute the rapid appearance (or reappearance) of evil forces that threaten the stability of democracy. In this regard, moral condemnation has been the order of the day, as seemingly all parts of the democratic spectrum rally around fighting this still developing threat. In July 2018, Michiko Kakutani argued in *The Guardian* that "[a]round the world, waves of populism and fundamentalism are elevating appeals to fear and anger over reasoned debate, eroding democratic institutions, and replacing expertise with the wisdom of the crowd" (Kakutani, 2018a). According to her, this signifies nothing less than *truth decay*, a fierce illness that should be combated:

> Without commonly agreed-on facts – not Republican facts and Democratic facts; not the alternative facts of today's silo-world – there can be no rational debate over policies, no substantive means of evaluating candidates for political office, and no way to hold elected officials accountable to the people. Without truth, democracy is hobbled.
>
> (Kakutani, 2018b, p. 172)

Democracy requires unanimous agreement on facts across the aisle. Otherwise, the system will collapse. This argument channels one of the predominant modes of retaliation from both the journalistic and political establishment against the state of democracy: moral condemnation of those daring to speak against singular orders of truth. While moral condemnation might not appear as a solution by the look of it, it structures a large part of contemporary post-truth worlds. Outrage is not just a way of negatively labeling certain groups or institutions: it also contains a series of imperatives – get in line, act otherwise, behave as you ought to.

The condemnation of not only fake news or misinformation but of the misinformed masses themselves – supposedly living outside society in alternative realities – establishes a troubling dichotomy between those who are worthy of political influence (the informed masses) and those who are deemed unworthy (the misinformed masses). Not only is one group in this narrative distinguished from the other by promoting a superior cause or rule of law, the other group is seen as not belonging to the democratic people. Post-truth worlds implicitly legitimize a viewpoint in which a large number of citizens could be removed from political influence without violating the egalitarian basis of democracy. As these people live in alternative realities, stripping their influence to secure truth becomes a legitimate resolution – at least if this line of reasoning is taken to its logical conclusion.

By framing calls for political change as cases of misinformed masses, post-truth worlds largely neglect popular demands and refuse to take them seriously. This form of inaction could have a profound political impact, as it might very well confirm the already lingering notion that citizens have little influence on the political system and the status quo. In this way, inaction becomes a performative act and not just a neutral absence of response. This will not do: in any democracy, popular demands cannot simply be disregarded as the voice of misinformed masses – they need to be taken seriously. By this, we do not necessarily mean accepting, condoning, or endorsing them; popular support is of course no apology for violence, hatred, xenophobia, or bigotry. Yet, serious efforts need to be taken to try to understand why and whence such disappointment and dissatisfaction emerges. Demonizing those who think otherwise or calling for their complete removal from influence does not help us in this regard.

Both Chantal Mouffe and Jacques Rancière have hinted at something similar in the past, arguing that moral condemnation of dissent has served to sediment post-politics as the order of the day. The moralizing language currently linked to issues of post-truth can be seen as yet another facet of post-politics itself. Long before the current truth crisis, the seemingly stable democratic order of the 1990s and 2000s started to crack. Already in the early 2000s, Mouffe (and others) observed how a peculiar paradox started to emerge. On the one hand, proponents of reason and rationality claimed that modernization and individualization led to "a unified and pacified world" (2005, p. 64), while on the other hand, "this is far from being the case and their post-political vision has increasingly been contradicted from many quarters" (p. 65). Thus, while it is true that "the frontiers between left and right have become increasingly blurred" (p. 65), this has *emphatically* not meant "a more mature democracy, [because] what we have witnessed in many Western societies is a loss of legitimacy of democratic institutions" (p. 65).

Public voices have often tried to explain away this paradox, not least with reference to the resurgence of right-wing populism across Europe, by relaying central tenets from their rationalist quiver. Voters are said to be "uneducated, lower-class ... susceptible to being attracted by demagogues" (2005, p. 65). Yet, as Mouffe makes clear, this is far from being supported by sociological analysis. Instead of seeing populism and right-wing politics as a return to a more primitive era, it must be grasped as a genuine product of our times and the democratic ideas perpetuated by the parties in power. For Mouffe, part of the explanation for the rise of anti-establishment and right-wing parties consists precisely in the fact that the existing political system has neutralized genuine conflict and privileged a consensus-based mode of democracy. All of this leads Mouffe to the following set of important observations:

> It is high time to realize that, to a great extent, the success of right-wing populist parties comes from the fact that they articulate, albeit in a very problematic way, real democratic demands which are not taken into account by traditional parties. They also provide people with some form of hope, with the belief that things could be different. Of course it is an illusory hope, founded on false premises and unacceptable mechanisms of exclusion where xenophobia usually plays a central role. But when they are the only channels for the expression of political passions, their presence to represent an alternative is very seductive. This is why I submit that the success of right-wing populist

parties is the consequence of the lack of a vibrant democratic debate in our post-democracies.

(Mouffe, 2005, p. 71)

Mouffe's observations seem to hold not only for populism, but also for post-truth politics. We might ask: is it not precisely the same desire for alternatives that far-right populists and their attacks on established truth-telling regimes and knowledge gatekeepers bring to the foreground? Again, we need not accept the vision contained in such movements to see these as a means of articulating a way beyond the impasse of democracy "as usual." When Donald Trump (2020) claims to "drain the swamp," when Recep Erdoğan claims globalization is "a new way of colonialism" (cited in Daily Sabah, 2016), or when Viktor Orbán (2022) claims to have "seen what the globalists ruling class has to offer, but we have a different future in mind," are they not reactivating a potential that has seemed otherwise obscured and foreclosed by post-politics? In these situations, what seems to take place is not a rejection of all forms of truth, but particular forms of truth, namely those provided by the gatekeepers of the old post-political system. What Trump, Erdoğan, and Orbán seem to promise, not unlike Marine Le Pen in France or Narendra Modi in India, is a *post*-post-political world: that is, one in which technocracy and depoliticized liberal democracy are once again rethought, bringing the discontent of "the People" to the forefront. Moral condemnation always reveals its own hand. In its negative critique of the other – the enemy – it showcases its own rationality and ideology. As Rancière (2014) notes:

[p]opulism is the convenient name under which is dissimulated the exacerbated contradiction between popular legitimacy and expert legitimacy, that is, the difficulty the government of science has in adapting itself to manifestations of democracy and even to the mixed form of representative system. This name at once masks and reveals the intense wish of the oligarch: to govern without people, in other words, without any dividing of the people; to govern without politics.

(Rancière, 2014, pp. 79–80)

As Rancière argues, populism has become a derogative term used by political elites to lament all politics, which falls outside of rational consensus and brings disagreement to the forefront. Could we not think something similar about the current post-truth predicament? From our perspective, the idea that uninformed masses are living in epistemic bubbles does – at least to some extent – carry an implicit wish for an undisputed government. By stating that people are disconnected from reality itself, post-truth discourses often seem to justify or even promote a form of governance that does not rely on or concern itself with the dispute of the people. Instead, it operates based on a rational order of unlimited expansion of the global market. From this position, the fact that people can no longer be trusted easily becomes a justification for removing them from the democratic equation, leaving decision-making in the hands of the few. This links directly to the rapid rise of anti-fake news laws and surveillance across the world.

Solution 2: policing the truth

Moral condemnation is not the only set of solutions currently being tested to combat fake news and post-truth. As detailed in Chapter 6, governments and policymakers around the world have become increasingly eager to legislate their way out of the current situation. Banning fake news and creating specialized units and taskforces dedicated to hunting down perpetrators have become the order of the day. To briefly mention some of the initiatives currently being launched, we can recall how dozens of governments across the world implemented free speech restrictions during the COVID-19 pandemic in the name of protecting society from fake news and the infodemic (Human Rights Watch, 2021). Already before COVID-19, a range of countries – from Germany to Kenya, Singapore to Venezuela – had limited free speech through legislation to combat fake news (Mchangama & Fiss, 2019; Neo, 2020). Despite being implemented by markedly different governments – some democratic and others non-democratic – political leaders have often legitimized such legal measures through remarkably similar lines of reasoning. To protect the societal stability and security, this line of argument goes, harsh measures are justified and will not have negative implications for fundamental civil rights.

To give a few examples, in 2017, in defence of its upcoming NetzDG law, the German government argued that hate speech, malicious gossip, and fake news were becoming an "ever more serious" threat to society and that, while "freedom of expression and press freedom are the cornerstones of open and free society… freedom of expression ends at the point where criminal law begins" (Federal Government of Germany, 2017). In 2019, with reference to NetzDG, Russian presidential spokesperson, Dmitry Peskov, defended Russia's upcoming anti-fake news bill in similar terms: "No doubt, one can hardly agree with the opinion that this is some sort of censorship. This sphere – the sphere of fake news – insults and so on, is under strict regulation in many countries of the world, even in European states. This undoubtedly has to be done in our country" (cited in Van Sant, 2019). During COVID-19, the Hungarian government similarly argued that its anti-fake news measures did not constitute any kind of government "power grab," since "only intentional false statements made to the general public that could obstruct or frustrate defense efforts would be sanctioned" (Varga, 2020).

As detailed in Chapter 6, these claims of necessity and benevolence have repeatedly been criticized by human rights groups and other free speech advocates (Human Rights Watch, 2018, 2021; Reporters Without Borders, 2017). Already in 2017, the United Nations and a series of regional human rights bodies warned about anti-fake news laws, "stressing that the human right to impart information and ideas is not limited to 'correct' statements, that the right also protects information and ideas that may shock, offend and disturb, and that prohibitions on disinformation may violate international human rights standards" (United Nations, 2017). Notwithstanding, the number of anti-fake news laws has only risen markedly since.

In addition to legislation, specialized task forces – by governments, intelligence agencies, and supranational institutions – have become a go-to solution for policymakers across the globe (Tenove, 2020). A prominent example is the European Union' East StratCom Task Force, launched in 2015 to counter the spread of fake news and propaganda, particularly from Russia. Not unlike the general set of interventions around fake news and disinformation, details are often scarce as to how this unit operates in practice. A good example of the problems this can cause came during COVID-19, when Reuters and *The New York Times* revealed that senior officials in the EU – according to internal sources – had pressured the East StratCom Task Force to tone down criticism of China in a report about COVID-19 disinformation (Apuzzo, 2020; Satter et al., 2020). As recounted by *The New York Times*, Chinese officials had gotten word of upcoming criticism from East StratCom and "quickly contacted the European Union's representatives in Beijing to try to kill the report, according to two diplomats with knowledge of the exchange and emails recounting the calls" (Apuzzo, 2020). As a result, the report was halted and revised at the last minute to tone down the criticism of China (Satter et al., 2020).

After these revelations came to light, leading EU officials vehemently denied the story. Josep Borrell, High Representative of the Union for Foreign Affairs and Security Policy, said that "no changes have been introduced to the report," while European Commission President, Ursula von der Leyen, stated that this was an "independent report done by the external service" (both cited in Ritchie, 2020). Whether or not – or to what extent – the EU had bowed down to pressure from China remained unclear. Yet, no matter the details, the debacle raised an obvious and unanswered question of how much independence East StratCom employees have from the interests of the EU (their employer), in this case in protecting a crucial trade relationship?

The rise of governmental, police, military, and supra-national task forces to combat fake news – a development seen across the world – has led to a new industry of top-down surveillance and communication. A strange mix of government officials, diplomats, military analysts, police officers, and communications specialists have all been tasked with monitoring digital media spaces and media outlets from foreign states and "bad actors." Not only do these operations often function without much transparency, raising questions about their inner workings. They also blur previously sedimented boundaries between journalism and other distinct fields within liberal democracies, such as government, police, and military. These agencies often perform duties traditionally associated with journalism (e.g., public factchecks, investigative reporting), yet without formal independence from the institution they belong to.

The problem with these solutions is that, once again, political elites seem to reuse already known means of political intervention, tightly linked to post-political and post-democratic currents. Instead of fostering new spaces of political dialogue, difference, and independent scrutiny of those in power, increased surveillance, policing, and monitoring represent a continuation of existing anti-democratic currents. Not only are such interventions rarely prone to public scrutiny or dispute, they also displace politics to internal governmental and legal mechanisms. As detailed in the previous chapter, this movement of politics from the sphere of popular dialogue to legal-constitutional frameworks is precisely indicative of the yet more authoritarian direction taken by advanced capitalist states. Indeed, to once again turn to Ian Bruff's (2014) critical analysis of contemporary democracy, we may note how

under authoritarian neoliberalism dominant social groups are less interested in neutralizing resistance and dissent via concessions and forms of compromise that maintain their hegemony, favoring instead the explicit exclusion and marginalization of subordinate social groups through the constitutionally and legally engineered self-disempowerment of nominally democratic institutions, governments, and parliaments.

(Bruff, 2014, p. 116)

In order to maintain the status quo of global capitalism, Bruff (2014) argues, disciplinary actions by political elites are often legitimized by reference to supposedly hard economic necessities demanded by the capitalist economy. This is especially the case after the global financial crisis in 2007–2008 where public discontent at massive bank bailout was largely rejected by references to market needs, as the banks had become simply "too big to fail" (Bruff, 2014). Since the rise of post-truth worlds, it seems that such disciplinary actions are increasingly premised on the *necessity of truth*. Public discontent is treated not as genuine calls for political change but as misinformed "noise" from irrational crowds. Indeed, keeping our account of post-politics in mind, it seems that the proclaimed destabilization of truth is synonymous with a destabilization of the fabric of expert-led, consensus-based politics, which has dominated liberal democracies since the 1970s. Seen in this light, it is hardly surprising that political and economic elites have turned to increasingly coercive and police-based modes of retaliation.

More often than not, prominent academics endorse such coercive mechanisms, as when astrophysicist Neil deGrasse Tyson (2018) calls for a governmental "Truth Force" to police public speech and combat "all enemies of accurate information, both foreign & domestic." Or when applied mathematicians Brody and Meier (2018) call for government censorship to "combat the domination of noise," presenting little to no reflection on how equating public voices to noise could lead to authoritarian consequences. Or when leading scholars at Oxford University, during COVID-19, call for "clear legislation and punishment of those who produced and disseminated false information" and state surveillance of "nefarious misinformation spread by local and foreign actors" (Mills et al., 2020, p. 26). Journalists have also contributed to these solutions, as when Sholto Byrnes, writing for *The New Statesman,* argues that anti-fake news laws "should be celebrated wherever they are introduced, whether that's in Germany, France, Malaysia and Singapore" (Byrnes, 2018).

Faced with the undermining of their authority, political, economic, journalistic, and academic elites might see disciplinary and coercive strategies like these to be the only way out. What we need to recognize, however, is that the overall idea that falsehoods, untruths, and fabrications can or should be limited through legal-coercive means is in itself deeply political. It is based on the normative claim that democracy only has room for Truth in the singular, and that dispute, conflict, and the voice of those who think otherwise should be eradicated. In this way, post-truth worlds present not only a normative description of the world, but also a normative infrastructure for how democracy *should* develop, which deepens existing post-politics trends. In this regard, legal and coercive mechanisms from political elites work in tandem with technological solutionism from market forces.

Solution 3: technological solutionism

In their analysis of post-politics and post-democracy, Mouffe and Rancière pinpoint how the hollowing out of liberal democracies, which has been taking place since the 1970s, has consistently been legitimized through ideas of rationality and market logics. Free capitalist markets have continuously been seen as more effective, balanced, and fair than popular rule. Instead of leaving political decision-making in the hands of citizens – with ambiguous, conflicting, and shifting opinions – systemic problems are best left up to the market to solve. Remarkably, this discourse has even prevailed in the wake of the financial meltdown of 2007–2008. While this led to massive state bailouts of banks, few profound changes to the economic system followed, thus preserving the already established slogan: *there is no alternative* (TINA). With this in mind, it is perhaps little to no surprise that the contemporary post-truth worlds also consistently cast capitalist market actors – more specifically the world's largest tech companies – as key to solving the proclaimed post-truth crisis. While companies such as Meta and Alphabet might often be described as the villains of the post-truth era – as discussed in Chapter 4 – political, journalistic, and academic elites simultaneously present these companies as potential saviors: "Technology Is a Big Part of the Problem, But It's Also a Solution" (Gent, 2016).

Across the political spectrum, political leaders argue that tech companies are key to re-establishing Truth and saving democracy. To a large extent, tech CEOs have happily embraced aspects of this rhetoric, emphasizing their own importance and indispensability in the struggle against fake news. This is exemplified by Meta CEO Mark Zuckerberg: "It's an arms race, and it will take the combined forces of the US private and public sectors to protect America's democracy" (cited in Boland & Titcomb, 2018). Within this narrative, contemporary liberal democracies are characterized by a fundamental lack or deficit, meaning that they cannot be saved through democratic politics alone. The only way to re-establish stability, rationality, and consensus is to rely on the generous support of private actors – in this case tech companies, such as Meta. Without these corporations, there cannot and will not be any democracy to save. In this way, tech solutionism represents a direct extension of the TINA paradigm: democracy cannot be imagined as existing without relying on the deregulated circuits of global capital.

As with many other facets of post-truth worlds, what seems like unanimity on the surface quickly becomes contradictory at closer inspection. While a number of political actors argue that tech companies are key to restoring democracy from its impending demise, the exact role of such companies differs to say the least. Nowhere is this perhaps better exemplified than in the United States, where the Democratic and Republican parties have presented remarkably different solutions. While both parties point to private tech companies as key for saving democracy, their identification of challenges and opportunities diverge. Democrats have argued that the immense democratic threat posed by fake news and disinformation, especially from Russia, has largely been neglected by Republicans, leaving all hope in the hands of private tech companies. As Senator Schumer (D-NY) argued during the Trump administration:

> I think they [tech companies] should do more on their own for sure. That's the antidote to government regulation and also the antidote to a lot of this stuff. Now they've had some successes. Facebook took off 50,000 fake accounts before the French election and it was relatively free . ... I don't think the Trump administration will do a thing. The amount the Trump administration is doing against Russia is appallingly, zero almost. It's up to tech to do more, and I do think they're making an effort not only because it's the right thing to do, but because I think they know down the road their survival depends on it.
> (Senator Chuck Schumer cited in Recode Staff, 2018)

Tech companies are the only contemporary actors, Senator Schumer (D-NY) argues, who are powerful and rational enough to save democracy from its prevailing crisis of Truth, as leading politicians are both unwilling and incapable of acting. Platforms such as Facebook instil hope for the future, as they are not only resourceful, but also have rational incentives to save democracy, not for democracy's sake but to ensure their own prosperity. From this perspective, tech companies' mode of operation is in many ways superior to that of democracy. Reproducing existing vocabularies of post-politics and post-democracy, democracy's key goal is to accommodate ever-increasing market growth.

While Democrats argue that companies should ramp up efforts against fake news and disinformation – saving democracy as well as their own continued prosperity – Republicans have presented a quite different position. Instead of arguing for increased actions against fake news and foreign interference, Republican lawmakers have called for tech companies to combat a different imminent threat to democracy: bias against conservative viewpoints. As Republican Governor, Ron DeSantis (R-FL), stated in 2021, social media companies originally empowered citizens by enabling them to circumvent "those legacy outlets that many Americans grew to distrust and rightfully so" (cited in Pearce, 2021). Increasingly, however, tech companies have become "enforcers of orthodoxy... suppressing ideas that are either inconvenient to the narrative or that they personally disagree with" (DeSantis cited in Pearce, 2021). To protect democracy, in other words, social media companies need to re-enable the flourishing of "good" information (that is, Republican voices).

As in the Democratic line of argument, tech companies are in this narrative cast as both villains and potential saviors: they have caused political turmoil but can also stabilize democracy. The means for doing so, however, are vastly different, as saving democracy requires the strengthening of conservative worldviews in digital media. As argued by Donald Trump, search engines like Google needs to algorithmically ensure that when people search for "Trump News" they are not only presented with the "reporting of Fake News Media" (Trump, 2018), here synonymous with CNN and other traditional media outlets.

Paradoxically, Democrats and Republicans thus seem to agree that democracy needs tech companies in order to limit the menace of fake news. Yet, since they define fake news in completely different ways, their calls for action point in completely opposite directions. While this highlights how fake news has increasingly become a floating signifier lodged between hegemonic discourses, it also underlines a fundamental weakness of this kind of solution: namely that technological removal of fake news rests entirely on which political actors get to define fake news in the first place. Additionally, it provides yet another example of how prevalent solutions in post-truth worlds predominantly rely on post-political measures. By this we mean that, instead of taking popular dissatisfaction seriously, acknowledging that citizens feel neglected by market-based consensus, people's dissatisfaction is dismissed as nothing less than the result of a lack of consensus. The masses have been exposed to too much bad information (whether from Russia or CNN, depending on the party) and so they need to be brought back to reality. In this way, solutions are cast as merely technological rather than political: if only Alphabet or Meta could promote real news and limit the irrational type, the power of consensus would be restored. If successful, we can all finally return to a "truth era" or "make America great again."

Solution 4: re-establishing centers of truth-making

The fourth set of solutions that will be discussed here revolves around reclaiming the authority and capacity of certain fields to once again produce and maintain truth-telling power. Indeed, as showcased in Chapter 6, there have been numerous calls for making science, journalism, and politics capable of speaking truth again. In some cases, such as that of the sciences, this argument is made against those who claim climate change and vaccines are little more than a conspiracy or hoax. Here, it is argued that there is a need to acknowledge that the claims made by the scientific field are not of the order as those made by "laymen." Because science has established certain institutional structures and procedures for validating truth claims, this line of argument goes, this field should be guarded against conspiracy theories, economic interests, and partisan politics. While part of the logic is similar for journalism and politics, the underlying arguments are different. For journalism, it is not only climate or vaccine denial that fuels a desire to reclaim truth, but the supposed demise of journalistic practices themselves. It is because of a changed media ecology, new reader habits, and skewed economic structures that journalism is in decline. If democracy is to prosper, it is said, journalistic practices must once again be made able to speak against power (and the lies spun by those in power).

What is at stake with these developments is a series of difficult questions. Part of the problem is that these discussions about truth often take place as if the context did not matter. However, to speak of Truth – and the need to reclaim Truth – in terms of science, journalism, and politics is imminently not the same. Each field has its own internal logic of what counts as true and what does not. Adding to this, solutions have often been underpinned by an implicit, zero-sum assumption: if you do not accept that politics is solely about truth, then you are a relativist skeptic, or climate denier. Part of the problem is that acknowledging that scientific practices, understood as a semi-autonomous field of practice, can produce certain truth-claims through institutional and practical arrangements does *not* mean acknowledging that such claims are universally accepted or beyond dispute. Thus, while science does produce something it labels true, there is nothing to suggest that such claims can simply be transferred unaltered into all other domains of society. Part of the problem might even be that, all too often, it is assumed that the things produced as true in the scientific field can be neatly moved into the field of politics. The field of politics also produces truths, however, but it does so through completely different mechanisms. What is at stake here is often *not* the politicization of science, but the reverse: an inability to politicize science (*if* by politicize we understand a translation of the categories of truth employed in the scientific field to those in politics). The issue is that all too often this does not take place. If anything, the reverse seems to have taken place: the increasingly persistent depoliticization of politics (ruling through hard economic necessities rather than popular sovereignty) has created a democratic deficit. This radical lack has turned into an *excess* of truth: in the absence of any space for difference in the core political order, the boundaries start to overflow with *other* truths, other ways of thinking, and other ways of claiming a voice. It is this excess of truth in politics that seems to be spilling over to the field of science when citizens reject scientific consensus.

We are obviously not against the production of truth in the scientific system, but we are against the idea that the field of politics can be ruled by experts, necessities, and facts seemingly beyond dispute. While there might be good reasons to take note of how science informs us about the world, we cannot and should not expect this field to dictate democratic decisions. Like it or not, democracy can and does act against the supposedly better judgment of experts. To return to a quote from Chapter 3, it remains vital to note that just because

> a question remains unanswerable by science or that it does not attain the status of a truth that can be demonstrated does not mean that a reasonable opinion cannot be formed about it or that it cannot be an opportunity for a rational choice. Hannah Arendt was absolutely right to insist that in the political sphere one finds oneself in the realm of opinion, or "doxa," and not in that of truth, and that each sphere has its own criteria of validity and legitimacy.
>
> (Mouffe, 1993, p. 14)

All of this, then, is an argument for separating our discussions of truth in a way that is specific to particular contexts, spheres, domains, or fields of practice. Yet, to us, the idea that traditional centers of truth production – that is, those who traditionally held a monopoly on what could be counted as true – should be reinstated rings hollow. Critical voices rightly suggest that the notion of a post-truth era is first and foremost an attempt by those who used to hold power to reclaim and once again assert their dominance. In this context, the work of Mejia, Beckermann, and Sullivan (2018) stands out. These authors have sought to dismantle contemporary discourses of post-truth not only for what these discourses say, but also for what they fail to recognize:

> Post-truth criticism can be dangerous because: (1) it often fails to recognize the uneven benefits and consequences of our historical and contemporary truth-telling regimes; (2) it often expresses nostalgia for those supposedly simpler days when the truth meant something; and (3) it re-centers whiteness throughout. In essence, much post-truth criticism is concerning because in demarcating 2016 as the beginning of our post-truth era, it effaces the epistemological, ontological, and axiological danger experienced by people of

color throughout American history. From this perspective, it would seem that the wish to return to an era of truth is a wish to return to an era of uncomplicated whiteness.

(Mejia et al., 2018, p. 113)

As Mejia and colleagues (2018) argue, post-truth worlds contain a nostalgia for a simpler time, yet largely neglects the troubled history of democratic development. "It is troubling to suggest," Mejia and colleagues (2018) continue, "that we now live in a post-truth era when our history includes the three-fifths compromise, ongoing segregation, uneven drug policies, and other atrocities. It is also troubling to discuss the politics of the post-truth as if the problem is epistemology and not ideology" (p. 120). Similar concerns have been voiced as to the classed characteristics of post-truth discourses. For some, post-truth should not be understood so much as a sudden historical rupture in the fabric of democracy, but as a particular imaginary that calls forth and reflects certain almost existential class anxieties: "the rapid growth of post-truth anxieties is also a classed phenomenon. The liberal, educated middle class has not lost its claim to authority … . Nevertheless, contemporary conditions have produced feelings of instability for this class – and for some members, quite real precarity" (Zimmerman & Eddens, 2018, p. 968).

From this line of criticism, we can begin to see how conservative and liberal arguments around fake news and post-truth – while oppositional in scope – often share a similar nostalgia for the supposed heydays of liberal democracy, that is, a time where truth-telling was more centralized and knowledge gatekeepers had more power and authority. If only we could go back to the good old times, this line of argument goes, democracy could once again become truth-based. The problem, of course, with this type of argument is that the history of truth-telling in liberal democracies is also a history of exclusion and oppression. Journalism, science, and politics have all historically been fields dominated by White, male elites that both implicitly and explicitly excluded women and minorities from participating in supposed rational debate. From laws barring certain groups from voting or studying to more subtle forms of discrimination as well as legacies of past economic injustices. To this day, the traditional fields of truth-telling are not equal in any meaning of the word. Given this situation, rallies against fake news often carry an implicit whitewashed premise, namely the fantasy that democracy and truth used to function smoothly for the benefit of all people and that restoring past systems of truth-telling would automatically strengthen democracy.

To us, this will not do. Whitewashing democracy's history will not help us move forward and improve this form of co-habitation. Similarly, we do not believe that prescribing post-political measures – in the form of tech solutionism, government task forces, and anti-fake news laws – can "cure" the fundamental democratic deficit plaguing liberal democracies. In fact, we are deeply worried that such measures might entrench the current state of post-political dysfunction and growing authoritarianism across the world further. To us, democracy can only be saved through the deepening of democracy itself.

Concluding remarks

With this chapter, we have honed in on the solutions currently proposed to solve the supposed crisis of democracy and truth. Whether imagined or implemented, we have sought to critically showcase not only why the current solutions are interlaced with internal paradoxes – but also, and more substantially, that these are all too often based on the normative assumptions that has sought to undermine democracy in the first place. Indeed, building on the arguments presented in the previous chapter, it is our contention that existing solutions have often relied on tropes found within post-political and post-democratic registers: that is, the foundational idea that for democracy to prosper again, technocratic forms of governance, seemingly beyond dispute, must be brought to the foreground. Whether through the moralizing language of public voices or the implementation of fake news laws and specialized task forces, emphasis has been put on combating misinformation and fake news by eviscerating and policing it.

To our mind, reproducing the core tenants of post-politics will not bring us closer to more inclusive, participatory, and well-functioning democracies, but only serve to further entrench the hollowed out and capital-centric form of democracy dominating today. Rather than a counter-hegemonic set of strategies, the contemporary field of solutions have instead provided us with tools for further deepening the already existing hegemony. If this is indeed the case, then how are we to carve out other, perhaps more democratic and sustainable, solutions? This is precisely the question we turn to next.

References

Apuzzo, M. (2020, 24 April). Pressured by China, E.U. Softens Report on Covid-19 Disinformation. *The New York Times*. www.nytimes.com/2020/04/24/world/europe/disinformation-china-eu-coronavirus.html

Boland, H., & Titcomb, J. (2018, 7 November). Fake News at the Midterms: How Silicon Valley Defeated Efforts to Manipulate the Vote. *The Telegraph*. www.telegraph.co.uk/technology/2018/11/07/silicon-valley-may-breathing-sigh-relief-drama-free-midterms/

Brody, D. C., & Meier, D. M. (2018). How to Model Fake News. *Arxiv*, 1–17. https://arxiv.org/pdf/1809.00964.pdf

Bruff, I. (2014). The Rise of Authoritarian Neoliberalism. *Rethinking Marxism, 26(1)*, 113–129. https://doi.org/10.1080/08935696.2013.843250

Byrnes, S. (2018, 3 April). Anti-Fake News Laws Could be the Only Way to Counter Disinformation. *The New Statesman*. www.thenationalnews.com/opinion/comment/anti-fake-news-laws-could-be-the-only-way-to-counter-disinformation-1.718480

Daily Sabah (2016, 2 November). Globalization New Form of Colonialism, President Erdoğan Says. *Daily Sabah*. www.dailysabah.com/economy/2016/11/02/globalizat ion-new-form-of-colonialism-president-erdogan-says

Federal Government of Germany (2017). *Answers to the Special Rapporteur on the Promotion and Protection of the Right to Freedom of Opinion and Expression in Regard to the Act to Improve Enforcement of the Law in Social Networks (Network Enforcement Act)*. www.ohchr.org/sites/default/files/Documents/Issues/Opinion/Legi slation/GermanyReply9Aug2017.pdf

Gent, E. (2016, 27 December). Post-Truth: Technology is a Big Part of the Problem, But It's Also a Solution. *SingularityHub*. Retrieved from https://singularityhub.com/2016/ 12/27/post-truth-technology-is-a-big-part-of-the-problem-but-its-also-a-solution/

Human Rights Watch. (2018, 14 February). Germany: Flawed Social Media Law. *Hrw. prg*. www.hrw.org/news/2018/02/14/germany-flawed-social-media-law

Human Rights Watch. (2021, 11 February). Covid-19 Triggers Wave of Free Speech Abuse. Hrw.prg. www.hrw.org/news/2021/02/11/covid-19-triggers-wave-free-spe ech-abuse

Kakutani, M. (2018a, 14 July). The Death of Truth: How We Gave Up On Facts and Ended Up with Trump. *The Guardian*. Retrieved from www.theguardian.com/books/ 2018/jul/14/the-death-of-truth-how-we-gave-up-on-facts-and-ended-up-with-trump

Kakutani, M. (2018b). *The Death of Truth: Notes on Falsehood in the Age of Trump*. New York: Tim Duggans Books.

Mchangama, J., & Fiss, J. (2019). *The Digital Berlin Wall: How Germany (Accidentally) Created a Prototype for Global Online Censorship*. http://justitia-int.org/en/the-digi tal-berlin-wall-how-germany-created-a-prototype-for-global-online-censorship/

Mejia, R., Beckermann, K., & Sullivan, C. (2018). White Lies: A Racial History of the (Post)truth. *Communication and Critical/Cultural Studies*, *15(2)*, 109–126.

Mills, M., Rahal, C., Brazel, D., Yan, J., & Gieysztor, S. (2020). *COVID-19 Vaccine Deployment: Behaviour, Ethics, Misinformation and Policy Strategies*. https://royal society.org/-/media/policy/projects/set-c/set-c-vaccine-deployment.pdf

Mouffe, C. (1993). *The Return of the Political*. London: Verso.

Mouffe, C. (2005). *On the Political*. London: Routledge.

Neo, R. (2020). A Cudgel of Repression: Analysing State Instrumentalisation of the "Fake News" Label in Southeast Asia. *Journalism*, *23(9)*, 1919–1938. https://doi.org/ 10.1177/1464884920984060

Orbán, V. (2022, 25 August).*"The Globalists Can All Go To Hell!": Viktor Orbán Rips Progressivism*. YouTube. www.youtube.com/watch?v=nkz2kr153XM

Pearce, T. (2021, 24 May). Ron DeSantis Signs Bill Cracking Down On Big Tech: "These Platforms Have Become Our Public Square." *Daily Wire*. www.dailywire.com/news/ breaking-ron-desantis-signs-bill-cracking-down-on-big-tech-these-platforms-have-become-our-public-square

Rancière, J. (2014). *Hatred of Democracy*. London: Verso

Recode Staff (2018, 13 March). Full Transcript: Senator Chuck Schumer on Recode Decode. *Recode*. Retrieved from www.recode.net/2018/3/13/17114616/transcript-senator-chuck-schumer-washington-dc-trump-politics-democrat-minority-leader-rec ode-decode

Reporters Without Borders (2017, 19 July). Russian Bill is Copy-and-Paste of Germany's Hate Speech Law. *Rsf.Org*. https://rsf.org/en/news/russian-bill-copy-and-paste-germa nys-hate-speech-law

Ritchie, H. (2020, 1 May). EU Chief Denies Disinformation Report Was Watered Down for China. *CNN World*. https://edition.cnn.com/2020/05/01/europe/eu-ursula-von-der-leyen-amanpour-china-intl/index.html

Satter, R., Emmott, R., & Stubbs, J. (2020, 25 April). China Pressured EU to Drop COVID Disinformation Criticism: Sources. *Reuters*. www.reuters.com/article/us-hea lth-coronavirus-eu-china-idUSKCN227030

Tenove, C. (2020). Protecting Democracy from Disinformation: Normative Threats and Policy Responses. *The International Journal of Press/Politics*, *25*(3), 517–537. https:// doi.org/10.1177/1940161220918740

Trump, D. (2018, 28 August). Google search results for "Trump News" shows only the viewing/reporting of Fake News Media. In other words, they have it RIGGED, for me & others, so that almost all stories & news is BAD. Fake CNN is prominent. Republican/Conservative & Fair Media is shut out. Illegal? 96% of... . Retrieved from https://twitter.com/realdonaldtrump/status/1034456273306243076

Trump, D. (2020, 8 May). *DRAIN THE SWAMP!* Twitter. https://twitter.com/realDona ldTrump/status/1258720717258006530?lang=en

Tyson, N. deGrasse (2018, 20 August). I'm okay with a US Space Force: But what we need most is a Truth Force – one that defends against all enemies of accurate informa- tion, both foreign & domestic. *Twitter*. Retrieved from https://twitter.com/neiltyson/sta tus/1031556958153666561

United Nations (2017). *Joint Declaration on Freedom of Expression and "Fake News," Disinformation and Propaganda*. www.osce.org/files/f/documents/6/8/302796.pdf

Van Sant, S. (2019, 18 March). Russia Criminalizes the Spread of Online News which "Disrespects" The Government. *NPR*. www.npr.org/2019/03/18/704600310/russia-criminalizes-the-spread-of-online-news-which-disrespects-the-government

Varga, J. (2020, 27 March). No Power Grab in Hungary. *Politico*. www.politico.eu/arti cle/coronavirus-hungary-no-power-grab/

Zimmerman, H. & Eddens, A. (2018). Governing the Liberal Self in a "Post-Truth" Era: Science, Class and the Debate Over GMOs. *Cultural Studies*, *32*(6), 953–974. https://doi.org/10.1080/09502386.2018.1431301

9 Democratic alternatives to post-truth worlds

When thinking about the current state and potential future of liberal democracy, public intellectuals tend to downplay the contradictions and tensions built into this system of governance. In the long history of human evolution, liberal democracy is a fairly new form of co-habitation: it is moreover one that revolves around a number of opposing forces, not least a fundamental tension between capital interests and ideals of egalitarian participation (Brown, 2015; Mouffe, 2005). After the end of the Soviet Union, prominent voices in the West proclaimed the enduring victory of liberal democracy as a more or less monolithic order, hailing its superiority in ensuring peace and prosperity (Diamond & Plattner, 1996; Fukuyama, 1992). As is well known, Francis Fukuyama (1992) proclaimed the supposed "end of history." Indeed, for some, liberal democracy had become the *only* model for politics, as all other forms of political power and participation had been outcompeted in the marketplace of ideas. As history has gradually made abundantly clear, however, liberal democratic hegemony is not as clear-cut as some might have thought. Far from it.

In recent years, a growing number of researchers have explored how, why, and when liberal democracies die or start to erode. This work is illuminating insofar as it reminds us that the end of democracy is not a distant or unthinkable event. In bestselling books, scholars such as David Runciman (2018) and Steven Levitsky and Daniel Ziblatt (2018) challenge what they see as our often-times inherited and presupposed ideas about how political disorder and democratic decay take place. When picturing the end of democracy, they argue, there is a tendency in public discourse to think of a far-away moment of sudden violence. Through mixtures of civil war, economic meltdowns, public unrest, and military interventions, democracies are seen as imploding in highly visible and brutal *coup d'état*s, often limited to short bursts in time. This image, however, does all too often not match with historical reality. As Levitsky and Ziblatt (2018) make clear: "Since the end of the Cold War, most democratic breakdowns have been caused not by generals and soldiers but by elected governments themselves" (p. 5). Democracies still end, these authors remind us, yet the ways in which they do so is far from the image often associated with democratic decay.

DOI: 10.4324/9781003434870-12

The unthinkability of democratic demise – that is, our collective inability to picture the end of democracy, especially in the Western world – is intimately linked to our understanding of how democracies end. If we can only image democratic decay through a language of militaristic implosion, chaos, and financial meltdown, then the very notion of "stable" democracies dying seems far off and unrealistic. Yet, as recent scholarship points out, the death of democracy in our contemporary age often takes on an altogether different and less spectacular form. Rather than through rapid bursts of violence, another path to the end of democracy comes via an ever so gradual hollowing-out of democratic institutions. Far from a discrete event or torrent of disorder, we are instead treated to a highly complex and intertwined set of processes of de-democratization.[1] Such processes take place in a myriad of different and invisible ways – often over many years, if not decades. Frequently, we might not even sense that these layered processes have anything to do with democracies at all. They come in the form of declining trust in public institutions, increasing concentration of legislative power, growing inequality, decreasing voter turnouts, and the democratic election of anti-democratic forces. In Chapter 7, we have laid out the development of precisely these forces over the past number of decades.

Interestingly, the ascendance of public fear about fake news, post-truth, and infodemics owes much to these conceptions, merging supposed immediate chaos with long-term decay. On the one hand, we are often treated to an image of fake news and misinformation as sudden threats, standing outside the borders of democratic institutions threatening to undo these in a flash. On the other hand, we are treated to an image of the current crisis as one in which citizens are slowly becoming more and more uninformed, enclosed within their own filter bubbles. Indeed, it seems that post-truth worlds often see the collapse of liberal democracies as much as a coup of lies as a gradual process of decay. Yet, as the previous chapters have sought to document, these pervasive narratives of demise – suggesting that fake news and misinformation have suddenly entered the political scene, causing liberal democracies worldwide to collapse from within – are not only too simplistic, but also deceptively so. These contemporary post-truth worlds frame our current political predicament in a wholly one-sided manner. Not only do they neglect the important historical point that liberal democracies have already been in a state of gradual and pervasive institutional hollowing-out for a number of decades (as argued in Chapter 7). These narratives also tend to romanticize and whitewash democracy's past, downplaying exclusionary and oppressive aspects of liberal democratic history, such as the disbarring of women, people of color, and disabled populations from the *demos,* or the use of military interventions to quell democratic movements that might hinder capitalist interests.

By promoting the need for a return to "the good old days" of truth-saying, post-truth solutionists set up our collective imagination for interventions that are all too often de-democratizing in their own right. By equating democratic decision-making with notions of reason, rationality, and truth *tout court*, we are treated to not only a poor rendition of both past and present-day democracy but also a normatively risky set of solutions for how we might improve it tomorrow. As such, existing post-truth worlds offer us little in the way of genuine alternatives to the current democratic deficit and – ultimately, possibly – end.

With this chapter, we want to suggest that there are other ways of dealing with our current democratic moment. Not only so. We want to argue that these are urgently needed if we want genuine democratic alternatives. To do so, however, we must put the question of democracy and politics center-stage once again. Rather than assuming that liberal democracies have ever been fully democratic, it seems to us that we need to muster an altogether different conception of what democracy ought to be. In a sense, we need to respond to the so often posed question, *are we seeing the end of liberal democracy as we know it?* with a well-timed provocation: yes, please!

Drawing on the work of Chantal Mouffe, as we have so often done throughout this book, as well as a range of other critical scholars, this chapter will argue that, in order to think of solutions for our contemporary democratic moment, we first need to re-center the *demos* as the core foundation of democratic governance. Rather than blindly focusing on restoring truth, we need to shift our attention to questions of how to strengthen popular sovereignty, egalitarianism, participation, and dispute. We do so by building on Mouffe's distinction between *the political* and *politics*, foregrounding the ideal of *radical democracy*. Through a call for deepening the political and agonistic dimensions of democratic politics, we argue that in order to combat de-democratization, we need to radicalize democracy in the process.

Politics as dispute

The meaning and content of democracy as a political system has developed over time. It has continued to be disputed, as both its meaning and concrete manifestations have changed considerably (Held, 1989, 2006; Müller, 2011). As ideas, both democracy and politics are highly contested concepts that have historically been imbued with widely different normative concerns. This also means that there is today an overflow of normative positions, seeking to outline and claim the supposedly proper nature of these concepts. Our intention here is not to review these multitudes of normative positions nor offer a complete guide to democratic theory. Instead, the present chapter focuses on thinking through democratic alternatives to the truth-based solutionism seen in post-truth worlds. Keeping within the core arguments presented throughout the book, we draw extensively on Chantal Mouffe's (1993, 2013, 2018) work on so-called *agonistic pluralism* or *radical democracy*.

Mouffe's work is, of course, situated in a broader intellectual as well as historical conversation that in large part revolves around the role of *agonism* in contemporary democracy. Indeed, since the 1980s, prominent political theorists such as William E. Connolly (2002), Bonnie Honig (1993), Aletta Norval (2006) and (not least) Chantal Mouffe have presented different takes on how democracy might be reconceptualized in a so-called agonistic manner (Tønder & Thomassen, 2014; Wingenbach, 2016). As Mark Wenman (2013) has argued, these approaches have substantive conceptual differences, yet also share certain characteristics. Indeed, contrary to mainstream approaches in normative political theory, "the theorists of agonistic democracy do not seek to ground their respective vision of politics in substantive accounts of human nature, in teleological assumptions about the good life or concerning the movement of history" (Wenman, 2013, p. 6). Instead, taking as a point of departure what we described in Chapter 3 as a *post-foundationalist* ontology, agonistic democratic theory takes the "ultimate groundlessness of all claims to political legitimacy" as a starting point (ibid.). Doing so means acknowledging the role of dispute, dissent, and disagreement as central to democracy and politics altogether. While doing so might seem like an uncontroversial move, it actually goes against large parts of the mainstream political theory – liberal, republican, and otherwise. Indeed, for the large part of normative approaches, it is far from the constitutive role of dispute and dissent to democracy that is highlighted, but rather the need for supposed rational dialogue, consensus, and evidence-based policymaking. The agonistic approaches thus provide a decidedly different – and in our view much needed – set of arguments.

Drawing on a post-foundationalist ontology, it is hardly surprising that Mouffe sees the search for foundations as an obstacle, rather than asset, for understanding contemporary forms of democratic struggles. As she writes:

> Political philosophy in a modern democratic society should not be a search for foundations but the elaboration of a language providing us with metaphoric redescriptions of our social relations. By presenting us with different interpretations of the democratic ideal of liberty and equality, it will not supply metaphysical foundations for the liberal democratic regime (they cannot exist and it does not need any), but it could help us to defend democracy by deepening and extending the range of democratic practices through the creation of new subject positions within a democratic matrix.
>
> (Mouffe, 1993, p. 57)

If we are to think of other solutions to our current democratic moment, beset with struggles as to what the meaning of truth and democracy should be, then we need to think through the question of politics and the political.

In Chapter 7, we engaged with Mouffe's historical analysis of contemporary democracies and the democratic tradition. We showed how she, to understand the peculiar compromise located at the core of liberal democracies, foregrounded what she called "the democratic paradox." Liberal democracies are a contingent articulation between two seemingly opposite political traditions: one that focuses on individual rights, rationalism, and legality (liberalism) and another centered on equality, popular sovereignty, and community (the democratic tradition). For Mouffe, as well as a number of other critical voices, what starts to take place in the 1970s and 1980s is a new articulation of this paradox. The liberal side increasingly comes to dominate, not least in a form that is driven by market-based and competition-oriented demands of economic elites. As a consequence, popular sovereignty and the voice of the democratic people have increasingly been subsumed to expert knowledge, so-called evidence-based policymaking, and hard economic necessities. The voice of the people has become an obstacle to generating cross-border flows of capital accumulation. Mouffe is highly critical of these developments. She is so in large part due to the inability of these changes to properly grasp the dynamics of politics and the political. According to her, this hegemonization of liberal dogmas places an emphasis on two conceptual and highly normative vectors: individualism and reason. It is precisely these two vectors – that is, these two ideas about what politics *is* – that seem so infeasible to her.

Mouffe's starting point for this critique is what we might call an expanded understanding of what is usually meant by the terms *politics* and *the political*. She argues that we need to make a sharp distinction between these two: "By 'the political', I refer to the ontological dimension of antagonism, and by 'politics' I mean the ensemble of practices and institutions whose aim is to organize human coexistence" (Mouffe, 2013, p. xii). By *politics*, then, she refers to the historically shifting bundle of institutions and practices that make up what we in collegial terms understand as politics: parliament, congress, elections, municipal councils, and so forth. This is a fairly autonomous part of society that has been historically tasked with carrying out a particular function – namely rule on behalf of and for the democratic people. However, strictly speaking, there is nothing necessary about how these institutions look or that they should be present at all. Indeed, we could well imagine societies without politics in this sense of the term.

Against this relatively narrow understanding of politics, Mouffe posits something else. She argues that merely looking at politics does not get us where we want. Instead, we must look to *the political*. For Mouffe, the political is not the same as politics. For whereas politics is a contingent set of institutions and practices, the political applies to *all* relations. Contrary to the contingency of politics, the political is strictly speaking necessary. The political seeks to capture the underlying conditions of possibility – that is, the quasi-transcendental foundations – for any and all meaning to come into being. Her argument here is, like Laclau, that all relationality, all meaning, all identity-formation is based on a constitutive lack. This constitutive lack can be understood as antagonistic distinctions between inside and outside, us and them, friend and enemy. For Mouffe, it is precisely this underlying antagonism that she calls the political. The political is, in other words, the always-present (yet not always visible) series of exclusions, otherness, and demarcations that make any order possible. This also means, as she makes clear, that contrary to politics, the political is an ontological matter. It is always there, since "every order is political and based on some form of exclusion. There are always other possibilities that have been repressed and that can be reactivated. The articulatory practices through which a certain order is established and the meaning of social institutions is fixed are 'hegemonic practices'" (Mouffe, 2005, p. 18).

The political, thus understood, means that conflict and exclusion are not erad-icable. They cannot be surmounted: "The political in its antagonistic dimension cannot disappear by simply denying it or wishing it away" (Mouffe, 2013, p. 4). Beginning to think through democracy via the notion of the political radically challenges the tenets of post-political, neoliberal, and more procedural ideas of democracy. It does so on several accounts.

Against the idea of post-politics, claiming that liberal democratic societies have moved to a greatly progressed point of consensus and harmony, Mouffe's account suggests that such consensus will not only falter in the long run, but that it is in itself the product of hegemonic struggles. Indeed, any attempt to make conflict and political dispute go away is premised on silencing differences, otherness, and those who think otherwise. Against more liberal and procedural ideas of democracy, *the political* dislocates both assumptions of individuality and reason. Against reason and rationality – these Enlightenment values that are so often channeled in post-truth worlds – Mouffe's account foregrounds con-flict, antagonism, and hegemonic struggles as the foundation of all relations. Rather than presupposing any shared human essence – such as rationality – focusing on hegemonic struggles prompts us to focus on how different orders or foundations have historically been dominant. From this perspective, ration-ality and reason are in themselves contingent political articulations, seeking to fixate how and in what ways relations should be organized. Thus, "[t]he political cannot be grasped by liberal rationalism by the simple reason that every con-sistent rationalism requires negating the irreducibility of antagonism. Liberalism has to negate antagonism since, by bringing to the fore the inescapable moment of decision – in the strong sense of having to decide in an undecidable terrain – what antagonism reveals is the very limit of any rational consensus" (Mouffe, 2013, p. 12).

Yet, more than that, conceiving of the political as an antagonistic drawing of a frontier between us and them calls into question the individualistic bend of post-politics. It does so by suggesting that collective identities cannot be aggregated or counted together from a series of discrete, individual entities. If we are to understand collectives, we cannot simply add up individual atoms. To do so would be to misunderstand how collective identification functions, namely by establishing itself collectively as being in opposition to others. Such differentiation is always affective, atmospheric, and embodied: it grips us in a way that cannot be reduced to neat logical arguments. As Mouffe (2005, p. 6) argues (we quote at length):

> The mistake of liberal rationalism is to ignore the affective dimension mobilized by collective identification and to imagine that those supposedly archaic "passions" are bound to disappear with the advance of individualism and the progress of rationality. This is why democratic theory is so badly prepared to grasp the nature of "mass" political movements as well as phenomena such as nationalism. The part played by "passions" in politics reveals that, in order to come to terms with "the political," it is not enough for liberal theory to acknowledge the existence of a plurality of values and to extol toleration. Democratic politics cannot be limited to establishing compromises among interests or values or to deliberation about the common good; it needs to have real purchase on people's desires and fantasies.

Beyond being affective, however, collective identification is also genuinely collective. What is articulated in the frontier between us and them is not an aggregated totality of discrete entities, but a collective *we*.

From these arguments, then, we can begin to see that any emphasis on democracy as bound up with capital *T* Truth is difficult to maintain. The image offered by Mouffe is precisely the opposite. We cannot presuppose that any Westernized and Enlightenment notion of humanity and subjectivity acts as the transcendental foundation of democracy. We cannot take rationalism, reason, or truth for granted. Instead, we must come to terms with democratic practices as conflictual, affectual, and intimately bound up with dispute. There is no going beyond the drawing of frontiers, no proper political practice that is beyond exclusion. From this, it does not follow that all democratic practices should turn into chaos or conflict. Much more modestly, the question becomes as follows: how can we envision a democratic politics that does not seek to eradicate antagonism and contingency, but acknowledges the constitutive character of exclusion, difference, and undecidability? And, given that all such politics depends on the drawing of frontiers between us and them, how can we create political institutions that can contain, transform, and generatively use such differences while simultaneously recognizing pluralism, diversity, and care?

Radicalizing democracy

What Mouffe sets out to do, then, is to provide a new vocabulary that is at one and the same time a dire critique of the status quo and an attempt to think and act otherwise. Against the status quo – that is, the increasingly depoliticized and post-political climate of today – Mouffe seeks to carve out other modes of pursuing democracy that can foster deeper engagement, political difference, and proper popular sovereignty. She does so, as outlined above, by discarding essentialist conceptions of human rationality or reason. Instead, following the contours of a post-foundationalist agenda, she suggests that the only thing that can be taken for granted is the always-fragile decision or act of exclusion that underlines all relations. Such exclusion establishes a ground or partial foundation – but one that is always open to dispute, conflict, and change.

The big issue, then, is reconciling these seemingly opposing ideas: how can we deepen democracy while simultaneously insisting on the antagonistic nature of the political? Mouffe's answer to this is the idea of *radical democracy* or *agonistic pluralism*. This model rests on the idea that, rather than eradicating antagonism – an impossibility – it must be used generatively, as a basis for vibrant clashes of opinions and forms of life. The way of doing so is to reformulate and reconceptualize what is at stake in the production of antagonism as such. Indeed, whereas antagonism and collective identities are often formulated around an idea of *us* and *them*, in which the *them* is an *enemy to be destroyed*, Mouffe argues that the *other* must become an adversary to be disputed yet cared for:

> Conflict in liberal democratic societies cannot and should not be eradicated, since the specificity of pluralist democracy is precisely the recognition and the legitimation of conflict. What liberal democratic politics requires is that the others are not seen as enemies to be destroyed, but as adversaries whose ideas might be fought, even fiercely, but whose right to defend those ideas is not to be questioned. To put it another way, what is important is that conflict does not take the form of an "antagonism" (struggle between enemies) but the form of an "agonism" (struggle between adversaries).
>
> (Mouffe, 2013, p. 7)

Mouffe's model centers on the distinction between antagonism and agonism invoked in the last part of the quotation. For her, it is precisely by reformulating the relation between us and them that a new and deeper form of democracy can be created. This is one, as she makes clear, that does not dispute the other's right to think otherwise, but that seeks to build political dialogue around this act of thinking otherwise. This is also imminently a call for including and thinking with the affective and embodied dimensions of politics. Instead of hiding the affective, it can be put center stage in dialogue and conflict over the very stakes of how society should and ought to be structured. As Mouffe will go on to suggest, it is precisely in such struggles for hegemony – for establishing different and alternative orders – that democracies can once again begin to thrive.

Defending this radical deepening of democracy does not mean accepting capitalism as the only game in town. Far from it. The questioning of the post-political climate and the effort to reclaim the democratic tradition goes against a number of the core tenets of the capitalist mode of production. However, far too often, she argues, the Left has assumed the struggle against capitalism should be principally linked to its economic exploitation. People do not struggle against capitalism as an abstract historical system, she argues. They struggle in concrete situations and against concrete forms of oppression, destitution, and disenfranchisement.

In calling for a radicalization of democracy and political institutions, not least as an argument against capitalism, Mouffe has certainly not been alone. Indeed, Wolfgang Streeck, whom we also encountered in the previous chapters, also maintains the dire necessity of once again reclaiming the role of democracy over capitalist markets and economic elites. For Streeck (2016) one of the main tasks of contemporary democratic struggles is to – in his words – "reverse the institutional devastation wrought by four decades of neoliberal progress, and as far as possible to defend and repair what is left of the institutions with whose help social justice might be able to modify or even replace market justice" (Streeck, 2016, pp. 173–174). This also means actively engaging with the institutions that underpin our democratic societies, thus "building institutions through which markets can be brought back under the control of society: labour markets that leave scope for social life, product markets that do not destroy nature, credit markets that do not mass-produce unsustainable promises" (Ibid.). Far from an easy task, however, this will – according to Streeck – imply "years of political mobilization and lasting disruption of the social order that is today taking shape before our eyes" (ibid.).

It seems to us that these ideas have a direct consequence for how we think about the current moment. As shown in the previous chapter, existing solutions to the supposed post-truth era have tended to reproduce or rely on post-political tropes perpetuated since the 1970s. In doing so, these solutions have not only failed to acknowledge what might be at stake in contemporary struggles over questions of truth and democracy, they have also come to consolidate and entrench precisely that which has come into question: the hollowing out of democracy itself. This leads to the peculiar situation, observed a number of times throughout this book, in which (a crisis of) post-politics is combated with more post-politics. Whether such measures have taken the form of state policing or corporate tech solutionism, to name just two of the solutions considered in the previous chapter, they have nonetheless attempted to move us back in time. Rather than promising better conditions for popular dispute, social justice, and conditions of living, they have ordained experts who "know better," punishment for difference, restrictions on dispute, and the fortification of that which is claimed to be under siege. To our mind, these solutions do not suffice. While they might serve to ban, remove, and stigmatize certain voices, they will not solve the underlying democratic deficit. Condemnation, laws, and police do not make democracies democratic. Democratic practices do.

By engaging with the work of Mouffe, we suggest that we need to leave idealized conceptions of democracy as bound to truth and rationality aside and come to terms with the contingency of politics itself. For any order to be fixated and consolidated, there is always exclusion, conflict, and that which cannot be contained. The political involves the drawing up of frontiers between us and them, adversaries and friends. Now, the core question, it seems to us, is not how such frontiers can be navigated through the construction of rational chains of policy making. More substantially, we follow Mouffe in arguing that reconciling the always-antagonistic dimension of the political requires the open, willing, and purposeful creation of spaces for vibrant clashes of conflicting alternatives. We need to create new spaces for the enactment of politics. For other voices to be heard. For the demos to once again claim its legitimacy against the market. In short, we need deeper, more egalitarian, and open democratic institutions. For democracy to claim superiority once again over supposed necessities of capitalist markets, real actions are needed. This takes time. It requires democratic mobilization and the will to fight for sustainable worlds that do not subordinate either the life of humans or other species to that of capital accumulation. Far from being a question of truth or lack thereof, this is an issue of equality, recognition, and care.

Indeed, rather than ordaining more truth, expert knowledge, and supposedly universal reason, Mouffe's work prompts us to ask a series of hard questions: how can new spaces for the enactment of agonistic politics be created and maintained? How can new modes of democracy, which do not rely on essentialist claims to truth or rationality, be constructed, including people that think and act otherwise? What would it mean to work through the challenges posed by misinformation and blatant lies through strengthening the voice of those who have traditionally been silenced, rather than resorting to policing, surveillance, and legal restrictions? In other words, if what is to be combated is not a sudden erosion of truth, but a sustained attack on democracy as rule of the people, then how can popular sovereignty, egalitarianism, and the conflictual voice of the people be reclaimed?

Solutions or strategies? Pointers for other ways out

What we have tried to outline up until this point is how we might take a decidedly different approach to the question of democracy than what is offered by post-truth worlds. Rather than taking a rationalist or essentialist understanding of democracy as our starting point, we have instead mobilized core concepts from Mouffe's work on radical democracy and agonistic pluralism. Doing so has prompted us to reformulate democracy in terms of conflict, dispute, and disagreement – not as negative factors to be eradicated, but as constitutive to the functioning of democracy as such. To our mind, doing so also provides us with a very different starting-point for understanding our current predicament and suggesting solutions for how to combat it.

Arguing for a radicalization of democracy does not mean importing a neat and already fixed set of institutions, practices, and modes of participation. We are certainly not suggesting any easy fixes. What we take from Mouffe, rather, "is a specific strategy of construction of the political frontier and not a fully fledged political programme" (Mouffe, 2018, p. 80). In this sense, we occupy an intentionally paradoxical position. On the one hand, we are staunch defenders of the need for academic research to go beyond merely analyzing our present social structures and engage actively in normative questions. In a way, academics cannot avoid doing so – although many researchers will claim so in the name of objectivity and scientific practice. All research is, willingly or not, part of the very reality it seeks to understand, and so all research is always-already normative. On the other hand, we also reject the nonsensical blackmail often leveled against researchers engaging with normative questions – namely that unless one can present neat and fully-fledged solutions, so technical in design that they could be implemented tomorrow, one ought not to speak at all. This is a political strategy designed to silence those who think otherwise by insisting that new ideas are acceptable *only if* formulated in the terms resembling those of current policymakers and political elites.

Against this monopolization of solutions – and firmly based on the key arguments presented above – we want to offer a series of strategic pointers or devices in the following. These pointers might help us to engage with developing novel political strategies – new grammars and languages – that can offer us hope for thinking and doing otherwise. At the very least, they may offer an entry-point for further discussions on how we might develop democratic alternatives to the all too often post-political – and even anti-democratic – solutions currently offered by scholars, policymakers, and journalists alike in response to fake news and post-truth.

To reclaim our democratic institutions, allowing us to put the constitutive role of difference, affect, and otherness at the core of these, we need to first acknowledge the interlinked crises underpinning contemporary capitalism. As we have detailed in the previous chapters, liberal democracies are facing a range of profound and escalating problems. Inequality grows, trust in authorities decline, growth rates stagnate, human-made climate catastrophe intensifies, far-right movements seize power, while our media landscapes are increasingly commodified. While these issues might seem disconnected or, at least, only tangentially related, we argue that they fundamentally arise from the same democratic deficit. Moreover, these interconnected issues often form the basis of many of the problems identified as constituting the post-truth era.

Take, for example, a crucial political issue such as climate change. In recent years, a growing number of people, especially in the US, have started questioning the scientific credibility of climate change research (Milman & Harvey, 2019). In post-truth discourses, this development has often been seen as yet another case of filter bubbles, low-quality content, and increasingly misinformed masses. As argued by *The Economist* (2022): "Fake climate news can spread faster than a California wildfire." Importantly, climate change denial among citizens have also been portrayed as a leading cause for political inaction against climate change: "Climate misinformation can confuse the public, contribute to political inaction, and stall support for effective climate policy" (Ibid.).

Despite popular belief, however, an overwhelming majority of people – also in the US – support decisive political action against climate change. As found in a 2022 study in *Nature Communications*: "80–90% of Americans underestimate the prevalence of support for major climate change mitigation policies and climate concern. While 66–80% Americans support these policies, Americans estimate the prevalence to only be between 37–43% on average" (Sparkman et al., 2022, p. 1). The main problem is not that the masses deny climate change, but that politicians do not listen to popular demands. How could this be, we might ask?

Rather than looking towards recent problems with fake news and digital media, understanding political inaction against climate change – which is a decades old problem – first and foremost requires us to look into the deep-seated problem of corporate influence in liberal democracies. Going back to at least the 1980s, the oil and gas industry have known about human-made climate change and used their massive wealth and influence to prevent political action against it (Franta, 2021; Maxwell & Miller, 2016). Using tactics mirroring those of the tobacco industry, the oil and gas industry have spent billions bankrolling public intellectuals to deny or downplay the existence of climate change as well as lobbying politicians into quelling proposed legislation that could limit fossil fuel profits (Brulle, 2018; Maxwell & Miller, 2016). As detailed in the book, *The Petroleum Papers* (Dembicki, 2022), the fossil fuel industry already knew in the early 1990s that "stopping climate change was not only possible but economically feasible." Yet, since the industry feared "taxing carbon would kill its profits" (Dembicki, 2022), it successfully lobbied to stop meaningful action.

Between 2000 and 2016, lobbying spent in relation to climate change in the US amounted to more than 2 billion dollars (Brulle, 2018), with spending from environmental organizations and renewable energy companies being "dwarfed by a ratio of 10:1 by the spending of the sectors engaged in the supply and use of fossil fuels" (Brulle, 2018, p. 301). Infamously, the Trump administration had close ties to oil and gas companies, most prominently the Koch family (Zhang et al., 2017), owners of the second largest privately held company in the US (Murphy, 2022). In 2018, the year after Trump announced a US withdrawal from the Paris Agreement, Charles Koch boasted to allied political donors that they had "made more progress in the last five years than I had in the previous fifty" (Mayer, 2019).

Alongside political lobbying, the oil and gas industry has pushed to make sure news organizations include climate change denial in reporting on climate change, exploiting "journalistic norms for 'balance'… in an attempt to confuse the public" (van der Linden, 2023). In 2018, the BBC acknowledged that it had been "wrong too often" in its coverage of climate change, telling staff that going forward, "you do not need a 'denier' to balance the debate" (Carrington, 2018)

Given these observations about the political influence of the oil and gas industry, it is easy to see how political inaction against climate catastrophe has much more to do with corporate power in politics than it has to do with filter bubbles or misinformed masses. As long as the oil and gas industry asserts immense influence on established media and politics, acting against climate disaster will continue to be an uphill battle. As such, no amount of new fact-checking initiatives, media literacy programs, or anti-fake news laws are going to cut it. To address an issue like political inaction against human-made climate change – which has lasted for decades – we need to address the elephant in the room, namely the fundamental and structural problems at the heart of liberal democracies. These revolve around issues of corporate influence in politics, wealth centralization, lack of democratic media, and lack of public influence on political decision-making. In the following, we will offer some brief reflections on these key issues, directing our attention away from what we see as inadequate and flawed truth-based fixes, and towards much-needed structural democratic solutions.

Rather than regulating fake news, we need to regulate wealth

As we have shown throughout this book, post-truth solutionism often focuses on regulating, surveilling, and policing democratic discourse, for example, through anti-fake news laws that delimit the borders of what can and cannot be said in public debate. This is, to our mind, a completely flawed approach, as it suppresses differences, dispute, and otherness in favor of the kinds of speech deemed appropriate by those in power. As an alternative to such an approach, we want to direct the attention towards political solutions that revolve around limiting the extent of centralized wealth and corporate power in liberal democracies.

Economists such as Thomas Piketty (2014), Joseph Stiglitz (2015), and Ha-Joon Chang (2010) have clearly laid out how both income and wealth inequality have risen markedly across the US and many European countries for decades. As summarized by Stiglitz (2015) with reference to the US: "The upper 1 percent of Americans are now taking in nearly a quarter of the nation's income every year. In terms of wealth rather than income, the top 1 percent control 40 percent... While the top 1 percent have seen their incomes rise 18 percent over the past decade, those in the middle have actually seen their incomes fall" (Stiglitz, 2015, p. 74). Looking outside North America and Europe – towards Latin America and Africa – inequality is even more pronounced, with the United Nations Development Program (UNDP) designating Latin America as being "caught in a high-inequality, low-growth trap" (UNDP, 2021, p. 21). While 105 billionaires in Latin America own a combined wealth of $446.9 billion, 2 out of 10 people do not have sufficient food to eat (UNDP, 2021). Across Africa, inequality rose throughout the 1980s and 1990s and, despite leveling off in the 2000s, remains staggering (Shimeles & Nabassaga, 2018).

Key factors for the rise in inequality has been corporate deregulation, increasingly globalized capital flows, and tax cuts for the wealthiest (Chang, 2010; Piketty, 2014; Stiglitz, 2015). Through slogans of trickle-down economics, politicians across liberal democracies have continuously proclaimed to deliver a new era of abundance through liberalization of international trade, deregulation of the financial sector, privatization of public infrastructure, tax cuts, and lower spending on public welfare. History has shown that these concerted political efforts have in no way delivered on their promises. As Professor of Economics, Ha-Joon Chang (2010), succinctly notes:

> The result of these policies has been the polar opposite of what was promised. Forget for a moment the financial meltdown, which will scar the world for decades to come. Prior to that, and unbeknown to most people, free-market policies had resulted in slower growth, rising inequality and heightened instability in most countries... . The problems were bad enough in the rich countries, but they were even more serious for the developing world.
>
> (pp. xiv–xv)

The current unequally distributed concentration of wealth – both within countries and between countries – is not simply the result of "the market" (as a form of quasi-biological entity), Chang (2010) reminds us. Rather, it is the outcome of deliberate political decisions. Our current system of economic inequality is intimately tied to a global division of labor, in which the continuous concentration of wealth and seemingly unstoppable imperative for growth in Western countries happens at the expense of the poorest regions of the world, a state of affairs that has deep colonial and imperialist roots. Authors such as Stephan Lessenich (2019) and Zygmunt Bauman (2003) have shown this in detail, pinpointing how globalized capitalism is deeply interconnected: economic prosperity, consumption, and globalization *for some*, always-already implies a world that is unlivable *for others*.

This is not the place to present these arguments in-depth. But let us simply suggest the following: in order to solve some of the major problems currently facing liberal democracies, wealth redistribution is paramount. This can be achieved through well-known fiscal instruments, such as capital gains taxes, inheritance taxes, and wealth taxes (Chang, 2010; Piketty, 2014; Stiglitz, 2015). Coupled to that, as Ha-Joon Chang (2012) have pointed out, there is a need for combatting tax avoidance from multinational companies and economic elites: "Why do tax havens exist? Because rich countries allow them to. If the US came down on tax havens in the same way they come down on countries that trade with Iran and Cuba, we'd have no tax havens in the world" (Chang, 2012). It is not that combatting inequality and tax evasion is too complicated to do. Rather, political elites in liberal democracies have so far simply been unwilling to do so. This needs to change.

Rather than restricting difference and dispute, we need to restrict corporate power

Bringing the need to regulate wealth to the front also brings us to the problem of corporate and elite influence in politics. As Colin Crouch writes (2011), corporations have increasingly become "the main source of power over politics" (p. 165). Through lobby groups and political donations, corporations and wealthy individuals assert significant power – both direct and indirect – over supposedly democratic decision-making processes. In this regard, corporations' ability to threaten to simply move production and profits elsewhere in the global economy have often served as a convenient excuse for politicians to argue that "economic reality 'requires' it" (Brown, 2015, p. 211). As Crouch (2015) notes in the book, *The Knowledge Corrupters: Hidden Consequences of the Financial Takeover of Public Life,* "where those exercising large quantities of power can obfuscate, confuse, and corrupt popular knowledge, democracy becomes the prisoner of powerful interests" (p. 4). This has led to a situation where – as Gilens and Page document in a 2014 study – "the average American appears to have only a minuscule, near-zero, statistically non-significant impact upon public policy" (p. 575). In cases of disagreement between elite interests and majority interests, politicians overwhelmingly side with economic elites.

In the book, *The Price of Democracy,* French economist Julia Cagé (2020) documents the extent of corporate and private influence in contemporary liberal democracies. In numerous countries, she highlights, elite donations to political parties are effectively subsidized by taxpayer money. In France, Canada, Italy, Spain, and Germany, political donors can deduct campaign donations from their taxes. Through such tax schemes, funds from the majority of the population are effectively allocated to subsidize political lobbying from economic elites. This, she argues, is a fundamental democratic problem.

In order to make liberal democracies more democratic, Cagé (2020) calls for a "complete overhaul of the way in which political groups and election campaigns are funded; that and that alone will make it possible to end the corruption eating away at our electoral systems, and the representation deficit affecting the great majority of citizens" (p. 226). This includes the removal of tax deduction schemes for private and corporate political donations or, more radically, a complete ban on private donations in politics. In its place, Cagé proposes the introduction of new systems of public political funding, in which each citizen gets to choose a political party or cause they wish to allocate a small amount of public funds for. Only through such systems, Cagé (2020) argues, would it be possible to "switch our democracies away from 'one euro, one vote' to 'one person, one vote'" (p. 278).

Rather than media literacy, we need democratic media

As documented in Chapter 4, another prominent solution presented by politicians, scholars, and journalists to solve the post-truth era is media literacy. That is, the idea that people should be taught about the pitfalls of digital media and their manipulative potential, and – in so being – they might know how to avoid these. Such solutions might in specific circumstances have their merits. Yet, they tend to only provide surface level solutions to deep structural problems. Indeed, in prompting people to be taught particular skills and competences, they fail to address the fundamental problem that our current media landscape is both controlled by and aligned with elite interests and thrive on controversy, clickbait, and manipulation. As scholars such as Siva Vaidhyanathan (2018), Shoshana Zuboff (2019), Christian Fuchs (2018), and Victor Pickard (2020) have argued time and again, both the news industry and tech industry currently fail to support a well-functioning democratic discourse and citizen participation. This has led to calls for radically rethinking the democratic function and funding of media.

One proposal, put forth by Christian Fuchs and Klaus Unterberger (2021), is *The Public Service Media and Public Service Internet Manifesto*. This manifesto – signed by prominent thinkers, including Jürgen Habermas and Noam Chomsky – lays out 10 principles for how to strengthen democratic media. It calls for "the creation of the legal, economic and organisational foundations" for new public service media – both online and offline – built for "citizens, not consumers" (p. 8). This means establishing new media institutions that can serve as non-profit alternatives to both commercial news conglomerates and surveillance-based tech giants.

Public service media, the manifesto reminds us, have historically played a key role for the functioning of liberal democracies. Yet, due to decades of austerity politics, commercialization, concentration of ownership, and lack of political visions for public service media in the digital age, surveillance-based tech companies have had little difficulty in monopolizing our online experience. As an alternative, democracies urgently need a public service internet that can help to support more diverse, equal, and just forms of political debate and communication.

In *The Media Manifesto* by Natalie Fenton, Des Freedman, Justin Schlosberg, and Lina Dencik (2020), we find similar lines of thought. Unpacking the deep-seated problems riddling global capitalism and its commercial media landscapes, the authors point out how, "in the majority of countries around the world, the trend is for media ownership at both local and national level to be more concentrated on ever fewer hands… creating an ever-more impoverished public sphere" (p. 103). To counter this development, these authors propose a number of concrete policy solutions, revolving around the establishment of new public service media, strengthening of press freedom, and limiting of corporate online surveillance. Overall, they conclude, there is an urgent need for imagining new forms of "media systems that prioritize the value of the public over profit.... to formulate mechanisms of inclusive citizen participation and democratic control of the spaces we inhabit" (Fenton et al., 2020, p. 117).

Taken together, we can begin to see how a number of scholars in recent years have presented serious policy proposals that go far beyond the notion of re-educating or realigning the misinformed masses through inoculation and media literacy. As these scholars make clear time and again, the problems of our current media landscapes cannot simply be tackled at an individual level but have to be addressed structurally. Simply put, there is a grave need to change the overarching economic structures that currently support corporate mass sur-veillance, clickbait, manipulation, and elite interests. We cannot do full justice to these debates or proposals here. Our point is not to imply that there exists any easy set of fixes or that, by adopting new forms of communication, we will suddenly have flourishing and prosperous democracies. Our point is rather that democratic media provide a fertile infrastructure for proper democratic practices to emerge. They are a starting point for deepening our democratic institutions, providing a potential alternative to ever-declining trust in knowledge gatekeepers and dwindling levels of political participation.

Rather than more Truth, we need more democratic participation

Finally, it seems to us that if we genuinely wish to strengthen democracy, we cannot do so by continuously fetishizing Truth with a capital T: that is, a singular and supposedly universal conception of truth. Such a conception is, as we have tried to demonstrate throughout this book, itself a product of historical struggles for hegemony, and it is one that is closely interwoven with ideas about ration-ality, reason, and administrative rule, rather than popular sovereignty and plur-alism. Hiding behind its own supposed objectivity, such a discourse is deeply political and ignores the fraught history of its own making.

In pursuing strategies for more democratic democracies, we need genuine political reform focused on making democracies more participatory, inclusive, egalitarian, and agonistic. As many political scientists have noted, the distance between politicians and citizens have been growing steadily across liberal democracies, as party and union membership has declined, while the number of constituents of each elected official has increased significantly over time (Crouch, 2011; Mair, 2013). Adding to this, supranational institutions, such as the European Union, have not only expanded the physical distance between citi-zens and politicians, but also increased the number of unelected officials. As pol-itical power has gradually shifted towards obscure and administratively dense legislative processes, participating in politics can not only seem futile, but down right impossible for many.

To our minds, if we are to stop the gradual hollowing out of our democratic institutions and once again build up public trust in these, we need democratic institutions that are actively based on the participation of citizens. This has to start at a local level, with community and citizen-councils being included into not only the development of new policies at a municipal level, but also actively involved in delineating which problems are constructed and framed as problems at all. It should also develop all the way up to national and supranational policies with an increased focus on public hearings, deliberations, and transparency throughout all stages of policymaking. The point here, surely, is not to develop a fully formed catalog of ideas; rather it is to say that building genuine spaces for difference, dispute, and pluralism does not simply imply fake democratic hearings designed to legitimize already-decided policies and bulldoze whenever real public concern is raised. Instead, it forces us to reimage our democratic institutions from the ground up. How can we, the big question goes, design these so as to maximize the potential for public deliberation by all parts of the citizenry?

Closing thoughts

Democracy needs continuous care and renewal if it is to prosper and be(come) vibrant. Our collective ability to articulate not just suitable analyses of the existing state of affairs, but also potential ways of moving beyond this, is tantamount to such a project. Indeed, if we are to deepen our democratic practices and institutions, allowing for vibrant clashes of meaning and inclusive spaces of political difference to emerge, we need to provide suitable – and, not least, desirable – options for change. We need to offer counter-hegemonic discourses that can help us drive social and political alternatives.

With this chapter, we have sought to lay out precisely this: other ways of thinking through and beyond our contemporary democratic moment. In so doing, we have sought to offer other narratives and discourses than those currently dominating amongst policymakers, academics, journalists, and economic elites around the world. What we need is not moral condemnation, policing, and new surveillance measurements, all erected in the name of singular orders of truth, reason, and rationality. Instead, we need to accept the fundamental heterogeneity underlying all these concepts, coming to terms with the powerful, yet so often misunderstood, notion that dissent, dispute, and difference are not things to be eradicated, but to be embraced and nurtured within our democracies. Indeed, against the temptation to recline into ever more narrow conceptions of truth, we need to open up our democratic institutions for politics proper to appear – that is, the role of the democratic people as not only "voters" to be addressed every few years or consumers who "vote with their wallets," but integral in a much more radical sense to the functioning of democracy.

In proposing this shift in our approach, we do not deny that democracies are in danger. They most certainly are – and have been so for several decades. Yet, we want to forcefully stress that any such danger is not – at least not primarily – due to a withdrawal of truth or reason; rather, it is to be attributed to a deep (and deepening) democratic deficit, which has been propelled and intellectually legitimized by the hegemony of the market, technocracy, and economic reason since at least the 1980s. If we understand the roots of our current democratic deficit solely in terms of a lack of reason and truth, we are not only treated to a poor rendition of our actual state of affairs; we are also left unable to understand the complex historical paths that have led us here. Moreover, we are – implicitly and unnoticeably – led to believe that democracy can only function in tandem with singular orders of truth. This is not the case. It should not be the case. Yet, the incessant belief that it is indeed the case has led to a series of problematic solutions that are supposed to cure the ills facing democracy, yet in reality seem to do just the opposite. The modest claim advanced in this chapter has been that there are other pathways – opportunities leading us beyond our current impasse. We just have to seize them.

Note

1 On the issue of de-democratization and de-politicization, there is a growing and hugely important body of literature that we can only mention in passing here. On the former, which is also studied under terms such as "backsliding" and "regression," well-known contributions include Charles Tilly's 2003 article, *Inequality, Democratization, and De-Democratization*, Wendy Brown's 2006 article, *American Nightmare: Neoliberalism, Neoconservatism, and De-Democratization*, and Nancy Bermeo's 2016 essay *On Democratic Backsliding*. On the latter, that is the issue of de-politicization, one might start with the edited volume *Anti-Politics, Depoliticization, and Governance* (Fawcett et al, 2017), or the work by Ernesto Laclau on this exact issue (1990).

References

Bauman, Z. (2003). *Wasted Lives: Modernity and Its Outcasts*. Cambridge: Polity Press.

Bermeo, N. (2016). On Democratic Backsliding. *Journal of Democracy*, 27(1), 5–19. http://doi.org/10.1353/jod.2016.0012

Brown, W. (2006). American Nightmare: Neoliberalism, Neoconservatism, and De-Democratization. *Political Theory*, 34(6), 690–714. www.jstor.org/stable/20452506

Brown, W. (2015). *Undoing the Demos: Neoliberalism's Stealth Revolution*. New York: Zone Books.

Brulle, R.J. (2018). The Climate Lobby: A Sectoral Analysis of Lobbying Spending on Climate Change in the USA, 2000 to 2016. *Climatic Change*, 149(3–4), 289–303. https://doi.org/10.1007/s10584-018-2241-z

Cagé, J. (2020). *The Price of Democracy: How Money Shapes Politics and What to Do about It*. Cambridge, MA: Harvard University Press.

Carrington, D. (2018, 7 September). BBC Admits "We Get Climate Change Coverage Wrong Too Often." *The Guardian*. www.theguardian.com/environment/2018/sep/07/bbc-we-get-climate-change-coverage-wrong-too-often#:~:text=The%20BBC%20has%20accepted%20it,to%20report%20on%20global%20warming.

Chang, H.-J. (2010). *23 Things They Don't Tell You About Capitalism*. London: Penguin.

Chang, H.-J. (2012, 14 December). How Effective is Overseas Aid? *The Guardian*. www.theguardian.com/commentisfree/2012/dec/14/how-effective-overseas-aid-coversation

Connolly, W.E. (2002). *Identity/Difference: Democratic Negotiations of Political Paradox*. Minneapolis: University of Minnesota Press.

Crouch, C. (2011). *The Strange Non-Death of Neoliberalism*. Cambridge: Polity Press.

Crouch, C. (2015). *The Knowledge Corrupters: Hidden Consequences of the Financial Takeover of Public Life*. Cambridge: Polity Press.

Dembicki, G. (2022). *The Petroleum Papers: Inside the Far-Right Conspiracy to Cover Up Climate Change*. Vancouver: Greystone Books.

Diamond, L., & Plattner, M.F. (Eds.). (1996). *The Global Resurgence of Democracy*. Baltimore: John Hopkins University Press.

Fawcett, P., Flinders, M., Hay, C., & Wood, M. (Eds.), *Anti-Politics, Depoliticization, and Governance*. Oxford: Oxford University Press.

Fenton, N., Freedman, D., Schlosberg, J., & Dencik, L. (2020). *The Media Manifesto*. Cambridge: Polity Press.

Franta, B. (2021). Early Oil Industry Disinformation on Global Warming. *Environmental Politics*, 30(4), 663–668. https://doi.org/10.1080/09644016.2020.1863703

Fuchs, C. (2018). *Digital Demagogue: Authoritarian Capitalism in the Age of Trump and Twitter*. London: Pluto Press.

Fuchs, C., & Unterberger, K. (Eds.). (2021). *The Public Service Media and Public Service Internet Manifesto*. London: University of Westminster Press. http://doi.org/10.16997/book60

Fukuyama, F. (1992). *The End of History and the Last Man*. New York: Free Press.

Gilens, M., & Page, B.L. (2014). Testing Theories of American Politics: Elites, Interest Groups, and Average Citizens. *Perspectives on Politics*, 12(3), 564–581. https://doi.org/10.1017/S1537592714001595

Held, D. (1989). *Political Theory and the Modern State: Essays on State, Power and Democracy*. Cambridge: Polity Press.

Held, D. (2006). *Models of Democracy*. Stanford: Stanford University Press.

Honig, B. (1993). *Political Theory and the Displacement of Politics*. Ithaca: Cornell University Press.

Lessenich, S. (2019). *Living Well at Others' Expense: The Hidden Costs of Western Prosperity*. Cambridge: Polity Press.

Levitsky, S. & Ziblatt, D. (2018). *How Democracies Die*. New York: Broadway Books.

Mair, P. (2013). *Ruling the Void: The Hollowing of Western Democracy*. London: Verso.

Maxwell, R., & Miller, T. (2016). The Propaganda Machine Behind the Controversy Over Climate Science: Can You Spot the Lie in This Title? *American Behavioral Scientist*, 60(3), 288–304. https://doi.org/10.1177/0002764215613405

Mayer, J. (2019, 13 August). "Kochland" Examines the Koch Brothers' Early, Crucial Role in Climate-Change Denial. *The New Yorker*. www.newyorker.com/news/daily-comment/kochland-examines-how-the-koch-brothers-made-their-fortune-and-the-influence-it-bought

Milman, O., & Harvey, F. (2019, 8 May). US is Hotbed of Climate Change Denial, Major Global Survey Finds. *The Guardian*.www.theguardian.com/environment/2019/may/07/us-hotbed-climate-change-denial-international-poll

Mouffe, C. (1993). *The Return of the Political*. London: Verso.

Mouffe, C. (2005). *The Democratic Paradox*. London: Verso.

Mouffe, C. (2013). *Agonistics: Thinking the World Politically*. London: Verso.

Mouffe, C. (2018). *For a Left Populism*. London: Verso.

Müller, J.-W. (2011). *Contesting Democracy: Political Ideas in Twentieth-Century Europe*. New Haven: Yale University.

Murphy, A. (2022, 1 December). America's Largest Private Companies. *Forbes*. www.forbes.com/lists/largest-private-companies/?sh=3c987cafbac4

Norval, A. (2006). *Aversive Democracy: Inheritance and Originality in the Democratic Tradition*. Cambridge: Cambridge University Press.

Pickard, V. (2020). *Democracy Without Journalism?* Oxford: Oxford University Press.

Piketty, T. (2014). *Capital in the Twenty-First Century*. Cambridge, MA: Harvard University Press.

Runciman, D. (2018). *How Democracy Ends*. London: Profile Books.

Shimeles, A., & Nabassaga, T. (2018). Why is Inequality High in Africa? *Journal of African Economies*, *27*(1), 108–126. https://doi.org/10.1093/jae/ejx035

Sparkman, G., Geiger, N., & Weber, E.U. (2022). Americans Experience a False Social Reality by Underestimating Popular Climate Policy Support by Nearly Half. *Nature Communications*, *13*(1). https://doi.org/10.1038/s41467-022-32412-y

Stiglitz, J E. (2015). *The Great Divide: Unequal Societies and What We Can Do About Them*. New York: W. W. Norton Company.

Streeck, W. (2016). *How Will Capitalism End? Essays on a Failing System*. London: Verso.

The Economist. (2022, 4 February). Data Point: Trust Issues. *The Economist*. https://impact.economist.com/sustainability/social-sustainability/data-point-trust-issues

Tilly, C. (2003). Inequality, Democratization, and De-Democratization. *Sociological Theory*, *21*(1), 37–43. www.jstor.org/stable/3108607

Tønder, L., & Thomassen, L. (Eds.). (2014). *Radical Democracy: Politics Between Abundance and Lack*. Manchester: Manchester University Press.

UNDP (2021). *Trapped: High Inequality and Low Growth in Latin America and the Caribbean*. www.undp.org/latin-america/regional-human-development-report-2021

Vaidhyanathan, S. (2018). *Antisocial Media: How Facebook Disconnects Us and Undermines Democracy*. Oxford: Oxford University Press.

van der Linden, S. (2023). *Foolproof: Why Misinformation Infects Our Minds and How to Build Immunity*. London: 4th Estate.

Wenman, M. (2013). *Agonistic Democracy: Constituent Power in the Era of Globalization*. Cambridge: Cambridge University Press.

Wingenbach, E. (2016). *Institutionalizing Agonistic Democracy: Post-Foundationalism and Political Liberalism*. London: Routledge.

Zhang, H.B, Dai, H.C., Lai, H.X., & Wang, W.T. (2017). U.S. Withdrawal from the Paris Agreement: Reasons, Impacts, and China's Response. *Advances in Climate Change Research*, *8*(4), 220–225. https://doi.org/10.1016/j.accre.2017.09.002

Zuboff, S. (2019). *The Age of Surveillance Capitalism The Fight for a Human Future at the New Frontier of Power*. New York: PublicAffairs.

10 Conclusion

We are currently living through a democratic moment – a moment in which the once so settled borders of democracy are again opened for radical questioning and contestation. Indeed, whether we accept the current image of a post-truth condition or not, deep-seated conversations about the state and future of democracy are undeniably taking place in the Western world and beyond. Institutions, ideas, and ideals that once seemed clearly demarcated are being redrawn. With these changes, history is once again being written. Our democratic moment presents itself as much as a challenge to established institutions as an opportunity for renewing our commitment to creating a more inclusive society and a deeper democracy. It seems that we are at a time when the dislocating rhythm of globalized capitalism has reactivated the otherwise sedimented structures of our post-political institutions. The established political consensus is no longer viable. This opens up new opportunities for change – both negative and positive.

The modest intervention provided by this book has been to take a step back from the immediacy and self-explanatory nature of this moment. Our aim has been to carve out a map of the current political terrain by systematically investigating and unpacking contemporary post-truth worlds. We have wanted to unravel the anxieties, dreams, and ideals that are currently being negotiated, circulated, and contested. In doing so, we have showcased not only how a certain idea about democracy has been at the core of these worlds, but also how this model might end up reproducing and reinforcing developments broadly identified as *post-political* and *post-democratic* in nature. Indeed, this is the paradox or tension identified at the core of the contemporary political terrain: current calls for deepening democracy might in fact contribute to further hollowing out popular participation and the voice of the democratic people. Instead of providing a new vision for reinvigorating democracy in times of capitalist crisis and rising authoritarianism, post-truth discourses provide a nostalgic narrative about modern-day villains and a longing for the past. By doing so, we argue, they do not productively move us forward. On the contrary, they might add further ill to our already dire situation.

DOI: 10.4324/9781003434870-13

We have presented these arguments in several parts. In the first and second parts of this book, we tackled these issues by moving to the inside and interior of contemporary post-truth worlds. Here, we showed how a whole range of public figures – journalists, intellectuals, politicians, and commentators with access to international media outlets and journals – have come to lament the current state of liberal democracies. Concepts such as fake news, post-truth, alternative facts, infodemics, and misinformation have been seen as the latest manifestations of a profound crisis of truth. Indeed, according to these contemporary discourses, the formerly flourishing capacity to make decisions based on rational debate, reason, and evidence is waning. Post-truth, it has been claimed time and time again, is a disease that is rapidly spreading throughout the democratic body and must be stopped through protective counter-measures. We have furthermore shown how this basic narrative has become pivotal to a series of crisis narratives of our time. Indeed, it seems that post-truth discourses cling to and are continuously repurposed within a series of seemingly disparate events. Post-truth worlds have become a common discursive infrastructure that can seemingly be strategically mobilized within almost all crisis situations.

In this third part of the book, we suggested that the common representation contained in these discourses – a model of democracy that fuses technological solutionism with staunch rationalism – reinforces and further entrenches a very particular normative idea about democracy as a political system. This is one that values consensus over dispute, truth over affect, and stability over struggle, reproducing and amplifying existing attempts to neutralize and dismantle the democratic tradition from within. Our argument has been that these discourses fit hand in glove with the kinds of anti-democratic and anti-political currents demanded by the capitalist system and its market-premised conception of political participation. From this, we further suggested that if democracy is in a state of crisis – which certainly seems to be the case – then this need not be a crisis of truth. Perhaps it is simply a crisis of democracy itself; that is, the crisis of a system that claims to be democratic, yet gradually has dispelled the elements that formerly made it so. As a consequence, we argue that a way of saving democracy and the democratic tradition might be to create, nurture, and assemble genuine spaces for the enactment of politics proper again. Democracy does not need more truth but more politics and popular rule. We need to reclaim the democratic tradition by honing in on the constitutive role of both popular sovereignty and difference.

These are the arguments we have sought to advance throughout this book. We have empirically portrayed the coming of a new political terrain and placed this within a wider politico-historical context in order to interrogate and question its implicit normative ideas. It is our hope that neither our analysis nor critique of these contemporary post-truth worlds will be read or understood in too simplistic terms. We have emphatically *not* suggested that truth, evidence, and informed debates (whatever any of these terms may mean) are unnecessary for democracies to prosper. We have not claimed that climate denial or the brazen lies of right-wing demagogues should not be questioned or contested. In fact, one of our core critiques of post-truth discourses is that they do *not* provide any proper democratic alternatives to such anti-democratic tendencies. Instead, they end up longing back to a glorified time of proclaimed consensus.

To us, the ways in which we can and should contest the worrisome rise of authoritarian leaders is *not* by clinging to a supposedly universal idea of democracy as truth, reason, and rationality. Truth is a necessary but *not sufficient condition* for democracy. Informed debates are a necessary but *not sufficient condition* for mobilizing and building political alternatives. In this sense, our argument is not that truth should be thrown to the wayside or that there is no place for so-called evidence-based policymaking. What we have tried to suggest is that equating this capacity with democracy as a whole is a seriously one-dimensional view of history and the democratic tradition. It is precisely the strategic mobilization of this history cut in two that we object to, as have a range of critical scholars in the past. Arguing that what is currently under attack is solely truth and evidence – and that the solution is to police wrongdoers and give power back to traditionally privileged groups – is part of wider attempts at de-politicizing, de-democratizing, and hollowing out our democracies, taking power away from the people and placing it in the hands of the few. Against this backdrop, we have tried to say that other ways are possible and that it is time to reinvigorate democracy by installing genuine ideas from the democratic tradition again. These include notions of equality, voice, egalitarianism, common concern, and care.

These arguments have consequences for how we approach questions of post-truth, fake news, and alternative facts in the future. Indeed, with this book, we hope to have not only delivered a normative critique of contemporary post-truth worlds, but also a theoretical and conceptual one. The book has forcefully argued against what we perceive to be two major problems facing contemporary debates on the proclaimed post-truth condition of democracy, both in scholarly and public discussions.

First, there has been a strong tendency to reify the basic political concepts mobilized and used in the public and intellectual debate. As demonstrated in this book, post-truth discourses all too often take for granted that the meaning of notions such as "democracy," "truth," and "reason" are self-evident, collectively shared, and built around an essential relation. As this book has brought to the forefront, this is in many ways an unproductive premise. All of the terms used in contemporary post-truth worlds are deeply politically charged and often one-sided. They are not mere descriptions of a world that is already assembled and created "out there," but discursive tools used to intervene and shape both the state and potential future of democracy. This also means that future research would do well to take the normative and contested nature of such labels into account. Doing so means taking seriously the foundational role of discourses in understanding and shaping politics.

Second, there has so far been an absence of critical perspectives on post-truth politics. Critical voices have largely been missing from the picture, while those who have engaged in debates have all too often simply overtaken the dominant political narratives as well as the latest hyped terms, whether that be post-truth, fake news, or the infodemic. Our intention with this book has not been to point fingers at such perspectives, but rather to point to alternative ways of thinking about our contemporary democratic moment. We need to engage reflexively with the narratives and discourses produced and circulated about our contemporary political age.

This book thus hopes to have carved out a fundamentally different opening to discussions of post-truth and democracy. If we cannot take any shared meaning of key political terms for granted and if there are no neutral definitions of concepts such as fake news and post-truth, then we need to investigate their mobilization as part of political conflicts. If there is any common ground – that is to say an underlying understanding of contemporary democracy and its discontents – then this is the outcome of political struggles for hegemony rather than a neutral starting point. Only through such a perspective can we begin to link our political moment to wider political developments of democracies in advanced capitalist societies. From these arguments, it seems to us that the big questions remaining are these: How are we to understand and make sense of our current democratic moment? Is democracy doomed? Or are there potential prospects for change?

It seems to us that one way of thinking through our moment might be to (once again) borrow some conceptual tools from the work of Ernesto Laclau. In what largely appears as a throwaway remark, formulated in *On Populist Reason* from 2005, Laclau (2005) suggested a subtle reformulation of Antonio Gramsci's (1992) idea of the organic crisis. The author of the prison notebooks had originally thought of such a crisis as followed by a moment where "the old is dying and the new cannot be born" (1992, p. 276). This was an "interregnum," he suggested, where "a great number of morbid symptoms appear" (Gramsci, 1992, p. 276). Laclau reformulated Gramsci's idea somewhat by arguing that "the 'floating' dimension [of particular signifiers] becomes most visible in periods of organic crisis, when the symbolic system needs to be radically recast" (Laclau, 2005, p. 132). Indeed, for Laclau (not unlike Gramsci), an organic crisis and its subsequent interregnum designate a period in which the old symbolic systems are dying and any new hegemonic order has yet to take its place. It is a period of profound dislocation where the existing hegemonic order no longer exhibits the same kind of primordial desire and identification it used to. Things may be going on as before, but the ideological attachment or political engagement seems to have disappeared.

We see these ideas as providing one way of interpreting the contemporary flourishing of post-truth worlds. From this perspective, we can see them as both an outcome of *and* an answer to a contemporary organic crisis. Alongside resurgent populism, authoritarianism, and demagogy, the coming of post-truth discourses seems to represent or even constitute the contours of a societal contract that is coming undone. The old and established claims to truth are no longer considered valid and new yardsticks are called for. We need not accept the claims made by proponents of these worlds to recognize that these discourses are likely the morbid symptoms of a social structure that is starting to fracture. In this sense, post-truth worlds are as much a symptom of change as they are implicated in prescribing solutions to the state of affairs. It is this very tension that we have tried to foreground throughout this book. Technocratic dreams are a response to a world in which the old hegemonic systems no longer hold sway over the public imagination. They are attempts to rehegemonize the field of meaning.

Using the idea of an organic crisis to portray the current situation gives us clues as to how we might interpret it. It also opens up pathways for change. An organic crisis does not need to be a purely negative moment – of rupture and destruction – but can also create space for a renewal and reimagination of our current state of affairs.

Why are we seeing the emergence of an organic crisis now? A likely explanation could be that the existential crisis – the symbolic dislocation of existing master signifiers – has emerged as a delayed response or even symptom of the financial breakdown in 2007 and 2008. Indeed, the strange "non-death of neo-liberalism" (Crouch, 2011) – that is, its capacity to absorb the shocks, not least through government bailouts – seemed to forcefully demonstrate the unwillingness or even structural inability of the capitalist system to learn from crisis. What emerged from the crisis was not a global resurgence of solidarity and capitalist intervention by those holding power, but fierce austerity and scapegoating of the democratic people. Even though it became clear that rampant capitalism and ecological disaster could not go on, capitalism simply started to march on without blinking an eye. The repercussions of the economic meltdown hit those in already precarious positions the hardest through an aggressive form of trickle-down punishment and austerity. This has only added fuel to an already heated fire, causing disillusion and disappointment.

To our mind, the current need for new discourses and symbolic systems – the flourishing of new imaginaries intended to capture the fate of liberal democracies – comes precisely as a delayed response to the non-death and continued destruction created by the global capitalist system. Post-truth worlds, as they have been examined here, are a response to this crisis, though not necessarily one that is being formulated by and for those most disenfranchised and most disillusioned. Instead, it is a discourse crafted by those who benefit from the status quo.

Thinking through our current democratic moment in terms of an organic crisis and its subsequent interregnum offers more than merely cause for concern. It should also be viewed as a moment of potential engagement and intervention. Perhaps more than ever, there is a need for the formulation of proper alternatives that seek to overcome the rationalistic dreams currently attracting worldwide media headlines. In striving to formulate new alternatives, the Left is certainly not alone. But it has been formed by an important democratic tradition that gives it plenty of intellectual background to do so. It is precisely this tradition that needs to be renewed and reinvigorated. Negative critique – in the form of detailed analysis of existing structures of domination, inequality, and mistreatment, related to the intersectionality of labor, gender, age, ethnicity, religion, and much more – is important in this regard. There is a significant and vital task in insisting on the need to question those in power. Yet, negative critique is not enough. What we need are genuine alternatives to the current order. Social movements, transnational alliances, and political groups are in many ways already formulating these – and it is this work that should be continued and supported.

The rise of post-truth worlds – and the all too often post-political visions they contain – act as a stark reminder that democracy is a fragile social contract. It requires continuous renewal and rethinking. There is nothing necessary or inevitable about liberal democracy as a form of co-habitation. While it may appear as the only option for much of the world today, history teaches us that this can transform suddenly and with dire consequences. In this sense, we neither can nor should ever become complacent. Instead, we must strive to continuously deepen and enhance existing democratic institutions and practices. With this book, we hope to have carved out at least some space for thinking critically through these questions, offering intellectual ammunition for those striving to protect and develop democracy. The impact of this work is – as with all other political interventions – dependent on the mobilization and coming together of the people itself. The question is whether we are all up for the task.

References

Crouch, C. (2011). *The Strange Non-Death of Neoliberalism*. Cambridge: Polity Press.
Gramsci, A. (1992). *Selections From the Prison Notebooks*. London: Lawrence & Wishart.
Laclau, E. (2005). *On Populist Reason*. London: Verso.

Index